Solidarity

American University Studies

Series VII
Theology and Religion

Vol. 190

PETER LANG
New York • Washington, D.C./Baltimore
Bern • Frankfurt am Main • Berlin • Vienna • Paris

Kevin P. Doran

Solidarity

A Synthesis of Personalism and Communalism in the Thought of Karol Wojtyla/ Pope John Paul II

PETER LANG
New York • Washington, D.C./Baltimore
Bern • Frankfurt am Main • Berlin • Vienna • Paris

Library of Congress Cataloging-in-Publication Data

Doran, Kevin.
Solidarity: a synthesis of personalism and communalism in the thought of
Karol Wojtyla/ John Paul II/ Kevin P. Doran.
p. cm. — (American university studies. Series VII,
Theology and religion; vol. 190)
Includes bibliographical references and index.
1. John Paul II, Pope, 1920– . 2. Solidarity—Religious aspects—
Christianity—History of doctrines—20th century. 3. Sociology, Christian
(Catholic)—History—20th century. 4 Christian ethics—History—20th
century. 5 Personalism. 6. Communalism. I. Title. II. Series.
BX1378.5.D663   230'.2'092—dc20   95-26224
ISBN 0-8204-3071-4
ISSN 0740-0446

Die Deutsche Bibliothek-CIP-Einheitsaufnahme

Doran, Kevin P.:
Solidarity: a synthesis of personalism and communalism in the thought of
Karol Wojtyla/ John Paul II/ Kevin P. Doran. -New York; Washington,
D.C./Baltimore; Bern; Frankfurt am Main; Berlin; Vienna; Paris: Lang.
(American university studies: Ser. 7, Theology and religion: Vol. 190)
ISBN 0-8204-3071-4
NE: American university studies/ 07

Contents

Abbreviations

The titles of works, to which reference is made frequently, have been abbreviated in the footnotes, in the second and subsequent references, as follows:

Acting Person	"The Acting Person," in *The Yearbook of Phenomenological Research: Analecta Husserliana*, Vol. 10, 3-367. Dordrecht: D. Reidel, 1979.
AAS	*Acta Apostolicae Sedis*
CA	*Centesimus Annus*. Vatican City: Libreria Editrice Vaticana, 1991.
Caractère	*Traité du Caractère*, in *Oeuvres de Mounier*, Vol 2. Paris: Editions du Seuil, 1961.
Division	*De la Division du Travail Social*, 7th. ed., Paris: Presses Universitaires de France, 1960.
DM	*Dives in Misericordia*. London: CTS, 1980.
DV	*Dominum et Vivificantem*. London: CTS, 1986.
EN	*Evangelii Nuntiandi*, in *Proclaiming Justice and Peace*, eds. Michael Walsh and Brian Davies. London: Collins 1991.
Eternal	*On the Eternal in Man*, translated by Bernard Noble. London: SCM Press, 1960.
FC	*Familiaris Consortio*. London CTS, 1981.
Fondamenti	*I Fondamenti dell'Ordine Etico*, second edition. Vatican City, Edizioni CSEO / Libreria Editrice Vaticana, 1989.
Formalism	*Formalism in Ethics and non-Formal Ethics of Values*. A new attempt toward the Foundation of an Ethical Personalism, translated by Manfred S. Frings and Roger L. Funk. Evanston: Northwestern University Press, 1973.
GS	*Pastoral Constitution on the Church in the Modern World: Gaudium et Spes*, in *The Documents of Vatican II*, ed. Walter M. ABBOTT. London: Geoffrey Chapman, 1966.
HSSP	*The Holy See at the Service of Peace*, ed. Sr. Marjorie Keenan. Vatican City: Pontifical Council for Justice and Peace, 1988.

IGP2	*Insegnamenti di Giovanni Paolo II*
IP6	*Insegnamenti di Paolo VI*
JW	*Justice in the World*, (Document of the Third Synod, 30th. Sept. – 6th. Sept. 1971), in *Proclaiming Justice and Peace*, eds. Michael Walsh and Brian Davies. London: Collins 1991.
LE	*Laborem Exercens*. London: CTS, 1981.
Love	*Love and Responsibility*. London: Collins, 1981.
MCC	*Mystici Corporis Christi*. London: CTS, 1943.
MD	*Mulieris Dignitatem*. Dublin: Veritas, 1988.
MM	*Mater et Magistra*, in *Proclaiming Justice and Peace*, eds. Michael Walsh and Brian Davies. London: Collins 1991.
OA	*Octagesimo Adveniens*, in *Proclaiming Justice and Peace*, eds. Michael Walsh and Brian Davies. London: Collins 1991.
Osservatore	*Osservatore Romano*, Weekly Edition in English.
Participation	"Participation et Alienation," in *The Yearbook of Phenomenological Research: Analecta Husserliana*, Vol. 6, 61-72. Dordrecht: D. Reidel, 1977.
Personnalisme	*Le Personnalisme*, second edition. Paris: Presses Universitaires de France, 1951.
PP	*Populorum Progressio*, in *Proclaiming Justice and Peace*, eds. Michael Walsh and Brian Davies. London: Collins 1991.
PT	*Pacem in Terris*, in *Proclaiming Justice and Peace*, eds. Michael Walsh and Brian Davies. London: Collins 1991.
QA	*Quadragesimo Anno*, in *Proclaiming Justice and Peace*, eds. Michael Walsh and Brian Davies. London: Collins 1991.
Qu'est ce que	*Qu'est ce que le Personnalisme?*, in *Oeuvres de Mounier*, Vol. 3. Paris: Editions du Seuil, 1962.
Relations	*Relations Humaines et Société Contemporaine: Synthèse Chrétienne Directives de S.S. Pie XII*, eds. Alfred F. UTZ and J.F. GRONER (French edition translated by A. SAVIGNAT and H. Th. CONUS), 3 vols. Paris / Fribourg: Editions St. Paul, 1956/63.
Ressentiment	*Das Ressentiment im Aufbau der Moralen*, in

	Gesammelte Werke, Vol. 3, ed. Maria Scheler. Berne: Francke, 1955.
Révolution	*Révolution Personnaliste et Communautaire*, in *Oeuvres de Mounier*, Vol. 1. Paris: Editions du Seuil, 1960.
RH	*Redemptor Hominis*. London: CTS, 1980.
RM	*Redemptoris Missio*. Vatican City: Libreria Editrice Vaticana, 1991.
RN	*Rerum Novarum*, Centenary Study Edition, with introduction and notes by Joseph Kirwan. London: CTS, 1991.
SD	*Salvifici Doloris*. London: CTS, 1984.
SRS	*Sollicitudo Rei Socialis*. London: CTS, 1988.
ST	*Summa Theologiae*, in 3 Vols. New York: Benziger Bros. Inc., 1948.
Subject	"The Person: Subject and Community," *The Review of Metaphysics*, XXXIII, 2 , No. 30, Dec. 1979: 273-308.
Sympathy	*The Nature of Sympathy*, translated by Peter Heath, with a general introduction to Max Scheler's works by W. Stark, London: Routledge and Kegan Paul. New Haven: Yale University Press, 1954.
Teoria-Prassi	"Teoria-Prassi: Una Tema Umano e Cristiano," *Incontri Culturali (Rome)*, 10 (1977): 31-41.
Valutazioni	*Valutazioni sulla Possibilità di Costruire L'Etica Cristiana Sulle Basi del Sistema di Max Scheler*. Rome: Logos, 1980.
VS	*Veritatis Splendor*. Vatican City: Libreria Editrice Vaticana, 1993.

Abbreviations are used in conjunction with the author's name, to facilitate cross reference to the bibliography. I have used *ibid.* rather sparingly because of the number of references and the consequent possibility of confusion.

Introduction

Like many people, I suspect, my first contact with the concept of solidarity was through the medium of the encyclical letter of Pope John Paul II, *Sollicitudo Rei Socialis*. I had heard the word many times, most notably in connection with the Polish trade-union movement. While I had an ordinary common-sense idea of what *solidarity* meant, the encyclical letter was the first place in which I had seen the concept developed and used as if it had a concrete meaning. When I consulted the index to the early volumes of *Insegnamenti di Giovanni Paolo II*, I discovered to my surprise that *solidarity* was not listed there. This suggests to me that, while John Paul II was using the concept from the beginning of his papacy, those responsible for the publication of his addresses had not yet adverted to the significant place of *solidarity* in his personal philosophical vocabulary. Neither had they readily recognised it as a concept which already had a certain currency in the social teaching of the Church.

My concern has been to establish what Karol Wojtyla / Pope John Paul II means when he speaks of solidarity. In order to provide a background against which Wojtyla's thought can be examined, and with which it can be compared, I have attempted to trace the origins of the concept of solidarity in Social Philosophy, in Sociology, and in the Social teaching of the Church prior to his election as Pope in 1978. I have made what I believe is the reasonable assumption that, in becoming pope, Karol Wojtyla did not cease to be a philosopher, but rather found a new context for the development of his philosophical thought.

The first chapter is a brief examination of the concept of solidarity as developed by the French sociologist Emile Durkheim, towards the end of the 19th. century. In Durkheim's view, the kind of social bond that exists in a society is expressed and can be read in its laws and its penal system. The complex modern society is governed primarily by contract and agreement, based on the awareness of interdependence. The end result would appear to be a solidarity of functions, based on the variety of available skills, rather than a solidarity of persons.

Chapter two is a study of the concept of solidarity in the thought of Max Scheler, and the related concept of communion in the thought of Emmanuel Mounier. The philosophy of Scheler, who belongs to the tradition of realist phenomenology, was a source of constant interest to Karol Wojtyla. His concept of social community is developed primarily in his ethical works, in the course of which he establishes that values are personal and not purely formal as Kant suggested. True solidarity between persons, which recognises the irreplaceable nature of every person, is found only in the highest social form, the person-community, in which the best elements of these group types are integrated.

Mounier, by contrast, rarely uses the concept of solidarity, and then only in a negative sense. His analysis of the intersubjectivity of persons in community is, however, quite similar to that of Scheler. The constantstruggle of every person is to remain open to communion and to avoid sliding-backwards into the individualism of the anti-personal society. Of particular interest for our study, is the question of whether Mounier, in pointing to the limitations of both Marxist socialist and liberal capitalist societies, intended to propose a *third way*, or simply an attitude which would facilitate co-existence and collaboration with others in either of the existing social systems. John Paul II frequently addresses the question of the destructiveness of opposing ideological blocs, each of which is in need of radical revision.

Chapter three is a study of the concept of solidarity as it is used in the social teaching of the church prior to Pope John Paul's election in October 1978. It transpires that the term *solidarity* was already quite current in the addresses of Pius XII. A central part of the work of this chapter is a comparison between the concept of solidarity and other concepts such as *friendship* (used frequenlty by Leo XIII), *social charity* (used frequently by Pius XII), and *civilisation of love* (found in the thought of Paul VI). These concepts are identified by Pope John Paul (in *Centesimus Annus*, § 10) as being essentially the same as *solidarity*.

Chapter four is a study of the concept of solidarity in the philosophical thought of Karol Wojtyla. The concept is developed almost exclusively in one work, *The Acting Person*, but against the background of a broader body of thought on the being and action of the person in community. *The Acting Person* is primarily concerned with a study of the human person through an examination of personal action. One aspect of personal action is co-action with others. Solidarity is presented as the attitude which ensures appropriate participation with others, having regard to the needs of the person and the good of the whole community.

Election to the papacy placed Karol Wojtyla on the world stage, and provided a new global context for his development and application of the concept of solidarity. Chapter five is a study of the use of *solidarity* in the addresses and writings of Pope John Paul II over the period 1978-1991. This chapter demonstrates a very clear continuity between the thought of

Wojtyla prior to and after his election as pope. There are also indications of some development in the concept of solidarity which can be traced to the more global context in which Wojtyla is thinking and acting.

Unless otherwise indicated, the translation of material cited, but not published, in English, is the responsibility of the author.

Acknowledgments

The preparation of any substantial work of research is in itself a useful context for the development of a practical appreciation of interdependence. While much is done alone and behind closed doors, the end result would not be possible without some very real solidarity on the part of others. I wish to take this opportunity to acknowledge that solidarity with gratitude.

My thanks goes in the first place to Prof. Alfred Wilder op., who generously made himself available to me for consultation while I was engaged in the research of which this work is the result. His advice and his constructive criticism, along with that of Prof. Rodolfo Garcia op., who also read the manuscript in its entirety, is greatly appreciated.

Home, for the past five years, has been Rome. I am grateful to the many good friends there who encouraged me, offered suggestions, and listened patiently when I needed to think aloud. A particular word of appreciation must go to my colleagues on the staff at the Pontifical Irish College, to the sisters of St. John of God, and to all the students who have passed through the college during those years. I have enjoyed their companionship, and valued their acceptance which is a particular mark of solidarity.

I am deeply indebted to my Archbishop, Desmond Connell, who was once my Professor of Metaphysics, and who kindly offered me the opportunity of pursuing this research. During my years in Rome, I have particularly valued his constant support and encouragement. Thanks is also due, on two counts, to Rev. Dr. Brendan Purcell of University College Dublin. His careful guidance of an earlier study of mine, on the concept of Person in St. Thomas, helped to prepare the ground for this study.[1] It was also he who put my thoughts into words, and suggested the title of this present work.

Last, but by no means least, I wish to record my thanks to my family whose support and encouragement, over the years has always been felt and appreciated.

Kevin P. Doran
2/9/'95

---

[1] Kevin P. Doran, *What is a Person*. (New York: Edwin Mellen Press, 1989).

Chapter One
THE ORIGINS OF SOLIDARITY IN SOCIOLOGY: EMILE DURKHEIM

1. Two Kinds of Solidarity

Jerrold Seigel suggests that the seeds of Emile Durkheim's theory of Solidarity are to be found in his graduation address to the students at the Lycée of Sens as early as 1883, in which he spoke of the fundamental distinction between two forms of society; a distinction which was later to be developed in his first book, *De La Division du Travail Social*.[1] It seems that Durkheim (1858-1917), when he moved to Paris to study, had a sense of being up-rooted and alienated in the city. This experience was shared by some of his close friends. Seigel believes that the personal experience of two types of society, the relatively stable and unchanging rural society in which he grew up and the more concentrated society of his student days in Paris, greatly influenced Durkheim's later work. He comments: "Durkheim's graduation speech was thus about a division of labour which he had experienced himself, and toward which he felt deeply ambivalent."[2]

Societies differ according to the kind of bond or solidarity that exists between the members, and Durkheim distinguishes two principal sources of social cohesion, namely similitude and the division of labour. The latter is to be understood to mean a tendency toward functional specialisation. The trend towards a greater division of labour has become accelerated in recent centuries, but Durkheim detects in society a certain ambivalence about this trend which may in some sense reflect his own feelings. "If public opinion accepts the rule of the division of labour it is not without a certain uneasiness and hesitation. While requiring people to become specialised, it seems, at the same time, to fear that they might become too specialised."[3]

The central thesis of Durkheim's first book is that, as less developed

---

[1] Emile DURKHEIM, *De La Division du Travail Social*, 7th. ed., (Paris: Presses Universitaires de France, 1960), hereafter referred to as *Division*.

[2] Jerrold SEIGEL, "Autonomy and Personality in Durkheim: an Essay on Content and Method," *Journal of the History of Ideas*, 48 (1987): 497.

[3] Emile DURKHEIM, *Division*, 6.

social types give way to more complex societies, so the kind of solidarity that is to be found in these societies changes from a solidarity based on similitude to a new and, in his considered view – apart from any possible personal inclination – a deeper kind of solidarity based on the division of labour or social utility. He envisages people as if participating in one immense work, not alone in any particular generation, but also united with their predecessors and their descendants. "It is, therefore, the continuous sub-division of the different forms of human labour which principally constitutes social solidarity and which becomes the fundamental cause of the extent and the increasing complexity of the social organism."[4]

The first part of the work is devoted to a detailed examination of these two types of solidarity and their causes. Given that, for Durkheim, solidarity is a moral phenomenon, it doesn't lend itself to direct examination. We must instead examine some external reality which symbolises or expresses it, using this as a means for studying solidarity itself. The kind of solidarity by means of which any society coheres is reflected in the law of that society.

> This visible symbol is law. . . . The life, in general, of a society cannot incorporate any aspect without the juridical life incorporating it at the same time and in the same relationship. We can, therefore, be certain that we will find reflected in law all the essential types of social solidarity.[5]

The best way to distinguish between types of law is on the basis of the kind of sanctions that attach to them. Broadly there are two categories under this heading: criminal law, to which punishment is attached, and civil law, which has more to do with restoring the balance of things than with inflicting punishment."[6]

2. Mechanical Solidarity

The most important concept for understanding the kind of solidarity based on similitude is that of the collective conscience, which Durkheim

---

[4] Emile DURKHEIM, *Division*, 27.

[5] Emile DURKHEIM, *Division*, 28/29. Durkheim accepts that, in exceptional circumstances, morals, to the exclusion of positive law, govern the relationships of society. He argues, however, that the law reproduces any type of social solidarity which we need to know.

[6] Cf. Emile DURKHEIM, *Division*, 34. Durkheim refers to these two types as "droit répressif " and "droit restitutif" respectively.

describes as "the ensemble of the beliefs and sentiments common to the average members of the same society."[7] In less complex societies which have a strong collective conscience the law tends to be penal in nature, and the penalties imposed for crime tend to be clearly codified. An act is considered criminal when it offends against the strongly held values of the society. It is not usually anything to do with the objective nature of the act that causes it to be considered criminal, but rather the perceived assault against the collective conscience. This may be something which threatens the security of the society in a real way or, perhaps, something which shows disrespect for the central institutions of the society.

Punishment is the reaction of a society against crime, and its nature will be determined by the extent of the offense against the collective conscience. Durkheim explains that there is a distinction to be made between punishment which is intended to protect society and that which seeks vengeance. The act of vengeance in primitive societies often embraces the innocent who are in some way close to the offender. Vengeance, in its own way, also seeks to protect society, but it has a tendency to be blind and irrational, excessive and ill-defined. Nonetheless, even in modern society, vengeance plays some part in our penal sanctions. Otherwise it would be difficult to explain why some crimes are so severely punished.[8]

Durkheim is anxious to make it clear that there is inevitably a social dimension to crime and punishment. Even though it may be an individual who is threatened, the society is affected and concerned. He argues that a punishment, properly speaking, is imposed by society and can only be remitted by society. In so far as this function, in more advanced societies, tends to be associated with particular offices, e.g., the executioner or the prison officer, it remains a social function. In Durkheim's view this may be because the origins of penal law are religious, and religion is a social phenomenon.[9]

We all tend to react strongly against anything that we perceive as an attack on the values we cherish most. What is significant in the matter of

---

[7] Emile DURKHEIM, *Division*, 46. Durkheim uses the term "conscience collective" which could literally be translated into English either as "collective conscience" or "collective consciousness." In the context, Durkheim's concept is closer to conscience in the moral sense than to simple reflective awareness.

[8] Cf., Emile DURKHEIM, *Division*, 56.

[9] Cf. Emile DURKHEIM, *Division*, 59-64.

crime and punishment is the fact that the values which are under attack are the most strongly held, universal or collective values of a particular society. Durkheim makes the point that the expiation required by society is sometimes attributed to some transcendent being or concept; be it God, honour, or duty. This, he says, is an illusion arising from the strength of the collective conscience. He remarks, however, that this is not entirely without foundation since the collective sentiment represents not just ourselves but society.[10]

When it comes to understanding solidarity in less developed societies, the essence of Durkheim's theory is that like sentiments attract and the stronger they are the greater the attraction is. This is not simply a matter of a preference for the company of persons who are like oneself; but a desire for their good as for one's own. In the less complex society there are to be found two types of conscience, the collective conscience and the individual conscience, but because of the value placed on similitude or collectivity in these societies, the two are closely linked even to the extent of being identical in some societies.

> Now, although distinct, these two consciences are linked to each other, because in effect they are only one, having one and the same organic substrate between them. They are, therefore, solidary. There arises, from this, a solidarity *sui generis* which, born of resemblance, attaches the individual directly to the society. . . . This solidarity does not consist simply in a general and indeterminate attachment of the individual to the group, but renders harmonious the detail of their movements... It is this solidarity that penal law expresses.[11]

In societies of this kind, there is a certain level of similitude required on the part of all the members, without which the individual would constitute a threat to the society. The punitive reaction of society to any offense against the collective conscience makes it possible for people to restate their values and to reassure each other that they are still in communion.

Durkheim argues, however, that it is not the crime or the punishment in themselves that prevent or give rise to solidarity. Rather it is how they are understood in terms of their relation to the collective conscience. Certain crimes do not in fact harm society, but they are interpreted as if

---

[10] Cf. Emile DURKHEIM, *Division*, 68/69.

[11] Emile DURKHEIM, *Division*, 74.

they did. This can happen particularly when the values of a society have changed but its laws have remained the same. As Serverin explains, Durkheim actually saw a certain utility in crime, partly because it allows for the expression of the collective feeling which is the motor of society, and partly in so far as it anticipates and even provokes change.

> I am referring to rule violations which anticipate, and prepare the way for the morality of the future.... The rules must be violated before they are solemnly abrogated. But this violation is not simply the sign of a failure to integrate the dominant moral conscience; it is the surpassing of the present state of the collective conscience, the anticipation of a future state, and, therefore, an element in a process of the dynamic integration of values.[12]

The value of punishment, then, is not in its capacity directly to benefit society in a practical way, but in the fact that it reinforces the sense of communion or solidarity which has been affronted. "It is a sign attesting that the collective sentiments remain collective, that the communion of spirits in the one faith remains intact and, in this way, it repairs the damage which the crime has done to society."[13]

3. Organic Solidarity

The nature of restitutive justice demonstrates that the solidarity to which it corresponds is quite different. This kind of justice is concerned with restoring the balance in society rather than with inflicting punishment. Restitutive justice is the product of a social relationship in which the collective conscience is less dominant and less pervasive. This is not to say that society does not enter into the relations between individuals, but simply that it does so in a different way.[14]

Durkheim explains that society intervenes in restitutive law either in a negative (abstentionist) way or in a positive (co-operative way) and that this distinction reflects a sub-division in the concept of solidarity between positive and negative solidarity. Negative solidarity exists both in less developed societies and in more complex societies, as a necessary accompaniment of positive solidarity, but it is not a true solidarity because

---

[12] Evelyne SERVERIN, "Propos sur l'Utilité: les Valeurs du Crime chez Marx et Durkheim," *Archives de Philosophie du Droit*, 26 (1981): 77.

[13] Emile DURKHEIM, *Division*, 77.

[14] Cf. Emile DURKHEIM, *Division*, 79-82.

it has more to do with keeping people apart than with contributing to any kind of co-operation between them.

> It is not, therefore, a positive social link; even the very expression negative solidarity, which we have used, is not perfectly accurate. It is not a true solidarity, having its own existence and special nature, but rather, it is the negative side of all kinds of solidarity.[15]

In the more complex society, this negative kind of solidarity is expressed in the law of property, and the personal relations which derive from it. But unless there is something more positive and fundamental governing the relations between people, negative solidarity on its own is impossible to activate. By contrast, the positive kind of solidarity is what is reflected by the other elements of restitutive law; namely, domestic law, contract and commercial law, and constitutional law. Durkheim explains that each of these branches of law determines the manner in which members of society should relate to each other in various essential areas. In each case he shows how the basis for the relationship is determined by the distribution of tasks and the taking on of specialised relationships, in the family, in business, and in the state. He concludes: "In summary, the relations which are governed by positive restitutive law, and the solidarity which they express, result from the division of labour."[16]

At this point Durkheim abandons any further consideration of negative solidarity on the basis that it does not, of itself, produce any social integration. He limits himself to discussing two positive types of solidarity which are distinguished as follows:

a. One links the individual directly to the society, while the other links the individual to the society through its intermediate parts.

b. The first or collective type sees society as a collection of more or less organised beliefs and feelings held in common. The second, by contrast, sees society as a system of different and specialised functions.

c. The third distinction arises out of the second. In the collective type, the society can only become strong according as the collective tendencies surpass those of the individual members. The members do not really belong to themselves. Rather they are parts of the whole, without any developed individual rights. The way in which they relate could well be expressed by

[15] Emile DURKHEIM, *Division*, 88.
[16] Emile DURKHEIM, *Division*, 96.

the analogy of mechanical parts.

Regarding the kind of solidarity found in the collective type of society, Durkheim says:

> I propose to give the name mechanical to this kind of solidarity. This word does not imply that it is produced artificially and by mechanical means. I give it this name only by analogy with the cohesion which unites the elements of inanimate bodies, by contrast with that which causes the unity of living bodies.[17]

One might question whether this analogy is satisfactory. While it is true that the collective conscience – the sense of identity – is dominant in this kind of society, Durkheim has failed to take account of the existence, which he has previously stressed, of the individual conscience, however strongly constrained. The very fact of crime and the need to respond to it in these societies would suggest that even in the case of the so-called mechanical solidarity, much depends on the will of the individual.

The second kind of solidarity, unlike the first, presupposes diversity of functions in society. The collective conscience withdraws and allows more scope for the individual conscience. The cohesion of the society is in proportion to the freedom of the individual, because the diversity of functions makes people more dependent on each other. Durkheim names this kind of solidarity organic, because it resembles the functioning of the organism in higher animals.[18]

4. Replacement of Mechanical Solidarity by Organic Solidarity

It is only when we look more closely at societies and social groups that we begin to recognise how much the division of labour in society is progressing. On the surface it may appear that nations are becoming more similar and that the old boundaries that rigidly separated the professions are being taken down. However, within societies and within professional groups there is greater diversification and specialisation than ever. This process of movement away from the collective is confirmed, according to Durkheim, by the way in which the thrust of law is away from the repressive and towards the restitutive.[19]

In comparing the two types of solidarity, Durkheim concludes that the

---

[17] Emile DURKHEIM, *Division*, 100.

[18] Cf. Emile DURKHEIM, *Division*, 101.

[19] Cf. Emile DURKHEIM, *Division*, 104-118.

kind which derives from the division of labour i.e., from specialisation, is stronger by reason of its complexity and more observable in modern society than the type of solidarity which derives from similitude. In support of this claim he argues that with the division into urban and rural societies, it has become almost impossible for a city to survive if separated from its hinterland. It could be argued that examples of the kind of thing to which Durkheim refers are, indeed, to be found in places where non-geographical frontiers have been artificially imposed e.g., in Ireland. It is far more difficult, according to Durkheim, to separate a region from an advanced society than from a primitive one. He also claims that it is more difficult for a foreigner to be absorbed into a modern society.[20] One only has to look at the immense legal machinery involved in regulating the freedom of movement and employment in the European Community to see what Durkheim means. By contrast detachment from one society and attachment to another would appear to have been far simpler in less complex societies.

Fernando Uricoechea holds that Durkheim is not comparing like with like in his discussion of the comparative strength of ties in each of the two social types. In the case of mechanical solidarity, he argues, Durkheim is talking about social ties, whereas in the case of organic solidarity, he is talking about functional ties. "These are examples of functional interdependence between aggregates and not examples of personal links between individuals and their society."[21]

A key element in understanding Durkheim's theory of solidarity is his belief that mechanical solidarity and organic solidarity are in some way opposed. Mechanical solidarity involves weaker links and is therefore, in his view, being gradually eroded as society progresses. "Not only does mechanical solidarity bind people together less strongly in a general sense than organic solidarity, but, as social evolution progresses, it grows steadily weaker."[22]

---

[20] Cf. Emile DURKHEIM, *Division*, 120ff.

[21] Fernando URICOECHEA, "La Theorie de Solidarité de Durkheim," *Cahiers Internationaux de Sociologie*, 66 (1979), no. 3: 120. Uricoechea suggests that the only example Durkheim uses, which could be considered a comparison of like with like, is that of the family ties. He argues, however, that Durkheim's claim that these are strengthened in modern society by the division of labour, is not borne out by the experience of widespread divorce.

[22] Emile DURKHEIM, *Division*, 124. In the following pages Durkheim shows how the gradual decline in force of the collective conscience is reflected in the decline in importance of whole sections of penal law; cf. 125-136. One area alone has remained unchanged – at

The weakening of the collective conscience and the growth of individualism and free thinking is not a modern phenomenon. It has been assisted by the advent of Christian scholastic philosophy, by the Reformation, and by the French Revolution, among other things, but there is no point at which it can be said to begin. Likewise there is no likelihood of the collective conscience ever being eliminated. It will simply become a thing of general and indeterminate expression.[23]

With the decline of the collective conscience we must assume that, unless there is to be a complete breakdown in social life, there must be some new social bond to take the place of the old one. Durkheim argues that this new bond is none other than the solidarity created by the division of labour.

> Furthermore, if we remember that, even where it is strongest, mechanical solidarity does not bind people with the same strength as the division of labour, and that, besides, it excludes from its action the majority of current social phenomena, it will become even clearer that social solidarity tends towards becoming exclusively organic. It is the division of labour which, increasingly, takes on the role which was in previous times performed by the collective conscience.[24]

In practice the two types of society are quite different. The "horde" is the name Durkheim gives to the kind of society based on similitude, and it is out of this "social protoplasm" that all other social types have developed. It is from mechanical solidarity that tribes and clans derive their principal psychological characteristics. This type of society has its own powerful idea of religion and its own particular communistic attitude to the ownership of property.[25]

The type of society in which organic solidarity is expressed is not like this. The structure is formed out of professional rather than hereditary relationships. Initially the division of labour takes the form of the development of various professional groups in each centre of population, but as time goes on we see greater specialisation determining the functions of towns and even entire regions. Durkheim explains that the basis of this

---

least in Durkheim's time – and this relates to the rights of the person. He argues that this is because, while the law regarding respect for the person appeals to the collective conscience, it is not so much to society as to ourselves that it binds us; cf. 147.

[23] Cf. Emile DURKHEIM, *Division*, 146.

[24] Emile DURKHEIM, *Division*, 148.

[25] Cf. Emile DURKHEIM, *Division*, 154.

kind of solidarity is functional. Sometimes the organs of society which are most in solidarity do draw closer for practical reasons, but this is not essential because organic solidarity derives from mutual dependence rather than from identification with any place or culture. "It is no longer consanguinity, real or imaginary, which dictates the place of each person, but rather the function which he fulfils."[26] One might ask if there is any place in such a society for someone who has no obvious social function to fulfil. The bond of organic solidarity based on interdependence would surely be weakened, in the case of someone who depends on others, but on whom nobody depends in turn.

The development from one kind of society to another is, according to Durkheim, something akin to what happens in biology. The simplest, most primitive organisms e.g., polyps, are linked in such a way as to be indistinguishable from others of the same genus, yet survival is not affected by separation. Higher organisms do not function in that manner, and even within one organism different organs are differentiated according to function. Many of these functions are essential to the survival of the whole organism. So, the more developed society, in which each one has his or her own function, but all depend considerably on each other, is analogical to the organic type of organisation.[27]

Uricoechea sees Durkheim's opposition between the two social types, and thus the two types of solidarity, as a fundamental error. They should not be considered, he says, as two different stages of the same process.

> He (Durkheim) fails to recognise that the two types correspond to different social processes which are not mutually exclusive, that they fulfil integrating functions which are different but necessary for the institutional organisation of the society... The first process responds to the problems of integration of the society as a social system; the second is necessary when the general question of integration and solidarity is viewed from the perspective of the society as a moral community.[28]

Durkheim takes issue with the British social philosopher, Spencer, who suggested that the centralisation of authority in primitive societies resulted in the annihilation of individuality. On the contrary, Durkheim says, the centralisation of authority in strong and sometimes despotic rulers and

---

[26] Emile DURKHEIM, *Division*, 158; cf. also 166, where Durkheim explains the relative unimportance of geographical proxmity for organic solidarity.

[27] Cf. Emile DURKHEIM, *Division*, 167.

[28] Fernando URICOECHEA, ibid., 120/121.

chiefs marks the dawning of the consciousness of personal individuality.[29] This point is important for Durkheim. It means that, when we want to ask why some ruler seems to have excessive power, we have to ask what kind of society it is that allows him to gain such power.

While Spencer is correct in stating that social harmony in organised societies derives from the division of labour, he is incorrect, according to Durkheim, in thinking that this happens spontaneously.[30] As penal law declines, we have seen that it is replaced by restitutive law. There is always some kind of explicit social organisation. We cannot foresee all possible eventualities, and it would be unacceptable to have to return to first principles every time we make a contract. It follows that there must be some specifically social element which forms the basis of a secure solidarity.

Durkheim argues that our contracts, which are an aspect of the division of labour are not, of themselves, sufficient to guarantee an adequate level of solidarity. This is because, while the contracts arise out of an individual act of will, they incur obligations which may eventually conflict with the will. This is the point at which spontaneity must give way to social organisation.

> It must not be forgotten that, although the division of labour contributes to interests becoming solidary, it does not confuse them; it leaves them distinct and in competition. Just as each organ within the organism is antagonistic towards the others, even while co-operating with them, each contracting party, even while having need of the other, seeks to gain what he needs at the least cost, that is to say, to acquire the greatest number of rights in exchange for the least possible number of obligations.[31]

The organising and sanctioning role of society recognises that there is more to the contract than simply the exchange of goods or services. There is also the social relationship which is established. But, for Durkheim, this remains a relationship of functions rather than a relationship of people. He argues, contrary to Spencer's view, that the progressive diversification of society doesn't reduce the significance of the role of the state. It is true that it's coercive power is diminished in intensity, but not in volume.

He explains, for example, that certain functions cease to be directly

---

[29] Cf. Emile DURKHEIM, *Division.*, 172.
[30] Cf. Emile DURKHEIM, *Division*, 177-180.
[31] Emile DURKHEIM, *Division*, 191.

performed by central government, such as the provision of health and education services. They are no less subject, however, to the influence of society in that the central authority moderates the activity of the specialised agencies which have taken on these tasks. The end result tends to be greater complexity and greater solidarity. That this is so can be observed, according to Durkheim, by noting how quickly an industrial dispute spreads in an organised society.[32]

With the division of labour, the social structures become more complex, and paradoxically, each organ in the organism becomes less distinct. There are less small factories and private operators and more large concerns. The larger organisation tends to take over the activities of the smaller which correspond with its own particular specialisation.

The conclusions of the first part of Durkheim's work on the division of labour, therefore, are that:

a. There are two types of positive solidarity, the mechanical type based on similitude and the organic type based on the division of labour, and the latter replaces the former as society progresses.

b. The division of labour alone cannot give rise to organic solidarity. It is the result of a combination of the division of labour and the moderating influence of society.

5. Causes of the Division of Labour

In the second part of his work, Durkheim sets out to discuss the possible causes of the division of labour. He rules out two possibilities, namely the quest for happiness and the quest for a greater variety in pleasure. He argues that there is a limit to the extent to which an organism can develop in any of its aspects, without becoming unbalanced and unhealthy. This is the case also with regard to the degree of happiness which people can absorb.

It would be fanciful, but incorrect, to think that our ancestors missed out on some of the happiness we have, and strove to attain it through the division of labour. They had the balance of happiness to which they were adapted, just as we have in our own time. In fact, he argues, if the search for greater happiness is what gave rise to the division of labour, the search was in large measure a failure. The ever increasing toll of suicides attests at least that the happiness of society in general is diminishing rather than

---

[32] Cf. Emile DURKHEIM, *Division*, 199-202.

increasing in proportion as society progresses.[33]

Neither is the desire for a greater variety in pleasure the cause of the division of labour. All peoples at all times naturally seek variety in pleasure as well as increase in its intensity, but not all societies progress in the division of labour. Furthermore, balancing the desire for variety in pleasure, is the desire for continuity in the pleasures we already have.[34]

Durkheim concludes, therefore, that the true cause of the division of labour is not something in man but rather something outside himself, in his milieu. Since there is not much change in the material milieu, it is more than likely that the catalyst for the division of labour is to be found in man's social milieu. The division of labour only occurs in a society as it becomes less segmented. The decline in segmentation must come first, although it is then stimulated further by the division of labour. For Durkheim, this decline in segmentation corresponds with a greater degree of contact and interchange within the social mass. In practice this growth in what Durkheim calls the "moral" or "dynamic density" of a society depends on a corresponding growth in "material density." Simply stated, the division of labour or progress in society and, consequently the development of organic solidarity, is favoured by urbanisation and centralisation.[35]

It is not simply growth in the volume of society, but the contact which this facilitates, that causes the division of labour, in Durkheim's view. I believe it must be acknowledged that, in many urban environments, the experience of people is one of isolation and alienation, rather than one of solidarity. This is due in no small measure to the fact that urban environments frequently are not conducive to real inter-personal contact, because people are known only on a superficial level, in terms of their functions. The failure to take account of this, I would argue, will prove to be a fundamental flaw in Durkheim's theory of solidarity.

Location and local conditions influence specialisation. For example fertile land supports agriculture, and a natural harbour facilitates fishing and trade. Specialisation also depends on the degree of contact that is possible between one area and another. An isolated society cannot afford the luxury of specialisation. In the final analysis, however, all these things simply permit and influence the direction of specialisation. What actually

---

[33] Cf. Emile DURKHEIM, *Division*, 211.
[34] Cf. Emile DURKHEIM, *Division*, 232.
[35] Cf. Emile DURKHEIM, *Division*, 237/238.

causes this division of labour is the combination of competition and the struggle to survive.

Unlike Spencer, Durkheim is adamant that the root cause of the division of labour is not something external to society, but something essentially social. In more advanced societies the prospect of competition is greater. Accordingly, as the dynamic and material density of society increases, so also does the likelihood of competition, and thus survival dictates the need to specialise.[36]

Durkheim presents the division of labour as something basically benign, in that it serves as a mechanism whereby rival members of society diversify rather than seeking to annihilate each other.

> Thanks to it, in fact, rivals are not obliged to eliminate each other, but can co-exist side by side. Furthermore, as it develops, it offers to an increasing number of individuals who, in more homogeneous societies, would be condemned to oblivion, the means to survive and to support themselves.[37]

Specialisation implies the production of goods and services for which there is a perceived demand. Durkheim argues, however, that economists have tended, while recognising the reality of the division of labour, to misinterpret it. The greater productivity that results from the division of labour is only a by-product of what is essentially a struggle to survive.[38]

It seems, therefore, that competition contributes to solidarity since it stimulates the progress of the division of labour. But this only happens, according to Durkheim, where there already exists a sense of society. This is why the more complex society develops out of the more homogeneous social type. It is worth noting, at this point, how fundamental it is to Durkheim's notion of solidarity in advanced societies, to refer back to the basis of sociality – in effect the "collective conscience" – which he regards as a characteristic of the less developed society. "The division of labour has sometimes, mistakenly, been seen as the fundamental fact of all social life....The collective way of life is not born of the individual, but rather individual life is born out of the collective."[39] This comment by Durkheim

---

[36] Cf. Emile DURKHEIM, *Division*, 249/250.

[37] Emile DURKHEIM, *Division*, 253.

[38] Cf. Emile DURKHEIM, *Division*, 259. Durkheim returns to this theme later in the work, accusing economists of having exposed the division of labour to unmerited criticism, cf. 364.

[39] Emile DURKHEIM, *Division*, 261, 264.

raises the question of whether he is not fundamentally inconsistent in opposing the two types of solidarity and, thereby opposing the values of sociality and of mutual dependence.

Durkheim, consistent with his theory, concedes that some form of international division of labour is possible, but only where narrow nationalism is transcended and where there is a genuine coming together of societies. There is a difference between the division of labour arising out of the merging of social segments, on the one hand, and mere mutualism, on the other. "Simply because two different organisms each find themselves with properties which are useful to the other, it does not follow that there is a distribution of functions between them."[40]

Apart from the struggle to survive, there are a number of secondary causes of the division of labour which Durkheim identifies. These relate to the weakening of the collective conscience, a necessary pre-condition for progress in the division of labour. One of these secondary causes is the gradual movement away from house gods and local gods of primitive societies to a God who is perceived as transcendent or other-worldly, who appears to impinge less on the everyday actions of people. There is no doubt that a significant stage in this process is the movement from a theocentric anthropology to an anthropocentric one, culminating in the rationalism of the enlightenment.

Another secondary cause of the weakening of the collective conscience is the weakening of tradition which is associated with the mobility of advanced societies. It is not merely the mobility that is significant, but the separation from the elders of the society which it entails, since it is in these that the tradition reposes for the most part. Because the trend is towards cities, it is here that the moderating influence of tradition is least strongly felt. Durkheim explains that the collective conscience is weakened in the city, by comparison with the smaller town. "Wherever the density of the conglomeration is in proportion to its volume, personal links are rare and weak: one easily loses sight of others, even those to whom one is closest, and, to the same extent one loses interest in them."[41]

Paradoxically, this comment would also seem to suggest, in conflict with Durkheim's own thesis, that the progress of the division of labour can actually contribute to a decline in solidarity in any truly human sense. In

---

[40] Emile DURKHEIM, *Division,* 266.
[41] Emile DURKHEIM, *Division,* 287.

his way of describing the progress of society, personal links seem to be more closely associated with mechanical solidarity, and functional links with organic solidarity. Progress and interdependence seem, at times, to be almost synonymous with the solidarity of organised societies which, however, seems to exclude any element that is truly personal.

Durkheim identifies one further secondary factor in the progress of the division of labour. This is the decline in the significance of heredity. Heredity, since it comes from the past, can act as a restraining force and thereby limit individuation. But Durkheim argues that, according as diversification progresses, the role of heredity becomes less significant. He also suggests that people are less ready to accept it as an explanation of human behaviour.[42] This may have been so in his time but, in the light of modern genetics, it is questionable whether this argument could be sustained today.

Durkheim's explanation of the causes of the division of labour has significant implications in that it means that society explains the individual. Social changes, such as the increase in density and volume of society, are what change individuals in so far as they are set free. Durkheim's view of the division of labour is, unlike Spencer's, a mechanistic one. He doesn't deny the possibility of a goal or an end, but argues that it is social change rather than any goal that necessitates the division of labour.[43]

6. The Division of Labour May Not Always Give Rise to Solidarity

There are undoubtedly situations in which the division of labour does not lead to the strengthening of social solidarity. Three examples of this are:

a. bankruptcy and industrial crises

b. the class struggle which, in Durkheim's time, was no longer merely the occasional dispute, but had become a state of more or less constant enmity.

c. the loss of a sense of the whole which seems to accompany the progress of specialisation.

A proper appreciation of the function of each organ of society is only possible where there is a sense of belonging to the whole.[44] This holistic emphasis in the thought of Durkheim is stressed by Matteucci, who points

---

[42] Cf. Emile DURKHEIM, *Division,* 295/296.
[43] Cf. Emile DURKHEIM, *Division,* 288; also 340-342.
[44] Cf. Emile DURKHEIM, *Division,* 344-348.

out that, for Durkheim, the social whole must be capable of being observed precisely as a whole.

> Durkheim adopts a holistic conception of society whereby the whole is thought of as an integrated collection of elements, endowed with its own reality *sui generis*. It is qualitatively different from the parts in that it is a subject of its own rules of formation, functioning, and change, which are not reducible to those which govern the behaviour of its components. The whole must be capable of being observed as distinct from the individual parts, and yet these parts all contribute to the organic growth of the whole; paradoxically their autonomy expresses the necessity of their mutual dependence.[45]

In support of this holistic vision of society, Durkheim refers to the view of August Comte who identified an independent organ within the social organism, namely the State, as having the role of keeping alive this awareness of the social ensemble.

It seems, therefore, that the essential difference between a condition of solidarity and a condition of *anomie* in a modern society is the organising role of the state. Solidarity, in that case, is not about values but about organisation.

> In order for organic solidarity to exist, it is not sufficient that there be a system of mutually necessary organs, which experience their solidarity in a general way, but rather, it is necessary also that the way in which they co-operate, if not in every kind of encounter, at least for the most part, should be predetermined.[46]

It is clear that Durkheim does not identify the State in any sense with the collective conscience. He criticises Comte for suggesting that the cause of anomy is simply the loss of ground on the part of mechanical solidarity. Instead he says that part of the process of social progress is a kind of hiatus between the decline in strength of the collective conscience and the full realisation of the conditions for organic solidarity. It is possible, in this assertion, to see that Durkheim, whatever his views about the decline of the collective conscience, saw serious problems in the advent of a society in which the freedom of the individual would dominate. The organising role of the state takes on the mantle of the collective conscience.

Seigel comments that by the time Durkheim came to write *Professional*

---

[45] Ivana MATTEUCCI, "Sull' Epistemologia Sociologica di Durkheim: note intro duttive," *Studi Urbinati B*, 61 (1988): 465.

[46] Emile DURKHEIM, *Division*, 356.

Ethics he had opted for a kind of dualism, after the manner of Kantian ethics, which placed genuine personal autonomy in opposition to individual differences and placed individuals in a state of perpetual inner warfare between fulfilling individual desires and responding to discipline by means of which are fulfilled certain deeply rooted "social sentiments" and "collective aspirations."[47]

This tendency to invest society with the characteristics of the collective conscience is to be found also in *Sociologie et Philosophie*, in which Durkheim says that, in the final analysis, it is society that creates the individual and not the reverse.

> The man that we seek to be is the man of our times and of our milieu. Undoubtedly each of us in his own way lends colour to this common ideal, the mark of his own individuality, in the same may that each of us, in his own way, practices charity, justice, patriotism etc., But it has so little to do with individual construction, that it is in this ideal that all the members of the one group are in communion; it is this above all that gives rise to their moral unity.[48]

It is essential to the production of solidarity, in Durkheim's view, that people maintain a lively and continuous sense of their mutual dependence, but in some circumstances this is made difficult as society progresses and becomes more centralised. An example of this occurs when the producer becomes distanced from his market and less able to determine what the market requires. This is not, however, a necessary or permanent consequence of the division of labour, as far as Durkheim is concerned, but can be addressed by means of progress in organisation and the development of new structures for realistic contact. Durkheim stresses that it is not necessary for every organ of society to have an explicit understanding of the whole, but simply that they have a sense of participation in a single great work.[49]

Another possible cause of the failure of the division of labour to produce solidarity is that this division does not always reflect peoples aptitudes. This means that society must take care not to allow a situation to develop in which people are forced to undertake functions for which they are unsuited. In this Durkheim seems to reflect the reservations of Marx about the division of labour. He appears to contradict his own earlier

---

[47] Cf. Jerrold SEIGEL, ibid., 491/492.
[48] Emile DURKHEIM, *Sociologie et Philosophie*, (Paris: Alcan, 1924), 99.
[49] Cf. Emile DURKHEIM, *Division*, 363.

criticism of Spencer when he says that the division of labour only produces solidarity when it is spontaneous. "Conversely, one can say that the division of labour does not produce solidarity except if it is spontaneous and to the extent that it is spontaneous."[50] This apparent contradiction is resolved, however, when Durkheim explains that society must guarantee the conditions for the exercise of this spontaneity. Solidarity is promoted when the internal inequalities (i.e., inequality of aptitude) of people are allowed the freedom to determine social roles by means of society's removal of external inequalities (i.e., inequality of opportunity). Whereas primitive society needs religion to survive, Durkheim argues that modern society needs justice.[51]

Finally, the division of labour can produce abnormal results in cases in which the sense of mutual dependence is not expressed regularly or consistently. So unemployment and under-employment tend to reduce the level of solidarity, even where the progress of the division of labour is well advanced.[52]

In his concluding comments in *De La Division du Travail Social*, Durkheim maintains that the moral value of the division of labour is in its capacity to remind the individual constantly of his dependence on society. The division of labour is not simply the basis of the social order; it is also the basis of the moral order. He argues that there are two duties to be realised in advanced societies:

a. to concentrate and specialise our activity.

b. to realise in ourselves as fully as possible the collective type of the society.

He argues that these two duties are not in conflict because the possibilities of the society are developed to the extent that the members specialise. "We must limit our horizons, choose a definite task and commit ourselves completely to it, instead of making of our being a sort of work of art, finished and complete, all the value of which is in itself and not in the service which it gives."[53] At first sight this could be interpreted as promoting a dynamic rather than a static conception of the person in society. However, in the context, it must be understood as a prioritisation, on Durkheim's part, of acting over being.

---

[50] Emile DURKHEIM, *Division*, 370.
[51] Cf. Emile DURKHEIM, *Division*, 374.
[52] Cf. Emile DURKHEIM, *Division*, 387.
[53] Emile DURKHEIM, *Division*, 396.

The social function of the individual takes precedence in his theory over the ontological reality. He would seem to argue, in his closing comments, that the real benefit of the division of labour is a benefit to society and that the benefit to individuals is only a secondary effect. "The division of labour does not present us with individuals, but with social functions. Now society is interested in the interaction of these latter: according as they either act together in a regulated manner or not, it will be health or unhealthy."[54] This interpretation is borne out by Durkheim's explicit rejection of any value in the individual person which is not derived from society.

> Analyse the empirical structure of man, and you will find there nothing of the sacred character with which he is presently invested and from which his rights are derived. This character is added to him by society. It is society which has consecrated the individual; it is she who has established him as the thing to be respected par excellence. The progressive liberation of the individual does not imply a weakening, but rather a transformation of the social link.[55]

7. Critique of Durkheim's Theory of Solidarity

I would criticise Durkheim's theory of Solidarity on a number of grounds. The principal criticism is of the way in which he opposes mechanical and organic solidarity as if they were in conflict with each other. This problem is due, I believe, in no small measure, to his use of the biological analogy for social development, though even using this analogy he need not have come to this conclusion.

I find Durkheim's analogy of biology and sociology unsatisfactory for both internal and external reasons. To begin with, his discussion of lower forms of society in terms of primitive organisms seems to conflict with his earlier contrast between mechanical solidarity (in less organised societies) and organic solidarity (in more complex ones). It would seem more correct to say that both types of society, and therefore both types of solidarity, could be considered according to the organic analogy, but that one is more complex and the other simpler.

If we are to accept an evolutionary model for society, we must also accept the fact that as evolution progresses towards higher forms of life the laws of the lower forms do not become any less important. They simply become less evident. The laws of chemistry, biology, and sensitive

---

[54] Emile DURKHEIM, *Division*, 403.
[55] Emile DURKHEIM, *Sociologie et Philosophie*, 106.

psychology still apply to humans, but new laws of a higher kind must be developed to explain the kind of activity which is specific to rational animals.[56] So, I would argue, the collective aspect of relationship does not cease to be important to people as societies become more complex. It simply becomes obscured and more difficult to identify.

Durkheim's view that organic solidarity replaces rather than complements mechanical solidarity removes the personal element of human sociality from his understanding of social cohesion. This leaves us with a concept of solidarity in advanced societies which is little more than an awareness of the interdependence of functions. I would not accept Durkheim's explanation that organisational deficiency is responsible for the failure of the division of labour to produce solidarity because ultimately solidarity is a moral phenomenon and the division of labour is purely pragmatic.[57]

The fact that Durkheim's sharp distinction between the two social types does not work is evidenced by the need, which he clearly felt, to make organic solidarity carry the burden of moral values as well as that of social organisation. As Uricoechea remarks: "Despite this very clear distinction between the functions performed by the two solidarities, Durkheim transfers the notion of personal relationships from mechanical solidarity to organic solidarity."[58]

As Seigel notes, Durkheim reacted in his later writings against the individualism which can become rampant in a society in which the collective conscience has been weakened. He distinguished the material individualising factor of the individual person from the spiritual factor – that part of the individual in which society established its presence.[59] In his *Les Règles de la Méthode Sociologique*, he argues against Spencer and Comte that social progress or utility is not enough to ensure social cohesion. A cause, as distinct from simply an end, is needed.

> In order that a government be given the authority it needs, it is not sufficient that the need should be felt; it is necessary to refer to the sources from which alone all authority is derived, that is to say to build up traditions, a common spirit etc. In order for this to happen, it is necessary to go further back along the chain of

---

[56] Cf. Bernard LONERGAN, *Insight*, (London: Darton, Longman and Todd, 1983), 256.

[57] Cf. Emile DURKHEIM, *Division*, 28.

[58] Fernando URICOECHEA, ibid., 119.

[59] cf. Jerrold SEIGEL, ibid., 484ff.

cause and effect, until one finds the point at which man can act effectively.[60]

Elsewhere, he says that the believer bows before God because it is God whom he believes to be the cause of his being, especially his mental being or his soul. In the same way, the individual in the more advanced society experiences the same response in the presence of the collective.[61] In reality I think it is true to say that the members of the more complex society, as he envisaged it, do not belong to themselves any more completely than those of the less developed society.[62]

The second significant criticism of Durkheim's theory is that it effectively reduces social cohesion to a relationship of functions. By placing all the emphasis on the specialisation of each organ of society in its activity, Durkheim isolates the individual in his ontological reality and renders him, precisely as a person, irrelevant to society. The truth, on the contrary, is that the individual member of society can exercise a social function only to the extent that he first exists as an individual person. He is not constituted by his function; rather he functions by virtue of his constitution.

Here again, the biological analogy may be a contributory factor to the problem in that there is a danger of its being taken too far when it comes to explaining social phenomena. The way humans act, individually or in society, must conform to the laws of biology, but human freedom cannot adequately be explained using rules which, even if not biological, resemble closely the laws of biology.

Durkheim argues that the cause of the division of labour is not identical with its end. He deduces this from a more general observation, pointing out that the organ is independent of its function.

> It is, for that matter, a true proposition in sociology as in biology, that the organ is independent of its function, that is to say that, while remaining the same, it can serve different functions. It follows that the causes which make it to be are independent of the ends which it serves.[63]

It does not appear to have occurred to Durkheim that this principle also

---

[60] Emile DURKHEIM, *Les Règles de la Méthode Sociologique*, (Paris: Alcan, 1919), 112.

[61] Cf. Emile DURKHEIM, *Sociologie et Philosophie*, 108.

[62] Cf. Emile DURKHEIM, *Division*, 100.

[63] Emile DURKHEIM, *Division*, 113.

applies to the individual person in the sense that his whole meaning is not exhausted by the acts he does or the functions he fulfils.

Chapter Two
SCHELER AND MOUNIER:
TWO INFLUENCES ON KAROL WOJTYLA

The link between Max Scheler (1874-1928) and the thought of Karol Wojtyla is well attested in the writing of Wojtyla himself. In a footnote to his introduction to *The Acting Person*, Wojtyla indicates that he has given much thought to the work of M. Scheler, in particular his *Der Formalismus in der Ethik und die materiale Wertethik*. He mentions that Scheler's critique of Kant contained in that work "is of crucial significance for the present considerations."[1] The extent of Wojtyla's interest in Scheler is, however, further underpinned by his earlier critical work on the possibility of constructing a Christian ethic on the basis of the system of Max Scheler.[2] While Wojtyla concludes that Scheler's phenomenological method makes his system unsuitable to sustain a Christian ethic, his critique is sympathetic and he recognises much that is of value in Scheler's system, especially the definition of value as personal. Hebblethwaite argues that, while Wojtyla's philosophical approach is not over-influenced by either Husserl or Scheler, there are grounds for suggesting that it has much more in common with Scheler than with Husserl, whose strand of phenomenology was firmly rooted in rationalist idealism.[3]

Karol Wojtyla does not acknowledge the influence of Emmanuel Mounier in the way that he acknowledges that of Max Scheler or of St. Thomas. There is ample evidence, however, both historically and in the writings of Wojtyla, to make a case for this influence. A number of Polish authors, among them Tadeusz Mazowiecki,[4] and Pavel Latusek,[5] mention

---

[1] Karol WOJTYLA, *The Acting Person*, in *Analecta Husserliana*, The Yearbook of Phenomenological Research, Vol. X (Dordrecht: D. Reidel, 1979), 302.

[2] Cf. Karol WOJTYLA, *Valutazioni sulla Possibilità di Costruire L'Etica Cristiana, sulle Basi del Sisetma di Max Scheler* (Rome: Logos, 1980).

[3] Cf. Peter HEBBLETHWAITE, "Husserl, Scheler, and Wojtyla: A Tale of Three Philosophers," *Heythrop Journal*, 27 (1986): 441/2.

[4] Cf. Tadeusz MAZOWIECKI, "Sur le Personnalisme et le Dialogue," *Esprit*, February 1974: 245/6. Mazowiecki comments that the personalism of Mounier, without becoming any less Christian, transcended confessional positions and constituted an opening to human values; thus facilitating the dialogue with Marxism.

the influence of Mounier and the journal *Esprit* of which he was the editor, in Polish philosophical circles in the 1930's and 1940's. Janusz Zablocki's contribution is interesting in that it details Mounier's contacts with Poland in a way which makes it possible to situate the young Wojtyla clearly within the sphere of influence of Mounier. In the 1930's, towards the end of which Wojtyla was a philosophy student at the Jagellonian University "*Esprit* embraced above all, those circles of young Catholic intellectuals which already found themselves within the sphere of French thought, and especially that of Maritain."[6] Mounier's *Manifesto in the Service of Personalism* appeared in Polish in 1942, while Wojtyla was a participant in the underground Theological faculty, and "the problems found in this work corresponded to the interests of many various self-education and discussion groups which were connected with different underground circles."[7] In May 1946, when Wojtyla was once more a student at the University, Mounier "gave a lecture in the main hall of the Jagellonian University on the spiritual and ideological problems of contemporary France."[8]

Jean-Marie Benjamin describes Wojtyla as a former student of Mounier and of Maritain, though he does not specify in what context this was so.[9] According to George Williams "the personalism of which the faculty of philosophy at KUL was most aware was that identified with Maurice Blondel...and Emmanuel Mounier."[10]

The most detailed case for the influence of Mounier on Wojtyla, however, is made by Dario Munera-Velez. Munera-Velez argues that "a global comparative analysis makes it possible to say that the majority of the components or personal structures of Mounier are to be found in

    [5] Cf. Pavel LATUSEK, *Incontro Tra il Personalismo e il Marxismo in Polonia*, Ph. D dissertation, Rome: Pontifical Gregorian University, 198?, 44/45. Latusek mentions Mounier's resonance among certain representatives of the anthropological strand of Polish Marxism.

    [6] Janusz ZABLOCKI, "The Reception of the Personalism of Mounier in Poland," *Dialectics and Humanism*, 5 (1978): 148; cf. also Mary CRAIG, Man from a Far Country (London: Hodder and Stoughton, 1979), 40.

    [7] Janusz ZABLOCKI, ibid., 149; cf. also Mary CRAIG, ibid., 52.

    [8] Janusz ZABLOCKI, ibid., 151; cf. also Mary CRAIG, ibid., 55-7.

    [9] Cf. Jean-Marie BENJAMIN, Jean Paul II: *L'Octobre Romain*, Paris: Editions France-Empire, 1979, 203.

    [10] George H. WILLIAMS, *The Mind of John Paul II: Origins of His Thought and Action*, New York: Seabury, 1981, 147.

Wojtyla."[11] Particularly interesting is the distinction that Munera-Velez makes between the narrower and the broader ways in which personalism can be understood.

> In the strict sense personalism is a philosophical approach which fixes its centre in the person. Its point of departure is the original metaphysical intuition of the person which is developed, explained, and situated in the plurality of concrete experiences, by phenomenological, existential, and historical analyses.[12]

The personalism of Mounier would be associated with this stricter understanding, while that of Maritain would be associated with the broader definition of personalism. Munera-Velez sees Wojtyla as belonging more to the tradition associated with Mounier than to that associated with Maritain.

> It is one thing to deduce behaviour from the arguments of a classical ontology, as Maritain did, and another to develop it in an original way from a lived personalist experience as did Mounier, and as subsequently Wojtyla did with his characteristic phenomenological method, integrating with it the personalist elements of Thomism.[13]

A. SCHELER'S PRINCIPLE OF SOLIDARITY

The Principle of Solidarity is a recurrent theme in the writing of Max Scheler. Simply expressed, it holds that persons are essentially social, and that all morally relevant personal acts have an essentially collective or communal dimension.

> The structure of social acts is such that in performing or in abstaining from performing them I assume a responsibility which cannot be limited to my own person and which necessarily extends to the presence or absence of reactions in

---

[11] Dario MUNERA-VELEZ, *Personalism Etico de Participacion de Karol Wojtyla* (Medellin: Universidad Pontificia Bolivariana, 1988), 112. Among the common elements identified by Muner-Velez in Mounier and Wojtyla are "the re-discovery of lost subjectivity," cf. ibid., 126; the emphasis on integration with the primacy given to subjectivity, cf. ibid., 127; the concept of the realisation of personal freedom through participation with others, cf. ibid., 127/8; the close correspondence between Mounier's notion of communication, and Wojtyla's concept of action, cf. ibid., 129; and the shared ideal of the "community in its historical form, in which the person arrives at his definitive realisation," cf. ibid., 130.

[12] Dario MUNERA-VELEZ, ibid., 114.

[13] Dario MUNERA-VELEZ, ibid., 115.

others corresponding to my attitude towards them: that is the simplest statement
of the principle of moral solidarity.[14]

Scheler maintains that the kind of solidarity that is possible is determined by the nature of the social grouping. This in turn is dependent on the
individual human beings who make up the social grouping, and the values
which they have in common. As a result, any study of Scheler's concept of
solidarity necessarily involves some consideration of his theories of man,
of values, of sympathy, and of social groups. According to Rainer Ibana,
"Scheler is perhaps the most important philosopher to have pondered the
principle of solidarity."[15]

1. Scheler's Theory of Person and Act

Scheler belongs to the phenomenological tradition and the method of
phenomenology significantly influences his theory of man. He distinguishes between events and functions on the one hand, and acts on the
other. Acts are strictly personal and have meaning. They can never be
objects of knowledge as functions or events can. This, however, does not
prevent us from having access to them phenomenologically. Acts can be
known in, and only in, their performance.

An act is a series of events, forming a unity, which has a particular
meaning. Since the essence of an act includes the meaning which it has,
and not only the events which it unites, an act can only be *given* in its
execution. Spader explains:

> You do not see such unity, such meaning, simply by blankly staring at the events.
> You see it by acting, by co-performing or post-performing an act unifying all
> these events in this one way.[16]

Scheler makes a parallel distinction between human beings and
persons. A human being performs functions and, like the functions he
performs, he can be an object of knowledge. A person, on the other hand,

---

[14] Maurice DUPUY, *La Philosophie de Max Scheler: Son Evolution et son Unité*, in
two volumes, (Paris: Presses Universitaires de France, 1959), 554.

[15] Rainer R.A. "The Essential Elements for the Possibility and Necessity of the
Principle of Solidarity according to Max Scheler," *Philosophy Today*, 33 (1989), No. 1/4:
42.

[16] Peter A. SPADER, " Person, Acts and Meaning: Max Scheler's Insight," *The New
Scholasticism*, 59 (1985): 207.

is an essential unity of acts, and as such cannot ever become an object of knowledge. Just as the acts can only be given in their performance, so also persons can only be known in their performance of acts.

> Persons, as the unifiers of acts which are themselves unifiers of objects, are, indeed, the most elusive of phenomena. This is not because we do not have access to them, but because it is so easy to mistake what is the person.[17]

In order to understand better what the person is, for Scheler, it is necessary now to examine his distinction between *life* and *spirit*. *Life* refers to the whole range of elements to be found in human beings, which they have in common with other types of living creatures.[18]

Spirit, however, is a uniquely human phenomenon, which completely transcends the competence of biology and psychology. It gives to man alone the power of objectifying the real environmental world, and of reflectively considering his own vital functions as objects of knowledge and of strictly scientific investigation. Ranly explains that

> only with the phenomenon of spirit do we reach the level that is distinctively and essentially human. With the presence of spirit in man, man has a most special place in nature, for spirit is evidence of a being that is essentially distinct from all forms of life.[19]

Spirit transcends *life* and this means that, for Scheler, the person in some sense transcends the man. However Scheler tries to avoid any kind of radical dualism, arguing that man experiences himself as one being, in which both the pull of the vital drives and the activity of the spirit are experienced.[20]

Scheler presents the image of the All-man (*Allmensch*) as the perfect model of humanity. He is the one who has achieved an adjustment in himself in the relation between *life* and *spirit*. Adjustment involves the inter-penetration of *spirit* and *life*. The difficulty, is that Scheler's concept of *spirit* is ambiguous. Sometimes it seems that it is a component in the substantial sense of the word. Elsewhere, it seems to have a more ethereal

---

[17] ibid., 211.

[18] Cf. Ernest W. RANLY, *Scheler's Phenomenology of Community*, (The Hague: Martinus Nijhoff, 1966), 20-21. These elements include a basic inner drive towards growth, reproduction and death; instincts and habits; and practical intelligence.

[19] Ernest W. RANLY, ibid., 22.

[20] Cf. Ernest W. RANLY, ibid., 34.

quality.

> He says that spirit is in the end essentially and solely a matter of the performance
> of spiritual acts ... Such acts are not to be thought of as carried out by a substance,
> by a part of man, or a more important part alongside other parts.[21]

Dunlop argues that, for its completion, Scheler's *adjustment* requires the performance of spiritual acts and that this "points inexorably ... to a spiritual principle in man which is already there and cannot simply be interpreted in terms of acts, but in something like substantial terms."[22] He notes that this seems to be contradicted elsewhere by Scheler. In fact, when he talks about the inter-penetration of *spirit* and *life*, Scheler is speaking of a spiritualisation of the Vital and a vitalisation of the Spirit, rather than of any mingling of two substances.[23]

Personal acts are the realm of the *Spirit* but the person can never be reduced to a "mere point of departure of acts" or to "a network of acts" as if he were no more than what he did.[24] This would suggest that, for Scheler, the person is more than just a collection of acts; indeed that it must be a separate entity in the way that a thing is. But here we come up against a quirk in Scheler's phenomenological method. We cannot know persons objectively, but only as they are given in their acts. Scheler argues:

> Surely the person is and experiences himself only as a being that executes acts,
> and he is in no sense "behind" or "above" acts, or something standing "above"
> the execution and processes of acts, like a point at rest.[25]

The upshot of all this is that, as far as Scheler is concerned, man is one, but it is only the vital element that is real and substantial. The person is

---

[21] Francis N. DUNLOP, "Scheler's Idea of Man: Phenomenology versus Metaphysics in the Late Works," *Aletheia*, 2 (1981): 221/2. Dunlop goes on to explain that adjustment involves the complementary processes of sublimation and re-sublimation which guarantee the correct balance of the spiritual and the vital in the ideal person. There is a tendency in Western culture to over-intellectualise things and to underestimate the value of hunches and instincts; cf. ibid., 225.

[22] Francis N. DUNLOP, ibid., 225.

[23] Cf. Francis N. DUNLOP, ibid., 227.

[24] Max SCHELER, *Formalism in Ethics and the Non-Formal Ethics of Values*, translated by Manfred Fring and Roger L. Funk, (Evanston: Northwestern University Press, 1973), 384. (Hereafter referred to as *Formalism*).

[25] Max SCHELER, *Formalism*, 393/4.

spiritual but not substantial. In this sense *man* and *person* are not synonymous. When it comes to resolving the problem of the unity of man, Scheler denies that there is any substantial bond of unity between *spirit* and *life*.

> Spirit is dependent upon and embedded in the lower life processes. But the type of unity between an individualised spirit (person) and its concrete centre of life activities is merely an experienced unity of dynamic relations.[26]

Any attempt to substantialise the person is not only false, but also unnecessary. There is no need to posit a substance to protect the integrity of the person. There are a number of reasons for this:

a. the whole person as a unity of acts is contained in every fully concrete act.

b. the person varies in and through every concrete act, because each concrete act is a unique correlation of abstract acts.

c. as the unity of these acts, the person is not exhausted in any of them.

d. since acts are non-durational, there is no question of the person, as the unity of acts, changing like a thing in time.[27]

However, to say that persons are non-substantial is not to say that they lack concreteness. "Scheler insists that persons are always concrete beings. They are always concrete because a person is a combination of more than one act of a different essence ... into a concrete essence."[28] In the final analysis, we can only gain access to Scheler's concept of person through the phenomenological method which he uses. This method admits the objective reality of the man and the events of his life, but allows only the serial experience of the person and his spiritual acts. We can say that every human person *is* a human being, but not every human being *experiences* himself or other human beings as persons.

2. Scheler's Theory of Value

For Immanuel Kant, value was non-material and the whole of ethics was rooted in the notion of duty. Scheler holds that Kant, by ignoring material (or non-formal) values, rendered his ethics purely subjective. In keeping with his phenomenological approach, Scheler sees value not as

---

[26] Ernest W. RANLY, ibid., 47.
[27] Cf. Peter A. SPADER, ibid., 210.
[28] Peter A. SPADER, ibid., 209.

some substance that is in itself good, but rather as a distinct quality borne by a thing. At the same time, the concept of value is not totally unrelated to that of being.

> A world of values would lose all of its meaning if it were, so to speak, radically cut off from being. In the final analysis every definition of value ... necessarily entails both a consciousness capable of living the value, or echoing it, and a reality which is susceptible of being modified as a result of the value. In brief, value has an intrinsic dependence with respect to being, which being does not have with respect to value.[29]

The fact that values hold or "obtain" and are not of the order of simple being does not make them any less objective, according to Scheler. Unlike feelings of pleasure or displeasure, they are established through the mediation of intelligence, rather than being directly related to sensations and perceptions, memories and images. That values are different from feelings of pleasure is also clear from the fact that it is possible for feelings of pleasure to be accompanied by strong negative feelings of value. Finally, what makes feelings of value normative is the fact that they are referred to objective values.[30]

Scheler distinguishes four levels on which it is possible to experience goodness; thus four levels of material values. Beginning with the lowest order of values, they are:

a. sensible (objects of pleasure, pain and utility),

b. life (the noble and the mean, strength and quality),

c. cultural (the beautiful, the ugly, the legal and the illegal, and true knowledge),

d. religious (beatitude, despair, feelings of holiness and unholiness).

The lower values would be those most readily identified with the vital drive in man, whereas the higher ones would be identified with the *spirit*. These four categories are distinguished by Scheler as a result of an investigation in which he applies five criteria.

> It appears that values are "higher" the more they endure and the less they partake in "extension" and "divisibility" . They are higher the less they are "founded" through other values and the "deeper" the "satisfaction" connected with feeling them. Moreover they are higher the less the feeling of them is relative to the

---

[29] Maurice DUPUY, ibid., 34/5.
[30] Cf. Maurice DUPUY, ibid., 38-41.

positing of a specific bearer of "feeling" and "preferring"[31]

Material values themselves are not in the realm of morality. For Scheler, moral value consists in the realisation of a material value. The absence of a good is in itself an evil. The important thing, as far as Scheler is concerned is

> that man must reunite himself in an intrinsic living way with the lower powers of life and of nature itself. The vital values are the lowest in the scale of values, but they are the most powerful, the most real. Man would undermine his own being if he cultivated only the spiritual and intellectual powers at the expense of the lower, vitalistic, emotional nature.[32]

Because it necessarily involves choice, moral value is always personal. What is interesting from the point of view of this study is why people choose to realise or not to realise certain values. According to Scheler, there is an objective world of values, but there is also, parallel to it a subjective system of eternal laws of axiological preference. This would seem to be some kind of "natural law." The problem is that the evidence of this inner preference can be masked from the conscience by factors which go beyond and perhaps even exclude the responsibility of the individual. When this happens, the person may live according to a consistent order of values as he experiences them, but an order which, as far as the absolute hierarchy of values is concerned, is perverse.[33]

Dunlop says that it was because of his belief that values are transmitted through human relationships, that Scheler introduced the concept of the *Allmensch*, to serve as a model value-type for the younger generation in the inter-war period.[34] Thus, for Scheler, human relatedness is crucial to morality. It can never be a purely individual thing, but must always have an interpersonal dimension. A major difficulty arises with regard to what exactly motivates the realisation of material values, out of which moral value is born. For Scheler, value, and this includes moral value, is grasped only on the level of experience. This is an outcome of the phenomenological method, which focuses on phenomena rather than on making judgements about the reality of things.

---

[31] Max SCHELER, *Formalism*, 90.
[32] Ernest W. RANLY, ibid., 81/2.
[33] Cf. Maurice DUPUY, ibid., 42.
[34] Cf. Francis, N. DUNLOP, ibid., 220/1.

Wojtyla argues that Scheler's system does not allow moral value itself to be the object of human action. In Scheler's own terms, this would constitute a kind of Pharisaism, because it would amount to desiring the experience of one's own goodness. One may only take material values as one's object.[35]

This distancing of moral value from material value, while it is not a denial on the part of Scheler that moral good comes from the doing of certain actions, does create difficulties when it comes to affirming the primacy of the person among the values to be realised. In this vision of things, morality is removed from the sphere of human efficacy, because the causal link between moral value and free human action is not established.[36] The person chooses to be good at this or that, but does not specifically choose to be a good person.

Scheler maintains that morality is personal, but if it is, then one of its essential elements must be the free act of the will which characterises the human person. Since this cannot be affirmed, the personal character of Scheler's moral theory would seem to be at least called into question. Wojtyla says: "I define moral value in the generic sense...as that through which the human being as human being becomes and is good or evil."[37] Further on he clarifies the essential link between moral value and the goodness of the person.

> To say that moral value – good or evil – is that which makes the human being good or evil as a human being, that through which the human being becomes good or evil, is, in a sense, to reduce moral value to humanity. The human being as a human being is good or evil solely and exclusively through moral value. No other value accounts for this. Other values only account for a human being's becoming or being good in one respect or another."[38]

---

[35] Cf. Karol WOJTYLA, *Valutazioni sulla Possibilità di Costruire l'Etica Cristiana Sulle Base del Sistema di Max Scheler*, (Rome: Logos, 1980), 131. (Hereafter referred to as *Valutazioni*)

[36] Cf. Karol WOJTYLA, *Valutazioni*, 131.

[37] Karol WOJTYLA, "The Problem of the Theory of Morality," in *Person and Community: selected essays*, Catholic Thought from Lublin, 4, translated by Theresa Sandok OSM (New York: Peter Lang, 1993), 143.

[38] ibid., 145.

3. Sympathy

It is possible to know human beings in an objective way, but we can only have access to persons as such, and their acts, in the co-performance of acts. Participation in the spiritual acts of another person is not knowledge; it is a matter of co-performance of, re-living and re-executing the acts of the other. It is about willing-with, feeling-with etc. It is through the act of sympathy that this participation is possible.

Before examining the nature of true sympathy, as Scheler understands it, it will be helpful to note the kinds of experience which he excludes from the definition of sympathy, properly speaking. To begin with, Scheler rejects any theory of sympathy which is merely empirical, or which accepts the body of the individual as the initial datum. He argues that we perceive the inner emotional states of the other directly, and not by any mediate act of analogy and inference. For the same reason, i.e., that sympathy can only be between persons, any form of participation in the emotional states of characters in books or films is not true sympathy.[39]

Scheler is equally critical of many metaphysical theories of sympathy, on the grounds that they are monistic. Some of these theories tend towards egoism and emphasise how a particular situation would feel for me, without any real going out to the other. The egoistic type of sympathy is on the level of *spirit*. By contrast with this, there is another type of pseudo-sympathy which Scheler calls *emotional identification*, in which one loses sight of oneself in the other. *Emotional identification* occurs on the level of some vital impulse. At an even more basic level, *emotional contagion*, such as when a number of people start to giggle or scream without any understanding of the emotion involved, is not a true act of sympathy.[40]

> Scheler rejected all forms of monism by insisting that authentic fellow-feeling necessarily entailed a 'distance' between individuals and an explicit awareness of this separateness .... Full phenomenological investigation discovers ample evidence for the unique individuality of the other, and for a realm of his absolute privacy, without destroying the intrinsic teleological relationship of mutual, social communication between ourselves and him.[41]

According to Kelly, phenomenological reflection reveals four essential characteristics of the true act of sympathy.

---

[39] Cf. Ernest W. RANLY, ibid., 41/2.
[40] Cf. Ernest W. RANLY, ibid., 43/44.
[41] Ernest W. RANLY, ibid., 45/46.

a. Pain is given to me as the pain of another person before I can perform the act of sympathy.

b. The otherness of the person is maintained in the act.

c. As a result, the emotional acts of the person with whom one sympathises ...are understood and possibly re-lived or re-performed by the sympathising person.

d. The act of sympathising with the emotion of another person is a cognitive act, whose material is given in the emotion of sympathy in which ... what is intended is not one's own feeling states, but the feeling states of another person.[42]

True sympathy is the act by which one person most perfectly and immediately enters into the emotional states of another. For Scheler, most of the theories of sympathy which he rejects are based on two erroneous pre-suppositions. The first is that it is one's own ego that is first given in experience. This is erroneous because

> what is immediately given in the human experience is a stream of conscious experiences at first undifferentiated between I and Thou. What is first experienced is the general experience of the "we" . It is in this sense that children and primitives at first tend to identify themselves with others. Only as a late phenomenon can they isolate themselves and identify their own Selves as individuals separate from the rest of the family community.[43]

It is in this context that Scheler develops his famous example of a Robinson Crusoe type of individual who finds himself alone on a desert island.[44] According to Scheler, even though Crusoe is living alone, there is an unmistakable emptiness or lack of fulfilment in his awareness which leads him to intuit the essence of community. To this extent he is immediately a social being. While insisting that all knowledge is derived from experience, Scheler argues that not all experience is factual (i.e., merely empirical). There is also the experience of emotional states. For this reason "intuition into an essence is possible, even when beginning from an empty experience ... an ever present element of man's consciousness is a

---

[42] Cf. Eugene KELLY, *Max Scheler*, (Boston: Twayne, 1977), 127/8.

[43] Ernest W. RANLY, ibid., 58.

[44] Cf. Max SCHELER, *The Nature of Sympathy*, London: Routledge and Kegan, 1954, 234/5, (Hereafter referred to as *Sympathy*); also Max SCHELER, *Formalism*, 521, where he uses the Crusoe image with specific reference to the principle of Solidarity.

reference to community."[45]

The second pre-supposition about sympathy which Scheler rejects is that the body of the other is the first datum in our experience of others. Obviously, as Ranly says:

The body-perception of the other is the condition under which our inner perception takes place, but neither my body nor the other's perceived body actually controls the total extent of the experience itself.[46]

Scheler's description of the fact and the manner of active participation between persons is a key doctrine in his ethics, with particular reference to man's relationship with others in person-community, and also in describing man's relationship to God. According to Ranly, the theory of sympathy "remains one of Scheler's most important contributions to contemporary thought."[47]

4. The Social Group Types and their Relatedness

The kind of social group that exists depends on the nature of the relationship that exists between the individuals who make up the group. Scheler identifies four essential social units which correspond to four types of human relationship, the degrees of sympathy and pseudo-sympathy. These four social types "are never purely and fully realised in factual experience,"[48] but they do function as the conditions of such experience. What is found in terms of priority-values in the individual soul can also be found in the corresponding social groups.[49]

a. The Mass. The first of the social group-types identified by Scheler is the *masse* (*mass*). In this kind of group the individuals are de-personalised, like a herd. It is a vital group-type and, because the individual does not exist at all as an experience, there is no solidarity in the group in the

---

[45] Ernest W. RANLY, ibid., 55. cf. also Max SCHELER, *Formalism,* 279. Scheler disagrees with the view of Spencer that man begins with individual egoism. He argues, rather, that egoism is a result of some early disappointment in community.
[46] Ernest W. RANLY, ibid., 59.
[47] Ernest W. RANLY, ibid., 54.
[48] Max SCHELER, *Formalism,* 526.
[49] Cf. Rainer R.A. IBANA, ibid., 43.

proper sense of the word.[50] All that is involved is involuntary imitation, devoid of understanding. What Scheler calls *psychic contagion*, substitutes for genuine solidarity in the social group of the mass. "No one can claim responsibility for the acts performed by these groups, because the events that they bring about are not willed, nor previously anticipated by anyone."[51]

b. The Life Community. In a *lebensgemeinschaft (life community)* the individual becomes aware of his experiences as his, but there is still a long way to go before they become personal experiences, because "there is no will which can be called purposeful which is able to choose, which is unitary and morally responsible, all of which would belong to a person."[52] The sympathetic-type response in the *life-community* is what Scheler calls *emotional identification.* Within the bounds of the various tasks or roles which are defined within the *life-community* one individual can easily be substituted for by another.

The solidarity found at this social level is called *representable* because each individual member of life-communities can represent any other member of the group. On this level however, the human being is still only a member and not a mature person. The *life community* is not much of an advance on the *mass* because the individual members of *life communities* are still immersed in the community's acts which hover among the individual members, like a stream of experience.   There are, however, stronger social bonds in the *life-community.*

> Their members are united by traditions, customs, and mores. Their shared experiences, feelings, and thoughts provide the context for the members of life-communities to aim for higher levels of values that transcend their individual levels of pleasure and pain.[53]

c. The Society. The social group which Scheler calls *gesellschaft (society)* is characterised, not by customs and mores, but by "autonomy,

---

[50] Cf. Max SCHELER, *Formalism,* 527.

[51] Rainer R. A. IBANA, ibid., 44.

[52] Max SCHELER, *Formalism,* 528.

[53] Rainer R. A. IBANA, ibid., 44. Taken together, Scheler's *mass* and *life-community* are quite similar to Durkheim's description of the primitive social group which gives rise to mechanical solidarity. Scheler's view of the life-community is, however, much more positive than Durkheim's view of the primitive social group.

equality and self-interest."[54] While the term *solidarity by interest* is sometimes used to describe the relationship between individuals in *society*, it is
not particularly accurate, because societal individuals relate on the basis of
clearly defined parameters rather than on the basis of co-feeling and co-
loving. Individuals "forge contracts and exchange commodities, in order
to maximise their own rationally calculated gains."[55] All that is required is
the capacity to make and keep agreements, and to have self-oriented needs
and desires. As Scheler says:

> All responsibility for others is based on unilateral self-responsibility, and all
> possible responsibility for others must be regarded as having come from a free
> and singular act of taking over certain obligations. There is no true solidarity (in
> some form of one-for-all and all-for-one) ... but only the similarity or dissi-
> milarity of individual's interests and the classes resulting from such interests.[56]

Scheler is quite critical of *society* which, he says, is far from being a
more general reality containing all communities. Rather, it is the detritus
or residue left over after the disintegration of every community. "Society,
the unity founded on contract, only appears when the vital unity of the
community is no longer capable of making itself respected." One of the
difficulties of *society* is the tendency to disagreement and lack of
consensus, and the risk of dependence on the use of force.[57]

Vacek explains that, while Scheler originally took a negative view of
society, this view was moderated over time. He criticised the Enlightenment for denigrating the values of the *life-community*, while at the same
time rejecting any reactionary Romanticism which disparaged the values
of *society*. For Scheler:

> Societies are permanently important because it is through societies that the
> human being first becomes free, mature, self-conscious and capable of an
> individual existence. It is here first that he lifts his head out of the stream of the

---

[54] E. VACEK, " Contemporary Ethics and Scheler's Phenomenology of Community,"
Philosophy Today, 35 (1991): 163.

[55] Rainer R.A. IBANA, ibid., 44.

[56] Max SCHELER, *Formalism,* 529.

[57] Cf. Rainer R.A. IBANA, ibid., 45; cf. also Max SCHELER, *Ressentiment,* 120/1.
The mistrust proper to mere society is, according to Scheler a characteristic of
contemporary morality. "This mistrust, so close to resentment, has contributed to the
formation of modern moral individualism, and the devaluation of the principle of
solidarity."

life-community.[58]

Society never succeeds in leaving behind entirely the social relationship of the *life-community*. While there can be *life-community* without *society*, the reverse is not the case. "All possible society is therefore founded through community."[59] In this sense the individual members of a society remain members of a community, and this community membership to some extent underlies their societal relationship. So, Scheler says:

> The duty to keep mutual promises that are in a contract, the basic form of the formation of a uniform will in society, does not have its source in another contract to keep contracts. It has its source in the solidary obligation of the members of the community to realise the contents that ought to be for the members.[60]

5. Person-Community and the Principle of Solidarity

According to Scheler, the principle of Solidarity rests on two central propositions, one of which makes it possible and the other of which makes it necessary. These two propositions form the basis for understanding the difference between the highest form of solidarity and any other form of social relatedness, so it is worth quoting Scheler at length. He says of the principle of Solidarity:

> Ultimately it rests on two propositions. The first is that a community of persons belongs to the evidential essence of a possible person ... and that the possible unities of sense and of value of such a community possess an a priori structure independent in principle of the kind, measure, place and time of the realisation of these unities. This is the foundation that makes moral solidarity possible. What makes moral solidarity necessary is the formal proposition concerning the (direct or indirect) essential reciprocity and reciprocal valueness of all morally relevant comportment and the corresponding non-formal propositions concerning the essential nexus of the basic types of social acts.[61]

a. The Possibility of Solidarity. As Ranly points out, there is some ambiguity in Scheler's use of terms such as *community, collective person* (*gesamtperson*), and *solidarity*.[62] Each of the social group types in its own

---

[58] E. VACEK, ibid., 163.

[59] Max SCHELER, *Formalism*, 531.

[60] ibid.

[61] Max SCHELER, *Formalism*, 535.

[62] Cf. Ernest W. RANLY, ibid., 70.

way reflects the values of the individuals who make it up, and their particular manner of relatedness. To that extent, the *life-community* is a collective expression of its members, just as the *society* is a collective expression of its adherents. Only the *person-community*, however, "fulfils the original definition of community and moral person."[63] Scheler, in fact, uses the term *collective person* as a synonym for *person-community*. This is the social group in which the most perfect form of solidarity is to be found.

It is important to be clear at the outset that, for Scheler, the *person-community* is not simply a community made up of persons, in which the whole is no more than the sum of the parts. The community is seen as fulfilling all the requirements of Scheler's definition of person as "a unity of all spiritual acts directed to a world in and for itself, including the entire range of values,"[64] and is given as a *collective person* with a being of its own.[65] Furthermore, the meaning and value of a community of persons has an a priori structure i.e., it is not dependent on location or size or even on the period of history in which it is realised.

The relatedness between the members of the *person-community* is a unique kind of solidarity which Scheler calls *unrepresentable solidarity*. By contrast with the solidarity of the life-community, this *unrepresentable solidarity* means that no one individual can represent another in taking responsibility for the community and for the other members.[66]

Corresponding to the highest level of values, Scheler identifies, as proper to the *person-community*, the highest form of love "which is a strictly moral love between persons. Personal love, a sense of moral solidarity and the knowledge of common salvation is the bond of unity in the *person-community*."[67]

Scheler's concept of unrepresentable solidarity, like his concept of personal love can be understood in different ways. As well as being a moral

---

[63] Ernest W. RANLY, ibid.

[64] E. VACEK, ibid., 166.

[65] Cf. Max SCHELER, *Ressentiment*, 139/40. Scheler argues that the Principle of Solidarity is contrary to what he describes as the Principle of Addition or Democratism. The latter "rejects the idea of a solidarity between the parts of humanity in virtue of which the fate of each member would have a repercussion on the whole." Solidarity is a completely different way of looking at community and, in a solidaristic relationship, "the individual feels and knows the community as something which penetrates him."

[66] Cf. Maurice DUPUY, ibid., 551/2.

[67] Ernest W. RANLY, ibid., 88.

concept it also has religious meaning. Even outside of any other social relationship the person can enter into relationship with God who "by definition is neither an individual nor a collective person, but one in whom both individuals and collective persons are solidary."[68]

b. The Necessity of the Principle of Solidarity. The members of the *person-community* relate to each other on the basis of transcendence, co-responsibility, and irreducibility. Social acts are inter-linked and moral acts affect the community of persons surrounding the acting person. "These effects and counter effects of human acts in the moral universe are what Scheler means by *essential reciprocity and reciprocal valueness of all morally relevant comportment*."[69] Persons transcend themselves by participating in the spiritual acts of the other members of the community. While there is relatedness at the level of other social groups, it is only at the strictly spiritual level that this transcendence of the person can be realised in any true sense.[70]

Co-responsibility goes hand in hand with the co-performance of acts. A favourite formula which Scheler uses to express this co-responsibility is "one for all and all for one."[71] He expands on this as follows:

> In the life community the bearer of all responsibility is the reality of the community, and the individual is co-responsible for the life-community; in the collective person every individual and the collective person are self-responsible ... and at the same time every individual is also co-responsible for the collective person (and for every individual 'in' it) just as the collective person is co-responsible for each of its members.[72]

At the level of the *person-community*, the reciprocal valueness of morally relevant behaviour has its roots in the fact that the spiritual acts performed call forth a response which is immediately to a person and not simply to a consequence or to a set of circumstances. If our acts of love, esteem, etc. were conditional on being loved and esteemed, this would be a false solidarity. It would be just another contractual arrangement such as

---

[68] Max SCHELER, *Formalism*, 563.

[69] Rainer R.A. IBANA, ibid., 48.

[70] Cf. Ernest W. RANLY, ibid., 70.

[71] Cf. Max SCHELER, *Ressentiment*, 120; also *Formalism*, 529.

[72] Max SCHELER, *Formalism*, 533/4. The ontological relationship between the persons on the person-community is what Scheler calls "connection in solidarity;" cf. also Rainer R.A. IBANA, ibid., 46.

we find in a *society*.[73]

A significant aspect of Scheler's concept of co-responsibility are the notions of collective guilt and collective merit. Writing in the aftermath of the 1914-18 war, Scheler uses the image of the people of Israel worshipping a golden calf to convey the sense of collective guilt for the destructiveness of war.

> From its sunbathed peak, you may look down into the maelstrom of Europe's common guilt, as into a valley of fearfulness, of sin and tears! Look down upon it as Moses saw the Jews dancing around the Golden Calf when, drunk with God, he strode quietly down the hillside; look down from your summit of conscience, still bathed in the splendour of your humble prayers, and see how Europe dances round its stupid ludicrous idols. Only one who does not dance in the depth of his soul, but who yet knows that his body is swayed by the rhythm, can discern the dance.[74]

Scheler is adamant that an acceptance of "collective guilt for the late war as an instance unique in history" can only become possible through "the religious moral principle of general Solidarity which western Europe has torn to shreds."[75]

The War is but an example. Collective guilt is an essential element of the *person-community* both as a moral concept and a religious attitude. Humanity rises or falls as a "morally compact mass" through the validity of the principle of solidarity.[76] Scheler says that the

> third great principle of ethics and religion is the principle of moral solidarity (or religious moral reciprocity). It means ... that we should feel ourselves truly co-responsible in all guilt. It means therefore that from the very beginning – even where the magnitude or extent of our actual participation are not clearly in view before our mind's eye – we must answer to the living God for all rise and fall in the moral and religious condition of the collective whole of the moral world, which is an intrinsically solidary unit.[77]

---

[73] Cf. Max SCHELER, *Formalism*, 534.

[74] Max SCHELER, *Eternal*, 125.

[75] ibid.

[76] ibid.; cf. also Max SCHELER, *Formalism*, 534.

[77] Max SCHELER, *Eternal*, 377. Scheler also speaks of co-responsibility in specifically religious terms. He talks of solidary responsibility for our faults and participation in the merits of the saints, and argues that the principle of moral solidarity "suggests a mysterious capitalisation of moral values in a Kingdom of God in which all men can participate," cf. *Ressentiment*, 119/20.

The irreducibility of the person is another aspect of co-responsibility. The very transcendence of human nature makes it impossible to find any basis of comparison between persons. On this spiritual level there is no "lowest common denominator." Moral solidarity is not, therefore, a statement of the equality of persons. The dignity and the absolute uniqueness of the other as person goes far beyond the notion of equality.[78] This is a reflection of the way in which values of the higher order, unlike those of the lower orders, although incapable of equal division, can be shared at a level which is beyond comparison. Ibana concludes that "the social structure of the highest form of solidarity can be fully understood only within the context of Scheler's ethical theory of an order of higher and lower ranks of values."[79]

6. Solidarity and Subordination

There is a further proposition which, according to Scheler, "confers on the Principle of Solidarity the complete fullness of its extension." This is the proposition that "there is no act whose execution does not change the content of the person's being and no act-value that does not increase or decrease, enhance or diminish, or positively or negatively determine the value of the person."[80] Scheler seems to make an analogy between this subordination of all personal acts to the meaning and value of the person, and the subordination of the lower social forms to the higher form of the *collective person.*

> Life community and society as essential forms of social unity are subordinated to this highest essential social form. They are determined to serve it and to make it appear but, to be sure, in their different manners. Although the highest form of social unity is not a synthesis of life community and society, essential characteristics of both are nevertheless co-given in it: the independent individual person, as in society; and solidarity and real collective unity, as in community.[81]

However, as Ibana points out, subordination is not to be taken to imply

---

[78] Cf. Max SCHELER, *Ressentiment,* 121/2. Scheler argues that the insistence that all men are equal is simply the expression of how much society resents those who are the bearers of higher values and seeks to cut them down to size. Such resentment does not belong in the person-community in which each person is valued as unique and irreplaceable.

[79] Rainer R.A. IBANA, ibid., 45/6.

[80] Max SCHELER, *Formalism,* 537.

[81] ibid.

destruction. It is a concept akin to subsidiarity.

> The solidaristic meaning of subordination precisely includes the preservation of the lower forms of social unities under the government of higher forms. The subordination of the lower forms of social unities under higher forms is precisely the guarantee for the existence of the lower forms.[82]

In the *person-community*, the values of the *life community* and the *society* are held in tension. The unity of the *person-community* is not a matter of territory, tradition or descent, but of its spiritual acts. "The unity of these acts means that a personal community exhibits the life-community's characteristic solidarity, and the spirituality of these acts means that it exhibits society's characteristic personhood."[83] By contrast, if one of the lower forms become the norm of social relatedness, the result is either the dominance of individualism or the repression of the individual. The key to solidarity as a principle of government is the voluntary service of the higher by the lower. None of the lower forms of social unity is capable of incorporating the others, precisely because none of them is the whole.[84]

Every social group has its ethos; its own values-to-be-realised, and this is no less true of the *collective person*, which has its own historically developing way of looking at and valuing world, spirit, and life. This has its practical implications in the relations that exist between nations. No one ethos is complete or supra-historical. "The necessary one-sidedness and incompleteness of one nation's ethos needs to be complemented by the ethoses of other nations. Pluralism is necessary for the whole, since the cultural individuality of one nation is irreplaceable."[85]

Looked at from a religious point of view, *love-in-God* overcomes the

---

[82] Rainer R. A. IBANA, ibid., 52. Scheler differs significantly from Durkheim in that, unlike Durkheim, he does not see that the development of the higher form of solidarity should or can require the erosion of the lower forms.

[83] E. VACEK, ibid., 167.

[84] Cf. Rainer R.A. IBANA, ibid., 52.; cf. also John H. NOTA, *Max Scheler, the Man and his Work*, (Chicago: Franciscan Herald Press, 1983), 119. Nota explains that Scheler was critical of Capitalism because, by viewing him as a separate isolated individual, it diminished the person and cut him off from his true selfhood. Marxism, by contrast, does the person an indignity because it only views him and deals with him as part of a whole. Solidarism is not just a compromise between the two, but a completely independent philosophy.

[85] E. VACEK, ibid., 168.

limitations of other ways of loving. Scheler is critical of the kind of humanism exemplified by Comte which promotes love of the other, simply because he is other, and which rejects all self-love as simply egoism.[86] On the other hand, he rejects Luther's idea of justification by faith alone which, he says, means in effect that all "love of neighbour must be absolutely subordinated to self-love and, in the final analysis, reduced to being nothing other than an instinctive sensible sympathy between men."[87] Love in the Christian sense is an act which refers to an ideal spiritual person, whether this happens to be one's self or another. It transcends the self/other division. "Christ commanded us to love our neighbour as ourselves"[88]

> By loving-in-God, the Christian can love all men individually and collectively, but without the cold universality of humanitarian benevolence. Through this love-in-God, there results the principle for the solidarity of all moral being, a moral love between persons, which is the basis for person-community.[89]

Scheler holds the primacy of the individual person and maintains that the value of the concrete individual person is not derivative from the group. However, rather than subordinating the community to the individual, he subjects both to God. Both exist for God and it is only in God that they too can exist for one another.[90] This meeting of self-love and other-love in God brings onto a spiritual level the idea of the constructive subordination of lower types of relatedness to the higher type of solidarity.

7. Critical Evaluation

As I mentioned at the beginning of this treatment of Scheler's Principle of Solidarity, his concept of person is of fundamental importance. This is doubly so because, in his view, the highest form of social group, the *person-community* is also a person. Scheler is adamant that man is one, and that the ideal man is the one who has achieved the appropriate adjustment of vital and spiritual values. This idea of adjustment is holistic and tolerant. It is realistic in the fullest sense of the term. The person transcends the vital

---

[86] Cf. Max SCHELER, *Ressentiment*, 105. Scheler also criticises Locke for the same kind of humanistic idea of love; cf. ibid., 119.

[87] Max SCHELER, *Ressentiment*, 133.

[88] Max Scheler, *Ressentiment*, 124.

[89] Ernest W. RANLY, ibid., 92.

[90] Cf. E. VACEK, ibid., 170.

man, but does not reject his values.

Scheler's criticisms of the short-comings of both the *life community* and the *society* are well founded. The social group reflects the values of its members, and the adjusted social group is the person-community in which the values and needs of the *life-community* and the *society* are preserved in balance, and transcended. Here also there is a sense of tolerance and openness, which is not found in Durkheim's theory of solidarity, which envisages the decline of one kind of social group so that another may come into being and develop. Scheler seems to have discovered in the *person-community* the integrating factor for which Durkheim in his later writings sought in vain.

All is not as simple as it seems, however, because there seems to be an ambiguity about the extent to which the person includes all that is human, and thus the extent to which the *person-community* can have any impact beyond the realm of the spiritual. The being of the person is the intrinsic end of all community and all evolution, according to Scheler. It is by no means certain, however, that his concept of person is the concept of a unified and distinct subsistent.

Despite the essential unity of man, Scheler insists that the person is constituted by its spiritual acts.[91] To this extent that the ontological reality of the *life* of man appears to have no direct bearing on the reality of the person. Instead, Scheler roots his concept of person in the ideation of man's spirit, a spirit which is not in itself substantial, but which is given in personal acts. It is true that the phenomenon of *spirit* is the evidence of a being that is essentially distinct from all forms of *life*, but this should not be taken to mean that, prior to the manifestation of specifically personal acts, there is no person.[92] This prescinding from the ontological reality of the whole man is not helpful when it comes to any attempt to understand and respond ethically to other individuals as unitary bearers of value.[93]

Scheler's concept of person is such that it precludes any consideration of a person who is devoid of many of the characteristic personal acts, or

---

[91] Cf. Ernest W. RANLY, ibid., 66/7.

[92] Cf. Ernest W. RANLY, ibid., 22.

[93] I assume here, for the sake of argument, the validity of Scheler's theory of value. One would, however, have to question the extent to which Scheler's values can properly be called objective. His denial that objects in themselves are values, even of a pre-moral kind, would suggest that ultimately man is the giver of all value, and it is only in the sense that value is given to objects that it is objective for Scheler.

even of all acts other than the act of being. Yet, for a creature who is, by nature, both vital and spiritual, a substantial act of being is, I would argue, fundamental to any spiritual activity. If Scheler's concept of person were to be accepted, it would certainly seem that many human beings, such as children and primitives and those generally who are "not of age" would, apart from their inability to enter into relationships of solidarity on their own behalf, be denied the possibility of being beneficiaries of the solidarity of persons who do have that capacity.[94]

Scheler's principle of Solidarity seems to founded on the belief that persons are only given in their spiritual acts. This is a fundamental problem arising from his phenomenological method. The difficulty is that, as Gorevan suggests, "Scheler separates existence from essence so radically that existence cannot be known at all, merely felt in resistance."[95] Added to this, Scheler seems to ignore the difference between the nature of the "being-one" of the individual man and the "being-one" of the community, even while denying that the community is a substance apart from or above the persons of whom it is formed. This means that, as far as both individual person and the collective person are concerned, the fact of being is irrelevant to the exercise of solidarity.

It is somewhat difficult to get to grips with what Scheler's solidarity actually is. It is clearly more than just the factual reality of a common life, or even an awareness of inter-dependence. The mere co-performance of spiritual acts in itself is not solidarity either. To perceive the meaning of a person's acts does not of itself imply a sharing of that person's values. Solidarity in its most perfect form, for Scheler, makes possible the acceptance of co-responsibility. It could be argued that, since there is an active freedom about un-representable solidarity, by contrast with the passive nature of representable solidarity, this highest form of solidarity not only brings about an awareness of co-responsibility, but is actually a constituent element of that being-responsible.

In the final analysis, solidarity in its most perfect form is an attitude of personal love specifically oriented towards the realisation of the good of each person in the community and of the whole community-as-person. As a means to this realisation, it promotes participation, that is co-acting with and co-performing with others. It takes the form of a free choice to realise

---

[94] Max SCHELER, *Formalism*, 529.
[95] Patrick GOREVAN, "Max Scheler, Phenomenology and Beyond", in *At the Heart of the Real*, edited by Fran O'Rourke, (Dublin: Academic Press, 1991), 293.

the values which constitute the "good-in-itself-for-me," thus not preferring either myself or the other.[96] For this reason it requires the acceptance of shared responsibility for the acts of the community, and also for any failure to act which results in the non-realisation of a value.

The problem, however, is that Scheler has removed the realisation of values from the realm of the will, by reducing the person to the experience of emotions. If a person experiences something as good, there is no need for commands originating either from within or from other persons. If he does not experience something as good, then there is a real danger that a command based on someone else's value experience will mean that the person commanded never arrives at a true, lived experience of value.[97] Common sense tells us, in fact, that the experience of value and the experience of duty co-exist and that the experience of value alone is not enough to realise a value in any practical sense. If Scheler's *person* were as integrated as he insists it is, then the will would have a part to play in the realisation of values which are recognised in the judgement of truth, even though they are not experienced as good. Scheler's notion of collective guilt must also be evaluated in the light of his rejection of duty as an element in his ethics. There are two senses in which we tend to speak of guilt. In one sense it is simply a bad feeling. In another sense it is a recognition of an obligation to make amends or to act differently in the future, in order to realise a certain good, or avoid a certain evil. This latter is inseparable from the judgement of truth which gives rise to the experience of duty and the related act of will. It seems that Scheler's notion of collective guilt, however strong it may be as a feeling, can not be discovered to have any such practical outcome.

Viewed as a principle of social organisation, the Principle of Solidarity meets with other problems on a practical level. We have to ask whether the solidaristic organisation of social groups can ever really be achieved. Scheler's answer to this would seem to be that the challenge must at least be taken up, because the alternative is unacceptable.[98] It seems that, in his later writings at least, Scheler recognised that his strong rejection of *society* and its structures as the "left-overs" of the *life-community* would have to be tempered if the Principle of Solidarity were to have any practical impact. The structures can be and often are defective, as Durkheim recognised. We

---

[96] Maurice DUPUY, ibid., 551.

[97] Cf. Karol WOJTYLA, *Valutazioni*, 168.

[98] Cf. Rainer. R.A. IBANA, ibid., 53.

can change them, but we cannot do without them.

Having failed to come to grips with the real through his phenomeno-logical method, Scheler focussed his attention on God as the ground of existence or *world-ground*, which alone gives existence to everything, including the human person. This provides the basis for Scheler's assertion that true solidarity is only possible through love-in-God. Understood in terms of each person's recognition of the finality of the other and of the community, this would be a completely valid insight and, I dare say, the basis for a sound spirituality of solidarity. Gorevan points out, however, that for the late Scheler, the creature is subsumed into God "not merely as the ultimate source of its existence but also for its very substantiality."[99] This means, in effect, that the human spirit is incapable of motivating or, at any rate, empowering any action. Community of feeling, the highest form of sympathy, reverts to being a form of monism because the human person, along with the freedom which alone gives meaning to his acts, is lost sight of in the divine Other. In such a view of things, solidarity fades into identity and loses its meaning as a moral concept.

B. THE PERSONALISM OF EMMANUEL MOUNIER

Emmanuel Mounier (1905-1950), editor of the journal *Esprit*, is a key figure in the French Personalist tradition. His significant writing was done in the period between 1930 and 1950, a period which saw the rise and fall of fascism in Europe, and the struggle to find a new equilibrium in the post-war era. It is against this background that he examines how the emergence of different forms of social organisation is related to the way in which persons respond to the challenge or vocation of their personhood.

Mounier uses the term *solidarity* very sparingly, and is more inclined to the use of the term *communion*. There are, however, significant simi-larities between Mounier and Scheler, particularly in their identification of different forms of sympathy and different social group-types, arising out of the extent to which individuals have achieved or maintained a genuinely personal mode of existence. There is a difference of emphasis in that Scheler writes more in terms of individuals achieving personhood, while Mounier – beginning with persons – sees the risk of persons betraying their personhood through individualism.

Mounier, like Scheler, recognises the need to find the appropriate

---

[99] Patrick GOREVAN, ibid., 292; cf. also Francis N. DUNLOP, ibid., 231.

balance between individualism and collectivism, in which the dignity of the person will be respected and promoted. Writing some time later than Scheler, however, he is more explicitly aware of the great historical struggle between capitalist individualism and Marxist communist collectivism.

1. The Person

Mounier rejects any rationalist or spiritualist conception of man which would deny or devalue the bodily aspect of his nature. Personalism is in conflict with the idealist tendency to make of the body nothing more than an appearance of the human spirit. "Man is a body to the same extent that he is a spirit, body through and through and spirit through and through."[100] There is no opposition between these two elements of man's nature, and Mounier sees a need to overcome elements of dualism, both in our life-style and in our way of thinking. Man's body is a prerequisite for all his personal activity, and a vehicle of his being in relationship with the world.

> I cannot think without being, and being in my body: I am exposed by it, to myself, to the world and to others; it is by means of it that I escape to the solitude of a thought which is only the thought of my thought. Refusing to leave me transparent to myself, it casts me ceaselessly beyond myself into the problematic of the world and the struggles of man.[101]

It is clear from the above that, for Mounier, the bodily nature of man is not something negative in itself as some philosophers would argue, but it is not without its challenges. "Incarnation is not a fall. But because it is the place of the impersonal and the objective, it is a constant occasion of alienation."[102] The bodily aspect of man's nature can act as a barrier, on one side of which man can lose his interiority and an the other side of which he can lose his exteriority.

Mounier identifies two kinds of alienation to which man is constantly a prey. The first is the gap that exists between the thought patterns of

---

[100] Emmanuel MOUNIER, *Le Personnalisme*, 2nd. edition, (Paris: Presses Universitaires de France, 1951), 19. (Hereafter referred to as *Personnalisme*).

[101] Emmanuel MOUNIER, *Personnalisme*, ibid., 4. The human body is specifically the body of a rational being, oriented towards thought and linguistic communication. For a useful account of this "personality of the body," cf., A. R. LURIA, *Higher Cortical Functions in Man* (London: Tavistock, 1966), 58-61.

[102] Emmanuel MOUNIER, *Personnalisme*, 21.

idealism on the one hand and the development of the techniques of expansion which condition the everyday lives of people, on the other hand.[103] In other words, man is alienated from himself, in the world around him. By defining man in material terms and proposing a kind of *solidarity of things*, Marxism sought to address this alienation. Mounier points out, however, that the materialist approach doesn't resolve the alienation of man because, in the midst of things man is simply another thing, swallowed up. "The materialists forgot just one thing, the ambivalence of material life."[104] There is a fundamental difference between a view of man which is purely functional and immersed in the material world, with a view of man as a unity of initiative in relation to the material world.

The second form of alienation is the opposite of the first. It is the loss of self within, through loss of contact with the exterior world. In this condition, human beings also lose any real interiority because

> they live in the absolute isolation of dreams without object.... They no longer live in exteriority and they no longer live in interiority. They speak of themselves in the third person, like the child who is not yet firmly planted in the world of things. ... Neither the interior life in itself, nor the exterior life in itself, brings us into the gulf, but rather a certain manner of allowing ourselves to be overwhelmed by either of them, or else the dissociation of the two.[105]

Mounier distinguishes between the *individual* and the *person*. The individual is the

> diffusion of the person on the surface of his life, and his readiness to lose himself there. My individual is the imprecise and changing image, presented in double-exposure, by the different personages between which I fluctuate, and in which I distract myself and take flight. ... The person contrasts with the individual in that it is mastery, choice, formation, and self-conquest. ...It is enriched by all communions, with the flesh of the world and of man, with the spiritual which animates it, and with the communities which reveal it.[106]

Mounier does not, however, imply any radical dichotomy between the

---

[103] Cf. Emmanuel MOUNIER, *Qu'est-ce que le Personnalisme*, in *Oeuvres de Mounier*, Vol. 3, (Paris: Editions du Seuil, 1962), 211. (Hereafter referred to as *Qu'est-ce que*).

[104] Emmanuel MOUNIER, *Qu'est-ce que*, 212.

[105] Emmanuel MOUNIER, *Qu'est-ce que*, 213/4.

[106] Emmanuel MOUNIER, *Révolution Personnaliste et Communautaire*, in *Oeuvres de Mounier*, Vol. 1, (Paris: Editions du Seuil, 1960), 176/7. (Hereafter referred to as *Révolution*).

person and the individual. The opposition between person and individual is an opposition of two attitudes, but not of two beings. Moix explains that

> if one were to separate the individual from the person, one would cut away from it its concrete attachments... It is important, thus, to avoid opposing them too brutally, but to see in them rather a bipolarity, a dynamic tension between two interior movements, one of dispersion, the other of concentration.[107]

Just as the person is not to be equated with the individual, my person is not simply the knowledge I have of it. Likewise, because it is broader than any image of it which I can have, and more interior than any reconstruction of it which I can make, my person is not just the same thing as my personality.

The fact that there are so many possibilities open to man has tended to make people reluctant to accept any kind of permanence in man's nature. Marx, Freud, and Nietzsche between them showed up the struggle and the incompleteness of the human condition, as did two world wars. However, according to Moix, we can refuse to accept the tyranny of formal definitions, without completely denying all sense of an essence or structure. "If every man is only what he does, then there is no humanity, no history and no community."[108]

a. Three Dimensions of the Person. Mounier says that there are three fundamental dimensions of the person; *vocation, incarnation,* and *communion.*[109] The person is the presence and the unity in me of a *vocation* that calls me to go beyond myself to transcend myself in *communication* with others. Communication, however, is fraught with difficulty because of the human tendency to control and to dominate others. This leads people to turn in on themselves in order to avoid suffering and risk. "Individualism is a system of morals, sentiments, ideas and institutions, which organise the individual around attitudes of isolation and defence,"[110] As a social attitude it proclaims the self-sufficiency of each citizen; it rejects mystery and the call of spiritual presences.[111]

---

[107] Candide MOIX, *La Pensée d'Emmanuel Mounier,* (Paris: Editions du Seuil, 1960), 144.

[108] Candide MOIX, ibid., 128.

[109] Cf. Emmanuel MOUNIER, *Révolution,* 178.

[110] Emmanuel MOUNIER, *Personnalisme,* 37; cf. also 35/6.

[111] Cf. Emmanuel MOUNIER, *Révolution,* 179.

Being *incarnate*, the person can never completely shed the human condition or the limitations of matter. Mounier subscribes to the Thomist conception of nature, but without thinking of it in fixed or rigid terms. Man has far from fully explored or exhausted the possibilities of his nature. For this reason, Mounier prefers to use the term *human condition*, rather than *human nature*, because it is more suggestive of freedom and possibility.[112] The human condition is not a static nature but something dynamic. The person transcends his human nature even while being limited by it.[113] In saying that man transcends his nature, it is not entirely clear whether Mounier means that man's finality is supra-natural, or rather that to be a person is to be more than *what* a man is, and includes also *how* he is.

Finally the person is only really found and realised in *communion*, i.e., in a true community of persons. For this reason, the problematic of the person cannot be resolved without reference to the problematic of the community. We are led to ask which form of community contributes to the integration of the person, and which forms conflict with it.[114] This approach helps us to recognise that Mounier's priority is the integrity of the person, and this is the criterion according to which he identifies a hierarchy of social group-types.

b. Three Exercises in the Formation of the Person. Corresponding to the three fundamental dimensions of the person are three essential exercises in the formation of the person. These are *méditation (meditation)* – in search of one's vocation; *engagement (involvement)* – the recognition of one's incarnation; and *dépouillement (detachment)* – initiation in the gift of oneself and one's life for others.[115]

By means of meditation, the vocation of the person is discovered. At the heart of the human condition there is an essential *solitude*, which is not the same thing as the solitude of individualism. It is an interiority which prepares the ground for and complements our movement towards others.[116] The man of distraction is alienated, or inauthentic. Personal life involves the capacity to break with the milieu. Conversion towards personhood calls for recollection; for silence – since it is in silence that life is prepared; and

---

[112] Cf. Candide MOIX, ibid., 126/7.
[113] Cf. Emmanuel MOUNIER, *Personnalisme,* 1/2.
[114] Cf. Emmanuel MOUNIER, *Révolution,* 182.
[115] Cf. Emmanuel MOUNIER, *Révolution,* 179.
[116] Cf. Emmanuel MOUNIER, *Qu'est-ce que,* 223.

for solitude, because that is where man is rediscovered.[117]

One aspect of this personal solitude is the secret dimension of every person. Personal life involves a recognition that the wholeness of myself or of another person can never be fully revealed or penetrated. The failure to recognise this gives rise to a false egalitarianism, which is really only an exercise in reducing every person to being a nondescript individual. Personalism is anti-egalitarian in the sense that it sees persons as unique and incomparable.[118] Respect for the other is fundamentally respect for the mystery of the other.[119]

"For a definition of the personalist position, it suffices to say that every person has a meaning such that he cannot be replaced in the position which he holds in the universe of persons."[120] The discovery of his meaning or vocation is the challenge of solitude for each person. It is out of the uniqueness and diversity of human vocation that a community of persons comes into being.

Privacy (la zone du privé) marks, for Mounier, the crossroads where the secret life and the public life of the individual meet. Privacy is constructive provided it is not purely an occasion for seeking security in isolation.

> Between my secret life and my private life, it (privacy) marks the field in which I seek to maintain in my social being, the peace of the depths and the exchanged intimacy of one person and another. But it is also the place in which I look for vital indifference, vegetative passivity, and biological dependence.[121]

The person is marked by a willingness to become involved. "Mounier regarded the will to involvement to be the central vocation of his generation."[122] What counts is not simply arbitrary activity, but personal acts, of a kind which are to be found nowhere else in the universe. These

---

[117] Cf. Candide MOIX, ibid., 145.

[118] Cf. Candide MOIX, ibid., 159. Mounier argues that the idea of a material and collective "measure" of person is an invention of bourgeois rationalism, and the idea of absolute equality of action is a product of bourgeois anarchism.

[119] Cf. Emmanuel Mounier, *Personnalisme*, 53; cf. also Emmanuel MOUNIER, *Traité du Caractère*, in *Oeuvres de Mounier*, Vol 2, Paris: Editions du Seuil, 1961, 478, and 515/6. (Hereafter referred to as *Caractère*.) The person who respects what is secret respects not only the intimacy of the one who entrusted it to him, he also respects his own.

[120] Emmanuel MOUNIER, *Personnalisme*, 60.

[121] Emmanuel MOUNIER, *Personnalisme*, 55.

[122] Candide MOIX, ibid., 163.

acts are:

    a. to go out from oneself,

    b. to understand (entering into the viewpoint of the other),

    c. to take to oneself the destiny, trouble, joys and tasks of others,

    d. to give, generously, freely, and without the pre-condition of a response, and

    e. to be faithful, because love and friendship are only perfected in community.[123]

While shallow, arbitrary acts are of no personal value, and make no contribution to community, it is difficult to respond to the challenge to act always in a truly personal way. The person who exposes and expresses himself often experiences hostility and, for this reason, the attitudes of refusal and opposition are written into the human condition. It is not possible to take every option. To be a person sometimes involves protesting and resisting, especially when it is a case of resisting oppression, which is man's ultimate recourse.[124]

> But the person confronts (reality?) and, if it is true to say that one poses (affirms) oneself by opposing, then one must acknowledge the value of ruptures. To exist is not just to say yes, it is also to refuse. Mounier frequently commented on the positive aspect of negation.[125]

There is a constant tension between saying *yes* and saying *no*. But even in saying *no* there is an ambiguity; some people never say anything else, and so their *no* becomes just another type of conformism. Ideal causes and ideal circumstances do not exist in the world. To defer acting; to refuse to engage in politics is already to act.[126] Likewise, some philosophers, e.g., Sartre, Heidegger and Kierkegaard, have carried refusal to the extreme, to the extent that they leave nothing but a vacuum.[127] "For Heidegger and Sartre, there would be no authentic community except that of despair; a solidarity of cavemen attached by the same chains."[128]

    From a personalist perspective, refusal is only justifiable as a prelude

---

[123] Cf. Emmanuel MOUNIER, *Personnalisme*, 39/40.

[124] Cf. Emmanuel MOUNIER, *Personnalisme*, 63-71.

[125] Candide MOIX, ibid., 151.

[126] Cf. Emmanuel MOUNIER, *Personnalisme*, 112.

[127] Cf. Emmanuel MOUNIER, *Personnalisme*, 67.

[128] Candide MOIX, ibid., 184.

to a further positive response.

> There is no justifiable refusal, except in view of a positive choice; the *no* is the
> time which precedes the *yes*. Involvement is an essential requirement of personal
> life, and this is why personalism accords it pride of place.[129]

The third exercise in the formation of a person is the process of *detachment*, by means of which an individual is converted from appropriation to disappropriation, from having to being. Being and having are two poles of personal existence. There is, however, a tendency in man to become pre-occupied with the quantity of his possessions, while what really counts about having is the disposition and use of goods.

> The flowering of the person implies an interior condition of disappropriation of
> self and of one's goods, which depolarises egocentrism. The person only finds
> himself in losing himself. His wealth is what remains his when he has detached
> himself from all having – that which remains his at the hour of his death.[130]

Mounier recognises that property is necessary to personal life, but argues that we must struggle against the burden of possession, in order to become free to go out to others. There are other forms of having besides the ownership of goods. Having is relevant also to the need for security, the ownership of ideas, and the possession of the moral "high-ground." In all its forms, having is unavailability. Every situation which breaks the hold of having in order to free the fertility of being is a situation of personalism.[131]

Freedom (*liberté*) is related to the dichotomy of being and having. There is an ambiguity about freedom. The freedom of individualism is an unrestrained freedom, such as inevitably conflicts with the freedom of others. There is something suspicious about the individual who insists too much on his own freedom, because ultimately the sense of freedom begins with the freedom of others. In a world where each freedom sprouts in isolation, the freedom of one person can only unite with that of another either to dominate it or to be dominated by it.

True freedom is not possessed, it is lived.[132] Personal freedom is such

---

[129] Candide MOIX, ibid., 164.
[130] Emmanuel MOUNIER, *Personnalisme*, 59.
[131] Cf. Candide MOIX, ibid., 147.
[132] Cf. Candide MOIX, 153/4.

that it creates freedom around it, just as alienation creates alienation. Far from isolating, freedom unites. There is always a gap between the freedom we seek and the freedom we attain in reality.

> There is no human situation which does not involve alienation to a greater or lesser extent; it is in the condition of man to aspire indefinitely to autonomy, to pursue it unceasingly, and to fail indefinitely to attain it. In order that we should be delivered from every occasion of alienation, it would be necessary for nature to be wholly intelligible, for communion to be permanent, universal, and perfect, and for the possession of our ideals to be total.[133]

2. Social Group Forms

Some social structures act as a haven for individualism. Others are more conducive to the growth of persons. Personalism recognises a hierarchy among collectivities according to the degree of their communitarian potential and, therefore, the extent to which they are personalised. Side by side with this recognition, there is an acceptance of the fact that social groups depend on the human relations which give rise to them. There is no intention on the part of personalism to denigrate any form of social group *per se*.

a. The Impersonal World. The first social group identified by Mounier is what he calls the *monde de l'on*, or the *masse*. This is a faceless, impersonal kind of society, a world of vague opinions, gossip and political and social conformism, in which personhood is renounced in favour of becoming ordinary or commonplace. Masses are more the rubbish of community than the beginnings of it.[134] According to Moix, this world of irresponsibility with its absence of real ideas, is not so much associated with any one kind of society. Rather, it is, in all of them, a way of being. In this world the other is objectified and this is the greatest crime against the person.[135]

> What kind of communion can take place in the midst of such confusion. ...Communion with others? There are no longer oneself and others. There are no longer any neighbours, there are only doubles....The *monde de l'on* is beneath the threshold which marks the first traces of community.[136]

---

[133] Emmanuel MOUNIER, *Personnalisme*, 80/1.
[134] Cf. Emmanuel MOUNIER, *Révolution*, 195.
[135] Cf. Candide Moix, ibid., 137.
[136] Candide MOIX, ibid., 186/7. cf. also Emmanuel MOUNIER, *Personnalisme*, 45.

b. The Society of We. Just above the level of the mass is what Mounier calls the *Société en Nous Autres.* This comes about when a group of people, dedicated to a common cause come together as a *we.* This kind of society is characterised by a collective consciousness of self, which is often associated with considerable mutual abnegation. Fascism is an example of the highest form of this type of society; a form which inevitably leads to depersonalisation. "Blind obedience to the directives of the party can, for example, be a way of escaping from one's personal commitments, and an abdication of one's duties as a human being."[137] "This conformism at the interior of the society tends to render the collective will progressively more brittle."[138]

c. The Vital Society. Although they lack the vague spirituality of the *société en nous autres*, the *sociétés vitales* (*vital societies*) are generally considered to be superior to the *société en nous autres*, because of their more structured organisation. They require greater initiative and community asceticism. Yet this social type is far from ideal. "They are in effect associations of interest in which the functions are distributed; associations which individualise but do not personalise, and in which the individuals are inter-changeable."[139] This type of social group would include economic societies and even families in so far as they have nothing more in common than a blood relationship. Mounier comments that a family like this can easily become a "nest of vipers." Careful social organisation of political and social structures does not constitute a community.

> Vital societies, being insufficiently personalised... tend towards hypnosis, arrogance, and war; the internal hierarchy of functions, if it reigns supreme, becomes hardened into a master-slave relationship ... They tend to be the kind of whole in which the element of *we* becomes corroded.[140]

In these vital societies, people become absorbed in their shared tasks, relating to one another always on a functional level, and never really encountering one another as persons.[141]

---

[137] Candide MOIX, ibid., 137.
[138] Emmanuel MOUNIER, *Révolution*, 198.
[139] Candide MOIX, ibid., 138.
[140] Emmanuel MOUNIER, *Personnalisme*, 45/6.
[141] Cf. Emmanuel MOUNIER, *Révolution*, 200.

d. The Rational Societies. Up to this point, the various social types
identified by Mounier bear a striking similarity to those described by Max
Scheler. Mounier, however, adds a further distinction with what he calls the
Société Raisonnable. This rational society derives from the efforts of
eighteenth century philosophers and jurists to overcome the problems of
irrationalism. This social type comes in two forms, according to Mounier.
The first of these is the *société des esprits* (*society of thinkers*) in which the
hope was to assure unanimity and peace through the serenity of universal
thought. But knowledge in itself is not virtue. When the jurists tried to
achieve the same end by means of a society based on convention and
contract – the *société juridique contractuelle*, they failed because

> the impersonality of contract is just as big a fraud as the impersonality of thought.
> The contracts were made between persons who were unequal in power. ...Even
> if their equality had been assured, it remains that a contract does not bring two
> people into communion; it sets up two egoisms, two interests, two mistrusts, two
> strategies, and unites them in an armed peace.[142]

Mounier recognised the essential contribution that reason and law make
to the development of community, but realised that they alone could not
give rise to the fullness of personal community. As Moix explains, the
philosophers and jurists overlooked the fact that one cannot construct
universality on the neglect of the person.[143]

3. The Community of Persons

The term *community* is reserved exclusively, in Mounier's works, for
the highest form of social unit, which is the unity of persons. This unity is
something of a paradox. Since, "by definition, the person is that which
cannot be duplicated," it must be a unity in diversity rather than the unity
of identity, such as we see in the mass or in the *société en nous autres.*[144]

Mounier sets out to define this ideal community, as a background
against which the essential inadequacy of the historical realisations can be
seen.

> We reserve the name *community* to the only community which we regard as
> valid, which is the personalist community, and which could be accurately defined

---

[142] Emmanuel MOUNIER, *Révolution,* 201.
[143] Cf. Candide MOIX, ibid., 138/9.
[144] Emmanuel MOUNIER, *Personnalisme,* 47.

as a person of persons. In a perfect personal community, each person would fulfil himself in the totality of a continually fruitful vocation, and the communion of the whole would be the product of each of these singular successes. Contrary to what is the case in the vital society, the place of each one would be unsubstitutable and essentially desired by the order of the whole. Love alone would be its bond, and not any constraint, vital or economic interest, or any extrinsic institution.[145]

Only persons give rise to a viable social order. Only they offer an adequate defence against totalitarianism. A type of social organisation which subjects parties to the whole and to each other, in view of certain complementary functions, cannot organise a society of spiritual subjects. Once the person and his vocation are no longer at the heart of a society, the society becomes simply a controlling mechanism, and the person its plaything.[146]

"The link between the person and the community is so organic that one could say of true communities that they are, really and not just figuratively, collective persons."[147] In reality, however, Mounier accepts that

such a community is not of this world. Christians believe it to be alive in the Communion of Saints, but the Communion of Saints has no more than a beginning in the Church Militant. It realises the perfect *person of persons*, gathering the whole of humanity into the Mystical Body of Christ, by means of a participation in the Trinitarian Society itself.[148]

Occasionally in a love relationship, in a family, or among a few friends, we may come close to this kind of personal community. Likewise, a country might come close to it during the best moments of its history but, for the most part, it is an ideal to be striven for. Every community is shadowed by a politic which exposes it to degradation.[149] For this reason,

---

[145] Emmanuel MOUNIER, *Révolution*, 202.

[146] Cf. Emmanuel MOUNIER, *Personnalisme*, 49.

[147] Candide MOIX, ibid., 132/3.

[148] Emmanuel MOUNIER, *Révolution*, 202/3. Mounier first published this work in 1935, eight years before the encyclical letter *Mystici Corporis Domini*, of Pope Pius XII. Mersch explains that the development of the concept of the Mystical Body began to spread originally under the influence of the Ecole Française. It was seen as a remedy for naturalist rationalism and for individualist and nationalist egoism, and was present implicitly in the social teaching of the church as early as the First Vatican Council. cf. E. MERSCH, *Le Corps Mystique du Christ*, (Paris: Desclée, 1936), Part III, Ch. XI, passim.

[149] Cf. Candide MOIX, ibid., 141.

in the real world, persons must live and seek communion within imperfect communities, and this involves a continual struggle to maintain an appropriate balance which avoids the excesses of individualism and collectivism.

4. The Person in Imperfect Societies

A number of factors are identified by Mounier as affecting, positively or adversely, the genesis of the sentiment of community. These are:

a. The family, and especially the maternal influence.

b. Life experience and circumstances. Great joy or great sorrow tends to dissolve egocentricity, while mediocrity in one or the other seems to contribute to individualism.

c. Professional environment seems to exercise a similar influence, depending on whether a person works in conditions which tend create a community of destiny among colleagues, or whether he works and struggles alone.[150]

Einfühlung (*affective penetration*) alone is not an adequate explanation of the interior structures of the sense of the other. Personality has an important contribution to make, in so far as the incapacity of some people to work with others, or the tendency of some to co-operate as a way of evading personal responsibility, may be the result of an emotional inability to adapt to a more constructive or personal mode of engagement with others. At times it may appear that people are genuinely accepting others and going out to them, whereas in reality one person may be using others as a form of escape, as a mirror for himself, or in order to project onto them complexes and failings which he does not wish to see in himself.[151]

True *sympathie* (*sympathy*) "consists in re-living in ourselves the state of the other as other, yet without becoming exactly as he is."[152] It is only on the basis of this kind of sympathy that a personal community can be established. The opposite of *sympathie* is *méfiance* (*mistrust*), which is a primary expression of the refusal of others, and which characterises individualistic societies, almost as if it were a virtue. For the mistrustful person the other is scarcely seen in personal terms, but simply apprehended as the threat from outside. Mistrust may go beyond mere defensiveness to

---

[150] Cf. Emmanuel MOUNIER, *Caractère*, 517/8.

[151] Cf. Emmanuel MOUNIER, *Caractère*, 473/4, 483-6, & 520/1.

[152] Emmanuel MOUNIER, *Caractère*, 521.

be realised as a form of selfishness, lack of availability and of hospitality.[153] Hospitality is the characteristic which most reveals the open society, not simply in terms of the attitudes of the members, but the attitude of society itself.[154]

Love is the bond that unites the *I* and the *you* in the community and, this only takes place when I have learnt to love the other precisely as a person. He is no longer *he*, a third person, or an object. "Love is the unity of the community, just as vocation is the unity of the person."[155] The nature of love is such that it has implications for the relationship of the person to the society which is aspiring to the quality of community. The sacrifice and abnegation which community demands of the person is to be understood as the most personal of acts, and not as abandonment of the person. Love for others requires that we place the society above the individual. But love is always personal and, for this reason, the society must always serve the person and, through the person, the growth of community.

> It is necessary to establish as an absolute rule that all temporal society exists only in view of the good of persons. ... The duty of societies towards persons is therefore presented in categorical form. The problem of the duty of persons towards societies entails a greater number of traps and uncertainties.[156]

Mounier identifies a hierarchy in the order of interests or values, which determines when it is justifiable to sacrifice them. He frequently refers to the importance, when we make choices, of knowing clearly what it is that we are choosing.[157] The values which Mounier identifies as significant are:

a. Happiness and Science, which together formed the ideal of recent centuries.

b. Truth, which is not impersonal, as the rationalists would have it, but which involves an attitude of conversion.

c. Moral values, by contrast with the pre-moral. Anything pre-moral is impersonal and unfree. Immorality by contrast is a condition of freedom.

d. Art.

e. A community of destinies. There is a common human destiny and history, because there is a common humanity. This is one of the highest

---

[153] Cf. Emmanuel MOUNIER, *Caractère*, 475.
[154] Cf. Emmanuel MOUNIER, *Caractère*, 522.
[155] Emmanuel MOUNIER, *Révolution*, 193; cf. also 191/2.
[156] Emmanuel MOUNIER, *Révolution*, 206.
[157] Cf. ibid, 206; cf. also Candide MOIX, ibid., 156.

values for a community, but is only possible when persons are free and history is not over-structured.

f. Religious values; involving trust in and intimacy with a transcendent person.[158]

The person is completed by giving himself to the values which draw him out from his individualism and call him to transcend himself. In this sense there seems to be an interdependence between persons and values. Persons without values do not exist in the fullest sense, but neither do values exist except in the choice of persons to realise them. To this extent, values are both subjective and non-subjective.[159]

In a similar sense, the *we* of a group "is not established finally as a community until the day when each person is engaged primarily in drawing each of the others above himself, towards the particular values of his own vocation, and is lifted up along with each of them."[160]

A theory of action is an essential aspect of personalism. Action completes the person, by seeking to realise the values of the person and of the community to which he belongs. There are four dimensions of action which indicate the manner in which it completes the person. As in the case of values and of social group-types, Mounier identifies a scale of different types of action, according to the extent to which they express or lead to the integration of the person. Action operates in view of

a. the modification of exterior reality.

b. self-formation.

c. gathering people together.

d. enriching our universe of values.

The modification of reality is to be found in *doing* and is called *economic action*. But man is not satisfied with doing unless he finds in it

---

[158] Cf. Emmanuel MOUNIER, *Personnalisme*, 91-99. Mounier places these values on a scale, attributing the lowest place to the material values, followed by the vital, and the cultural. Like Scheler he gives pride of place to those values which are accessible to all, joy, suffering, and daily love. For some, he says, these values are intrinsically linked to the existence of a transcendent God and to Christian values. Faith in a personal God leads to the personalisation of values.

[159] Cf. Candide MOIX, ibid., 162/3.

[160] Emmanuel MOUNIER, *Révolution*, 191. This understanding of communion in community is close to Scheler's idea of unrepresentable solidarity. It is not a question even of desiring values for the other as my own values, but of desiring them for him precisely as the values to which he is called.

his own dignity, fraternity, and elevation above utility.[161] Self-formation is to be looked for in *acting*. This is referred to as *ethical action*. It finds its end in authenticity; not in what is done, but how the agent does it, and what he becomes. Ethical action, when combined with economic action, becomes *political action*.[162]

The development of a kingdom of values enclosing all human activity is the goal of contemplative action, which is not directly focussed on the organisation of external relations. The affirmation of the absolute in all its starkness results from the combination of the contemplative and the practical (ethical) in *prophetic action*.[163]

Finally there is the collective dimension of acting. Community of work and of destiny, or spiritual communion, are essential for the integral humanisation of acting. Fascism and communism owe a lot of their following to the fact that many people experienced the lack of such a communal dimension in their lives and in their countries.[164]

In so far as the person and the community are mutually dependent for their growth and completion, there is an inevitable element of collective responsibility in the thought of Mounier. Each person has the "power to transform the world to some extent by his decisions, his acceptances and his refusals, breaking the chain of fate, and upsetting all the calculations."[165] However, the great emphasis on the right to choose has tended to obscure the responsibility to choose well, both for one's own sake and for the sake of all who are affected by the choices one makes.[166] If the Christian were to refuse to be involved, he would have a comfortable pharisaic conscience. However "he feels himself solidary with every fault, and engages himself, not just here and there, but wholly in each act."[167]

In an address, published originally in 1947, Mounier argues that responsibility for the acts of one person often has to be extended to others, including his opponents who may, through their own failures, have contributed to his crime. This kind of collective responsibility, Mounier calls the *solidarity of adversaries*.

---

[161] Cf. Emmanuel MOUNIER, *Personnalisme*, 105.
[162] Cf. Emmanuel MOUNIER, *Personnalisme*, 106/7.
[163] Cf. Emmanuel MOUNIER, *Personnalisme*, 108/9.
[164] Cf. Emmanuel MOUNIER, *Personnalisme*, 110.
[165] Candide MOIX, ibid., 156.
[166] Cf. ibid.
[167] ibid., 164.

> If, the day after tomorrow, it were necessary to judge the head of a provisional fascism, would it not be necessary, behind him, to extend the judgement to those of his adversaries whose failures would have opened the way for him, and who might, nonetheless, appear on the bench of judges.

> This analysis of the solidarity of adversaries in certain historic trials should not serve to dilute responsibility or to cover up faults under a fog of diffuse guilt.[168]

The highest form of acting would be a combination of the political and the prophetic, but these two temperaments rarely co-exist in one man. The prophet-philosopher often waits for ideal circumstances and causes, which do not exist in this world. The politician, on the other hand, is always at risk of abdicating the person and his values because of the need for action in some form.[169]

This brings us to the final stage of our discussion of Mounier's personalist and communitarian thought, namely its role as a critique of capitalist individualism and of Marxist communist collectivism. This will involve an examination of the suggestion that Mounier and his collaborators were actively promoting a *third way*, or alternative political ideology.

5. Personalism and the *Third Way*

Mounier is associated particularly with the search for a *third way* as an alternative to the ways of individualist capitalism and Marxist collectivism. In view of the limitations of both neo-liberal capitalism and Marxist communism, there have been many attempts to find a middle way which

---

[168] Emmanuel MOUNIER, *Le Communisme en Nous*, in *Oeuvres de Mounier*, Vol. 4 (Paris: Editions du Seuil, 1963), 148. (Hereafter referred to as Communisme). Like Mounier, Viktor Frankl, who spent the second world war in Auschwitz, has reservations about any notion of collective guilt that would conflict with personal responsibility. He says, "Totally explaining one's crime would be tantamount to explaining away his or her guilt and to seeing in him or her, not a free and responsible human being, but a machine to be repaired ...I personally think that it is totally unjustified to hold one person responsible for the behaviour of another person or a collective of persons." Viktor E. FRANKL, *Man's Search for Meaning*, revised edition, (New York: Washington Square Press, 1985), 173/4.

[169] Cf. Emmanuel MOUNIER, *Personnalisme*, 111-113. This may explain the difficulty which Mounier himself experienced, when it came to looking for some way of bringing his personalist theory to bear in the concrete reality of France, especially in the post-war period. The only party which seemed to be genuinely prophetic was the French Communist Party, which he could not endorse because of fears that it was totalitarian in tendency; cf. Ralph NELSON, "Emmanuel Mounier, between Proudhon and Marx," *Science et Esprit*, 31/2 (1979): 219.

would attract a broad consensus of support. However, the concept of the *third way* is susceptible of many mutations.

From the point of view of the West, Alfred Utz says that the *third way* is no more than a variant of the old system of the free-market economy, inspired by the philosophy of ethical liberalism. The social element of this approach is no more than a concession to pacify agitators. Similarly, the Marxist approach to the *third way* takes the planned economy as its starting point, and the concept of totality as its philosophical basis, simply recognising that personal interest plays a part in making the economy work. The whole emphasis within Marxism, however, remains on the concordance between individual interest and the common interest, and there is no real response to the fact that, in reality, there may be a gap between the two.[170]

The fact that the various attempts at a *third-way* were often no more than attempts to make capitalism or communism more broadly acceptable without changing them substantially, is borne out by Mounier's experience. In the pre-war period, in common with many people in the workers' movement, Mounier was attracted to fascism because it seemed to be a step in the direction of a greater socialisation of the economic order. As Campanini explains:

> It is not without significance that, in the nineteen thirties, fascism firstly, and then National Socialism, presented themselves precisely as a third way...The various fascisms were in reality no more than an ideological cover for a capitalism which, in the face of the advancing workers movement, had understood that its battle could only be won by means of a kind of cover-up, which involved the survival and strengthening of capitalism itself, presenting itself under the guise of a revolution, perceived at the outset, even by a significant part of the workers movement, as being of the Left.[171]

Similarly, in the post war period, an alliance of the MRP and the Socialists, in France, presented themselves as a *third force*, but they were in reality "too bourgeois and reformist." They were "anti-communist, and Mounier always refused to align himself with anti-communism, because for him that meant taking sides against the workers."[172]

---

[170] Cf. Alfred UTZ, *Entre le Neo-Liberalisme et le Neo-Marxisme: Recherche Philosophique d'une Troisième Voie,* (Paris: Beauchesne, 1976), 160-162.

[171] Giorgio CAMPANINI, "Capitalismo, Socialismo, Terza Via," *Quaderno Filosofico* (Lecce), 8 (1983): 215.

[172] Ralph NELSON, ibid., 218.

Mounier was strongly critical of the individualism associated with capitalism, and the pretence that capitalism was the defender of the person.[173] He argued that the influence of the major Western powers, especially the United States, was no more constructive or liberating than that of the Soviet Union.[174]

> The starting point for Mounier was the condemnation of capitalism, and more specifically, the capitalist system of exchange. The problem was to overcome the faults of this system by uniting the freedom (of the person) and the demands of collective life.[175]

In spite of some opinions to the contrary, Campanini argues that Mounier's *De La Propriété Capitaliste à la Propriété Humaine*[176] is of major significance when it comes to understanding his thought, because it embodies a transition in Catholic social ethics away from a position which stressed the primacy of private property.[177] Mounier re-presents St. Thomas, originally but faithfully, arguing for the superiority of the common good over the individual good, asserting the universal destiny of the goods of the earth, and criticising severely the capitalist method of production and accumulation.

> That which is superfluous, being no longer attached to the holder by personal necessity, falls back of itself into the common destiny of goods, and must be distributed, by the one who holds it, to the community....The distribution of what is superfluous is required either by virtue of the danger to life which threatens the needy *or* by virtue of the superfluity in which it is possessed. *Or*, *vel*, that is to say *as well as*. The fact of superfluity alone is enough to condemn it.[178]

---

[173] Cf. Emmanuel MOUNIER, *Révolution*, 179/80.

[174] Cf. Emmanuel MOUNIER, *Le Communisme Parmi Nous*, in *Oeuvres de Mounier*, Vol. 4, (Paris: Editions du Seuil, 1963), 152. (Hereafter referred to as *Communisme*); cf. also Ralph NELSON, ibid., 220.

[175] Ralph NELSON, ibid., 211.

[176] Emmanuel MOUNIER, *De la Propriété Capitaliste à la Propriété Humaine*, in *Oeuvres de Mounier*, Vol. 1, (Paris, Editions du Seuil, 1960). (Hereafter referred to as *Propriété*.)

[177] Cf. Giorgio CAMPANINI, ibid., 218, 220 & 223.

[178] Emmanuel MOUNIER, *Propriété*, 459; cf. also Saint THOMAS AQUINAS, *Summa Theologiae*, II IIae, Q 118 a.4, 2. Other relevant material from Saint THOMAS AQUINAS, cited by Mounier includes ibid., II IIae, Q. 66, a.1, ad 2; a.7. The argument that society is such that people must put aside superfluous goods against their own possible future need leads Mounier to suggest that, if society has become like this, then the challenge is to change it, not to reinforce it.

Because of his criticism of capitalism, Mounier was often accused of being a communist sympathiser. He undoubtedly had a preference for a socialist economic order and maintained the hope that communism could overcome its faults. This hope was encouraged by the participation of the French communists in the Resistance during the war but was dashed by various events shortly after the war, including the Prague Coup of 1948 and the trial of Cardinal Mindszenty in 1949.[179]

Marxism put man back in the real world and affirmed, against rationalism and a false spiritualism, the essentially corporeal dimension of human nature. The problem was the exclusion of the spiritual dimension as a result of which man became identified with the material world. In 1934, Mounier argued that the problem with Marxism is that it is not simply a method of investigation or a series of intuitions on the human condition. There is also a kind of Marxism which takes the form of a totalitarian philosophy which threatens man, even by means of the methods intended to free him. Marxism has ato be evaluated in terms of its historical expressions, which include dictatorship and banishment.[180]

In 1946, Mounier was saying that Personalism and Marxism have a lot in common.

> We share with the communists their mistrust of the "bourgeois spiritualism" , their fear of idealist derivations and fine thinking mystifications....But we don't want man to rediscover himself on one side, only to lose himself on the other. We look where they look, but elsewhere besides. Their pre-occupation concerns almost exclusively the political and technical means of the first revolution, that which affects the social and material structures. Ours is concerned centrally with the destiny which is possible for man within these new structures.[181]

Mounier felt that it would be a mistake to put communism together with fascism as if they were equally given to totalitarianism. He argues that a better comparison would be between communism and the Church, in so far as each is at risk from its own form of clericalism. The test for communism is ultimately whether it has the inner freedom to exclude or restrict its clericalism to the extent that the church has.[182]

Although there were ambiguities, after the war, about Mounier's

---

[179] Cf. Ralph NELSON, ibid., 208 & 220.
[180] Cf. Emmanuel MOUNIER, *Communisme,* 109; also Candide MOIX, ibid., 222/3.
[181] Emmanuel MOUNIER, *Communisme,* 123.
[182] Cf. Emmanuel MOUNIER, *Communisme,* 128/9.

concept of the personalist community and its relationship to the Marxist collectivity, Nelson says that there was never any equivocation in Mounier's basic criticism of Marxism as a philosophy. Marxism, in spite of its value as a social critique, rejected metaphysics, was devoid of any real anthropology, and rendered impossible any inwardness or transcendence. "There is no place for the person in Marxism"[183]

The only hope for Marxism would be that, in keeping with its own principles it would be open enough to transcend itself through a reflection on circumstances and experience, and to build on the vision of Marx, who recognised the alienation of persons and the possibility of their liberation through the management of society. A Marxism which was open in this way would not be too far removed from personalist realism.[184] On this point there seems to be something of a meeting of minds between Mounier and Arrigo Colombo, who brings to the discussion a non-Christian perspective. Colombo argues that there are not two or three ways, but only one way with a number of different historical phases. The first phase is capitalism and it was surpassed by Marxism, with its exaltation of work and its awareness of class and the class struggle. However, Marxism itself has also been surpassed because it has degenerated into totalitarianism and a totally mistaken idea of leadership.[185]

Colombo maintains that in the Catholic idea of the *third way* there is a fundamental misunderstanding of Marxism"[186] It is not correct to put capitalism and Marxism on the same level, for the purposes of creating an equal distance between each of them and a *third way*. He argues that the way forward in a continuous process involves taking as the base-model the *communità autogestita* (*self-directing community*), based around the district and the work-place, the two essential nuclei of human co-existence and co-operation. Among the means of achieving this, he mentions taking up once again the "personal revolution" of Mounier.[187]

---

[183] Ralph NELSON, ibid., 214; cf. Candide MOIX, ibid., 227. Mounier felt that it was the role of non-marxists to demonstrate, not by word but in action, the superiority of a doctrine which saves the whole man.

[184] Cf. Emmanuel MOUNIER, *Qu'est-ce que*, 227; cf. also Ornella POMPEO FARACOVI, "Riflessioni su *Esprit* e la Terza Via" , *Quaderno Filosofico*, (Lecce), 8 (1983): 209.

[185] Cf. Arrigo COLOMBO, *"La Terza Via*, Una Proposta Ambigua" , *Quaderno Filosofico*, (Lecce), 8 (1983): 174ff.

[186] ibid., 181.

[187] ibid., 183/4.

Roggerone explains that, in speaking of Mounier as a proponent of the *third way*, it is necessary to distinguish between various possible interpretations of this concept, and of its relationship with the other two. It could be understood in terms of a by-pass of certain ideological difficulties; a convergence of the two ways in a third; an alternative way in co-existence with the others; or an alternative way in place of the others. He argues that Mounier would not accept any of these descriptions exactly, though he might come close to the last of them.[188]

Mounier rejected the idea that one must choose from one of two opposing blocs.[189] There exists a strong body of evidence to support the view that neither he nor his collaborators had any intention of proposing a *third way* in the sense of establishing an alternative ideology or political structure. His commitment was to remain free of any label in order to be in a position to support any authentic revolution, no matter who was undertaking it.[190] Mounier's vision of a *third force* was that it should be "an arbitrator, a meeting ground of conciliation, an intermediate zone inserting itself in the angle between the two blocs."[191] Personalism was to be out in the open, rather than tied to any "prefabricated systems." In this sense it is not a *third way* "but rather a proposal-search of a metaphysical and ethical order.... which, applied to the socio-political dimension, can facilitate the existence of a new man within structures oriented by justice and equality between men."[192] The personalist state is, by definition, weak in so far as it is a state.

> The state ultimately remains a state in so far as it is not personalist, and is personalist in so far as it is not a state. This signifies that, for Mounier and his collaborators, communitarian personalism cannot be translated here and now into socio-political terms.[193]

---

[188] Cf. Giuseppe A. ROGGERONE, "Temi da Riprendere," *Quaderno Filosofico*, (Lecce), 8 (1983): 226.

[189] Cf. Emmanuel MOUNIER, *Communisme*, 110.

[190] Cf. Emmanuel MOUNIER, *Communisme*, 136.

[191] Emmanuel MOUNIER, *Les Certitudes Difficiles*, in *Oeuvres de Mounier*, Vol. 4, (Paris: Editions du Seuil, 1963), 219. The translation of this citation is taken from Ralph NELSON, ibid., 220.

[192] Antonio DELOGU, ibid., 194 & 196.

[193] Antonio DELOGU, ibid., 196; cf. also ibid., 199. Mounier argued that Christianity requires a particular spirit in politics, but not any particular form of political system.

6. Evaluation

The similarities between the thought of Mounier and that of Scheler are numerous, while their methodology is quite different. Mounier's emphasis on the aspect of personal mystery and solitude and the conviction that the person is not an object, probably owe more to existentialism than they do to phenomenology.[194] While the unity of man as proposed by Scheler is far from convincing, Mounier's man is more recognisably one. There are, nonetheless, difficulties arising out of a number of apparently conflicting statements which Mounier makes about the constitution of persons.

Mounier states, on the one hand, that "I am a person since (the moment of) my most elementary existence and, far from depersonalising me, my incarnate existence is an essential factor of my personal condition."[195] Thus, to be a person is rooted in the fact of corporeal existence. Yet he says that the person is only realised in community.[196] Further, "I only begin to be a person... when I begin to possess myself and to act as *I*. I am only completed as a person from the day when I give myself to the values which draw me above myself."[197] He describes the person as a "centre of acts,... more a presence than a being,"[198] and "not so much a being as a movement of being."[199] For Mounier, "only what acts, exists."[200]

If Mounier is using terms such as *existence, being* and *complete* in their strictest sense, then he would appear to be suggesting that a man who has not yet established for himself a frame-work of values is not a person in the proper sense of the word. This would seem to have serious implications for the kind of treatment a "pre-personal" man might expect to receive in society, and the value that might be placed on his life and dignity. Such a position would conflict with the thrust of Mounier's opposition to fascism and totalitarianism of every kind. To define the person as "more a presence than a being" would seem to move Mounier closer to a disjointed,

---

[194] Cf. Candide MOIX, ibid., 177/8.

[195] Emmanuel MOUNIER, *Personnalisme*, 28.

[196] Cf. Emmanuel MOUNIER, *Révolution*, 182.

[197] Emmanuel MOUNIER, *Révolution*, 191; cf. also Emmanuel MOUNIER, *Personnalisme*, 90. "We do not exist definitively until the moment when we have established an interior frame-work of values and dedications, against which we know that even the threat of death would not prevail."

[198] Cf. Candide MOIX, ibid., 168. Moix sees Mounier as holding a position, middle way between Thomism and Existentialism.

[199] Emmanuel MOUNIER, *Personnalisme*, 85.

[200] Emmanuel MOUNIER, *Personnalisme*, 102.

Schelerian, concept of person.

The alternative conclusion would be to assume that Mounier, in keeping with the relatively un-structured style of Personalism, uses language in a looser way. It would then be possible to interpret his comments on the constitution of the person in terms of the classical Thomistic distinction of first (central) act and second (conjugate) act, whereby every finite thing, although in act, is also in potency to a further act.[201] A person, in order to exercise the activity proper to its nature, would first have to exist.

> Being and operation belong to the person by reason of the nature; yet in a different manner. For being belongs to the very constitution of the person, and in this respect it has the nature of a term; consequently, unity of person requires unity of the complete and personal being. But operation is an effect of the person by reason of a form of nature.[202]

Finite persons are engaged in interpersonal relations consequent upon their being, and are undeniably further perfected by these relations in terms of conjugate act, but interpersonal relations are not constitutive of finite persons.[203]

Tadeusz Mazowiecki discusses the ambiguity of the concept of person within the personalist tradition, seeing it as an attempt to reflect the complementary aspects of permanence and dynamism.

> The person is not a closed being whose values are inherent only to itself, and which could only enter into relations with others by what it is externally. On the other hand, it is not just a reflection of social relationships, because the values coming out of these relationships have their source in the personalisation of man; in the possibilities which he has as a person.

> The two terms, person and personality, which in Polish are interchangeable, must nevertheless be distinguished, because they show two aspects: that which is given, which determines the nature of the human person, and that which develops in his existence, in the first place by his relations with other men. Each man is inimitable and unique in his dignity as person, but he is at the same time formed

---

[201] Cf. Saint THOMAS AQUINAS, *Summa Theologiae*, ibid., Ia., Q.9, 2 ans. cf. also ibid., Ia., Q.45, 2, ad 2.

[202] ibid., IIIa., Q.19, 1 ad 4.

[203] Cf. Bernard LONERGAN, *De Constitutione Christi, Ontologica et Psychologica*, (Rome: Gregorian University Press, 1964), 25.

by his relations with others; by the whole history in which he is implicated.[204]

A related issue is the question of the order in which we become aware of the self and the community. This is something about which Mounier seems to have had some doubts. However, it is clear that he believed that, on the level of experience, the sense of community is very closely linked with the sense of self. At one point he states:

> The *we* follows the *I*, or more precisely – since one is not constituted without the other – the *we* follows from the *I*. ... The person is preceded only by the appearance of the *we*, as it is by its own phantasm, the individual.[205]

Elsewhere, however, he seems to imply a certain priority of the sense of community over the sense of self, when he says, "the *you*, and with it the *we*, precede the *I*, or at least accompany it."[206] This apparent contradiction may possibly be explained by taking account of the fact that an individual would have a sense of self which precedes a true personal awareness of self. Understood in this way the experience of community could be said to occur simultaneously with the flowering of the awareness of self as person, and both experiences to be rooted in a certain prior self-awareness. Since, by definition, degrees of personal integration cannot be measured mathematically, it is scarcely possible to be more precise.

The other principal issue with regard to which the thought of Mounier must be evaluated is the attempt to respond fairly to the inadequacies of both Marxist communism and capitalist liberalism. An aspect of this discussion in the 1990's must be the question about the role and contribution of personalism in a post-communist world.

Campanini expresses the view that Mounier's own preference for a form of self-organising social-democratic society probably involves a certain element of utopia, but "offers the only serious alternative for a *third way* which is not reducible to the mere correction of the worst defects of capitalism on one side and state socialism on the other."[207] However, in so far as Mounier expresses a preference at all, it is no more than an acceptance of the reality that one must live and work within some system.

---

[204] Tadeusz MAZOWIECKI, "Sur le Personnalisme et le Dialogue," *Esprit*, February 1974: 244.

[205] Emmanuel MOUNIER, *Révolution*, 190.

[206] Emmanuel MOUNIER, *Personnalisme*, 38.

[207] Giorgio CAMPANINI, ibid., 219.

The fact that Mounier refused to endorse either capitalism or Marxist communism, does not necessarily imply that he should therefore be expected to offer an alternative third system. History has shown that both capitalism and socialism are capable of extremes in their concrete manifestations; extremes which we might, for convenience sake, refer to in terms of the Right and the Left. Yet even in these manifestations, the one never completely excludes the other. The extreme capitalist system, as fascism demonstrates, generally has at its head a small elite group. Likewise, the extreme socialist system has tended to be characterised by the presence of powerful individuals in leadership.

As we move towards the centre, we move towards a situation of greater balance between the individual and the communal, between public and private ownership. This is precisely the type of situation in which *communion* or *solidarity* is at its most developed; a situation in which persons are unrepresentable, in which every person acts with responsibility in freedom, and each recognises the unique value of the participation of the other. Of its very nature, such a situation could not be brought about or maintained, either by contracts and agreements on the one hand, or by force on the other hand. The third or middle way comes about through interior personal conversion, not through the setting up of new structures.[208] This is why Mounier always argued that Christianity does not impose any particular political system.[209] Whether we approach by way of the Right or of the Left, we draw closer to the ideal of community only in so far as the social structures support the integration of the person.

A pessimist would be inclined to conclude that Mounier's thought has, therefore, nothing to contribute to resolving the conflicts and tensions of the real world. However, I would argue that his contribution is in pointing to the person, rather than the individual or the society as the point of departure.

Just as the *monde de l'on* is more a way of being than a particular social structure, so also the communion of persons, in an imperfect community, is a way of being rather than a new type of social structure. In this sense Mounier's thought does represent a *way*; not a *third way*, but the *only way* in which either of the principal socio-economic systems can draw closer to the other and closer to the realisation of the ideal personalist

---

[208] Cf. Antonio DELOGU, ibid., 194.
[209] Cf. ibid., 199.

community.

The apparent demise of Marxist communism in Eastern Europe does not in any sense lessen the importance of the contribution of personalism although it tends to confirm the argument that a society which oppresses the person can not survive. The expectation has been expressed in many quarters that, since the states of eastern Europe have broken loose from the bonds of communism, they must now inevitably embrace capitalism as it is practised in the West. Looked at from the perspective of Mounier's thought, this would represent no improvement.

The destruction caused by the preference for profit over persons is very evident within capitalist society at the present time, in terms of high levels of unemployment, currency crises and a widening of the gap between rich and poor. It could reasonably be argued that the absence of a *second way*, would more than likely contribute to the development of greater excesses in the *first*. In 1947, Mounier argued that "strong communist parties were the only solid guarantee against a return of fascism."[210]

---

[210] Emmanuel MOUNIER, *Communisme*, 150.

Chapter Three
THE PHILOSOPHY OF SOLIDARITY IN THE SOCIAL TEACHING OF THE CATHOLIC CHURCH, 1891-1978

In order to see more clearly what is meant by the concept *solidarity*, as it is used in the writings of Pope John Paul II – both prior to and during his pontificate – it will be helpful to make a comparison with the use of the term in the earlier social teaching of the church, beginning with Pope Leo XIII.

Towards the beginning of his encyclical letter *Centesimus Annus*, John Paul II comments that there is a relationship between *solidarity* and other terms used by previous popes.

> In this way what we nowadays call the principle of solidarity, the validity of which both in the internal order of each nation and in the international order I have discussed in the Encyclical *Sollicitudo Rei Socialis*, is clearly seen to be one of the fundamental principles of the Christian view of social and political organisation. This principle is frequently stated by Pope Leo XIII who uses the term "friendship," a concept already found in Greek philosophy. Pope Pius XI refers to it with the equally meaningful term "social charity." Pope Paul VI, expanding the term to cover the many modern aspects of the social question, speaks of a "civilisation of love."[1]

A further objective of this chapter will, therefore, be to investigate the use of the three terms *friendship*, *social charity*, and *civilisation of love*, in the social teaching prior to John Paul II, with a view to establishing why Pope John Paul II understands them to be the same as *solidarity*.

Finally, there are a number of other concepts which one might reasonably expect to be in some way related to *solidarity*, given the manner in which they have been used in the teaching of the Church on society. Among the more important of these are *(mystical) body (of Christ)*, *common good* and *communion*. These are not referred to by John Paul II in the passage quoted above. Why? There may be something to be learnt about *solidarity*, by comparing it also with these terms as they have been

---

[1] POPE JOHN PAUL II, *Centesimus Annus* (Vatican City: Libreria Editrice Vaticana, 1991), § 10. (Hereafter referred to as *CA*).

used in the social teaching of the Church. In keeping with the overall objective of this work, the focus of attention will not be the theological implications *per se* of the use of any of the concepts mentioned above. The aim will be to assess how certain philosophical concepts are used and related in a theological environment, and particularly to see what *solidarity* means, and how its meaning may have developed, in this environment. At the outset, it should be said that some of the terms mentioned above, e.g., *common good* and *friendship* are more immediately recognisable as classical philosophical concepts than others.

An examination of the kind outlined above could become very cumbersome and take up a considerably greater proportion of the work than it merits, unless the material to be examined were kept within relatively limited parameters. I shall, therefore, – for the purposes of this chapter – limit the examination to documents readily recognisable as belonging to the social teaching of the Church. Editors vary as to what documents they include in collections of the social teaching, and I have opted for the relatively restricted collection found in *Proclaiming Justice and Peace*.[2]

One exception which I have felt justified in making is the inclusion of some material from Pope Pius XII, none of whose writings are offered in the above mentioned collection. There are a number of reasons for this exception. Chronologically Pius XII's papacy spans the middle of the century whose extremities are *Rerum Novarum*[3] and *Centesimus Annus*. It was during the almost twenty years of his papacy that there arose in Europe some of the most extreme forms of collectivist social organisation. While the encyclical *Mystici Corporis Christi*[4] is not about society in the generally understood sense of the term, it has a good deal to say about the visible social structures of the Church, from which something can be gleaned about Pius XII's understanding of the relationship between individual and society, person and community.

In view of John Paul II's inclusion of the concept *civilisation of love* among the synonyms of *solidarity*, a further exception will have to be made, because neither of the two texts in which this expression is used by

---

[2] Michael WALSH and Brian DAVIES, eds., *Proclaiming Justice and Peace: One Hundred Years of Catholic Social Teaching* (London: CAFOD / Collins, 1991).
    [3] POPE LEO XIII, *Rerum Novarum*, Centenary Study Edition, with introduction and notes by Joseph Kirwan (London: ICTS, 1991). (Hereafter referred to as *RN*).
    [4] POPE PIUS XII, *Mystici Corporis Christi* (London: CTS, 1943). (Hereafter referred to as *MCC*).

Paul VI are included in what is generally thought of as the corpus of the social teaching of the Church.

A. SOLIDARITY

The impression is sometimes given that the concept of *solidarity* suddenly appeared in the social teaching of the Church during the papacy of John Paul II. Rémi Parent suggests that, in view of the fact that the concept does not have a long tradition in the magisterium, it is not surprising that there are fluctuations in the way in which it is used by John Paul II. He then goes on to say:

> The term appeared relatively recently in the official documents of the Church: it is not to be found before the appearance of *Gaudium et Spes* (1964). It does not even appear in the Latin text of *Gaudium et Spes*; it is the French translation of this and of *Populorum Progressio*, (which appeared in the same year) which introduced the abundant use of the substantive *solidarity*. This substantive, however, translates different Latin terms. Beginning with *Gaudium et Spes*, "solidarity" becomes a term frequently used as a complement or a synonym for *conjunctio, communion*, or *friendship-charity*.[5]

It is true that the Latin versions of the encyclicals of Pope John XXIII and Pope Paul VI do not use the substantive *solidarietas*. Parent is not accurate, however, in so far as *Gaudium et Spes* is concerned. There are no less than four cases in which the Latin text of this document uses the term *solidarietas* in one form or another.[6] In the latin version of the Synodal document, *Justice in the World*, the adjective *solida* is used twice, once to qualify the substantive *conjunctio* and once to qualify *necessitudo*. In the English text both expressions are rendered as *solidarity*.[7]

---

[5] Rémi PARENT, "Solidarité, Communion, Parti-pris," *Studia Moralia* XXXI/1(1993): 105.

[6] SECOND VATICAN ECUMENICAL COUNCIL, "Gaudium et Spes," *Acta Apostolica Sedis*, 58 (1966): 1028, § 4; 1051, § 32; 1078, § 57; 1112, § 90. (*Acta Apostolica Sedis* is hereafter referred to as *AAS*.

[7] Cf. WORLD SYNOD OF BISHOPS, *Justice in the World*, in *Acta Apostolicae Sedis* 63 (1971): 936 & 939. It is important, furthermore, to enter a caveat at this point. A conversation with Don Anacleto PAVANETO SDB, head Latinist at the Secretariat of State, confirms that encyclicals and other major documents are first prepared in a modern language, usually French or Italian. An official Latin version is prepared subsequently. As a general rule, the term *solidarietas* is not used in these Latin versions, because it is a neologism. *Solidarity* is usually translated as *conjunctio* or *mutua omnia necessitudo*. While the Latin version may, therefore, be considered as the official one, it should not be regarded

1. A Note on *Solidarism* as a Catholic Social Movement

In the latter part of the nineteenth century and the first few decades of the twentieth century, there developed a current of thought in Germany, generally known as *solidarism*, of which one of the principal proponents was Heinrich Pesch, a Jesuit who had training in law and economics, as well as philosophy and theology. One of the principal differences between solidarism, as it manifested itself in Germany, and the French positivist school in which Durkheim had his roots, is that German *solidarism* was primarily a movement of Catholic social thinkers.

The German current of *solidarism* stresses the concept of the *group*. According to Mulcahy, "solidarism's opposition to individualism, and the kind of capitalism based on it, is recognised; but at times the dissimilarity between solidarism and the systems which over-emphasise the *whole*, socialism, state socialism, and universalism, is not appreciated."[8]

Solidarism is a system, but one which depends more on the person than on the structures.

> An important feature of Peschian solidarism is that the emphasis is not on the institutional framework, though the vocational groups are considered an essential of the system: the vital factor is the *spirit* motivating the men organised in these institutions. It is recognised that the vocational group organisation can be harmful for the nation. The proper spirit is the acknowledgement of the welfare of the whole as the goal of the economic strivings of the individuals.[9]

German solidarism rejects absolute freedom in the economic sphere, just as it rejects the compulsory planned economy. Where property is concerned, solidarism upholds the right of private property, but maintains that there is a social duty arising from ownership.[10] The goal of solidarism is the common welfare.

While the conceptual base of *solidarism* is similar in many respects to Wojtyla's concept of *solidarity*, I have not come across any evidence to suggest that Karol Wojtyla / Pope John Paul II, was directly influenced by Pesch or his school. Pesch was, however, a close contemporary of Max Scheler, to whose thought Wojtyla paid particular attention. Pesch was a

---

as the original.
[8] Richard E. MULCAHY, *The Economics of Heinrich Pesch* (New York: Holt, 1952), 8.
[9] Richard E. MULCAHY, ibid., 10.
[10] Cf. Richard E. MULCAHY, ibid., 164/6.

native of Cologne and Scheler held a professorship at the University of Cologne in the period immediately after the first world war.

It is also generally accepted that Pesch had a significant influence on the development of the social thought of Pope Pius XI, and in particular the encyclical *Quadragesimo Anno*, in which the pope outlined his celebrated Principle of Subsidiarity.[11] Subsidiarity, as we shall see, is an essential element of Pope John Paul II's concept of solidarity. It may also be more than mere coincidence that Eugenio Pacelli, who became Secretary of State to Pius XI in 1930, had served in Germany for the previous thirteen years, first as Nuncio to Bavaria and subsequently as Nuncio to Germany. During this period, when the influence of solidarism would have been quite strong in Catholic circles in Germany, Pacelli demonstrated a concern for the condition of workers, and challenged the totalitarian social theories of Nazism, through a constant appeal to Catholic social teaching.[12] Later, as Pope Pius XII, he became the first pope to make significant use of the concept of solidarity in his public interventions.

2. Pope Pius XII

The earliest reference to *solidarity* in the writing of Pius XII is to be found in the encyclical *Summi Pontificatus* at the beginning of his papacy. He argues there, that the first of two contemporary pernicious errors is the "neglect of the law of human solidarity and of charity dictated and imposed as much by the community of origin and by the equality of rational nature among all men .. as by the redemptive sacrifice offered by Jesus Christ."[13] He goes on to state that

in the light of (the) unity of humanity, both in law and in fact, individuals do not seem to us to be without mutual links, like grains of sand, but rather, united by organic, harmonious, and mutual links ... resulting from their destination and

---

[11] Cf. Exequiel RIVAS, "La Solidaridad en la Esenanza de Juan Pablo II," in *L'Antropologia Solidaristica nella Centesimus Annus*, papers of an international conference, 22-27 Oct. 1991, organised by ASCE / Diocese of Rieti, ed. Alfredo Luciani, 216/7. (Milan: Massimo, 1992); cf. also Richard E. Mulcahy, ibid., 8.

[12] Cf. Nazzareno PADELLARO, *Portrait of Pius XII*, translated by Michael Derrick (London: Catholic Book Club, 1956).

[13] Cf. POPE PIUS XII, *Summi Pontificatus*, AAS 31 (1939): 546. This encyclical is presented in a number of different languages in *AAS*. The reference above is to the official text in English. The text in Latin renders the corresponding phrase as *oblivione continentur mutuae illius hominum necessitudinis caritatisque*; cf. ibid., 426.

from their natural and supernatural impulsion.[14]

It is clear that Pius XII understood human solidarity as a secular concept which was compatible with, and had its roots in, Christian charity. In the course of an address to an organisation of Italian farmers, he says: "Human solidarity has no solid foundation outside this Christian charity, in which it equally finds its perfection."[15]

In the aftermath of World War II especially, Pius XII frequently comments that people everywhere have common interests, such as lasting peace, food and shelter, employment, and the recognition of their rights. At times it seems as if he uses *solidarity* simply to give a name to that state of common need and mutual dependence. It is implied that this situation of interdependence should evoke a co-operative response.

> Why should this solidarity with so many people, who find themselves dispossessed of their peace and in danger, not become for all, a sure way from which salvation may come. Why should this spirit of solidarity not be like a support for the natural social order in its three essential forms: family, property, state, to lead them to an organic collaboration.[16]

At other times, however, *solidarity* seems to be used not so much to name the fact of interdependence, but rather to describe a particular positive moral response to that reality.

> Recent events have again shown to what extent, even among the most humble and the least equipped, solidarity and devotion were expressed in gestures of heroic and moving generosity. It is one of the happy traits of the present time that it accentuates the feeling of interdependence between the members of the social body, and leads them to recognise more clearly that the human person does not reach his true potential except by recognising his personal and social responsibilities, and that many human, or simply economic problems will only find their solution by means of an effort at understanding and sincere mutual

---

[14] Pope PIUS XII, *SP*, 428.

[15] POPE PIUS XII, Address to the International Consultative Commission of the Entrepreneurs of the Chemical Industry, 10/1/'58; cf. Arthur. F. UTZ and J. F. GRONER, *Relations Humaines et Société Contemporaine: Synthèse Chretienne Directives de S.S. Pie XII,* translated and edited in three volumes in French by A. SAVIGNAT and H. Th. CONUS, 3218. (Paris and Fribourg: Editions St. Paul, 1956/63). (Hereafter referred to as *Relations Humaines);* cf. also idem. Radio Message to Participants in a Congress of Christian Associations of Italian Workers, Milan, 1/5/'56, ibid., 3442.

[16] POPE PIUS XII, Christmas Message, 23/12/1950, *AAS* 43 (1951): 55/6.

love.[17]

Solidarity is a generous attitude which seems to be found even among those who can ill-afford to be generous. It is also directed towards those from whom, by reason of their humble state, little or nothing in the way of material recompense can be expected.

Respectful of persons and of their inalienable rights, conscious of the profound solidarity which binds him to the humblest of his fellows, the man of heart, the Christian above all, refuses to accept the judgement of economic facts and social situations by the light of the determinism of blind laws, or of an inexorable historical evolution.[18]

There is no sure way to peace other than the re-education of humanity in the spirit of fraternal solidarity, and world leaders can bear witness to this through their own flexibility with regard to structures.[19] It is the mission of the "social forces" to promote "full reciprocal solidarity between men and between peoples." It is on the foundation of this solidarity, and not on "vain and unstable systems" that Pius XII issues the invitation to re-build society.[20]

Pius XII speaks of *solidarity* as if it were an established principle which serves to counteract the extremes of individualism, and leads to collaboration, not simply on a local level or within individual enterprises, but between enterprises and even between nations.[21] It is by means of *solidarity* that people are drawn together to work in harmony for a common end. One of the ends referred to by Pius XII, in the context of *solidarity* is the supporting of the natural social order.[22] A second is the maintenance of international peace. In his Christmas message of 1957, he envisages the

---

[17] POPE PIUS XII, Address to Participants at the First Congress of the International Association of the Economic Sciences, 9/9/'56, *AAS* 48 (1956): 673.

[18] POPE PIUS XII, *Relations Humaines*, 3517.

[19] Cf. POPE PIUS XII, Christmas Message, 24/12/'46, *AAS* 39 (1947): 13/14.

[20] POPE PIUS XII, Christmas Message, 24/12/'52, *AAS* 45 (1953): 39. Pius XII also insists that there should be a greater actuation of international solidarity, tending towards, if not reaching, the absolute equality of peoples; cf., ibid., 40.

[21] Cf., POPE PIUS XII, Address to Participants at the International Meeting of Catholic Organisations of Small and Medium-Sized Businesses, 8/10/'56, *AAS* 48 (1956): 798; also idem. Christmas Message, 23/12/'50, *AAS* 42 (1951): 55/6; and idem. Christmas Message, 23/12/'56, *AAS* 49 (1957): 18/19.

[22] Cf. POPE PIUS XII, Christmas Message, 23/12/'50, *AAS*, 42 (1951): 56.

establishment of international structures for the preservation of peace arising out of the *solidarity* of nations which seek peace. It would appear that Pius XII understood *solidarity* to be an expression or a manifestation of the divine law.

> The divine law of harmony in the world imposes firmly on all the governments of peoples the obligation of preventing war through international institutions suited to placing armaments under effective surveillance; to deter, through the solidarity between those nations which sincerely seek peace, those who would disturb it.[23]

3. Pope John XXIII

The references to *solidarity* in the social teaching of John XXIII are to be found principally in the encyclical *Mater et Magistra*.[24] Pope John, like his predecessor, refers to a *principle of human solidarity* as if it were something well established.[25] The sense of mutual *solidarity* is to be a guiding principle in the establishment of associations of workers, and in the relations between workers and employers.

> Both workers and employers should regulate their mutual relations in accordance with the principle of human solidarity and Christian brotherhood. Unrestricted competition in the liberal sense, and the Marxist creed of class warfare, are clearly contrary to Christian teaching and the nature of man.[26]

Human solidarity is, thus, not to be identified with either of the two existing models of socio-economic organisation, and at least certain aspects of both are incompatible with solidarity.

The other area of concern to which John XXIII applies the principle of solidarity is the issue of hunger and poverty, particularly on a global scale. He argues that "the solidarity of the human race and Christian brotherhood demand the elimination as far as possible of these discrepancies."[27] He

---

[23] POPE PIUS XII, Christmas Message, 22/12'57, *AAS* 50 (1958): 23.

[24] POPE JOHN XXIII *Mater et Magistra*, in Michael WALSH and Brian DAVIES, (Eds.), *Proclaiming Justice and Peace: One Hundred Years of Catholic Social Teaching*, 2nd. Ed, London: CAFOD / Collins, 1991. (Hereafter referred to as *MM*).

[25] Cf. POPE JOHN XXIII, *MM*, § 23; also idem, *Pacem in Terris, Proclaiming Justice and Peace*, Michael Walsh and Brian Davies (Eds.), London: CAFOD/Collins, § 107. *Pacem in Terris* is hereafter referred to as *PT*.

[26] Cf. POPE JOHN XXIII, *MM*, § 23; cf. also ibid., § 146.

[27] POPE JOHN XXIII, *MM*, § 155.

argues that "the solidarity which binds all men together as members of a common family makes it impossible for wealthy nations to look with indifference upon the hunger, misery and poverty of other nations."[28] It becomes clear that for John XXIII, *solidarity* is a relationship which finds its basis in human nature itself, and is not exclusively linked to membership of particular groups.

Finally, John XXIII points out that even those nations which are less well off, and more dependent, have a responsibility to exercise solidarity among themselves. "The problems which face the poorer nations in various parts of the world ... are caused, also, by the lack of effective solidarity among such peoples."[29]

4. Vatican Council II

The term *solidarity* is used in nine different locations throughout the Conciliar document *Gaudium et Spes*,[30] sometimes with a spiritual meaning and sometimes with reference to the organisation of society. The activity of dialogue in which the Vatican Council is engaged is seen as an expression of its "solidarity with, as well as its respect and love for the whole human family."[31] The Church is referred to as a "new brotherly community," the "body" of Christ, in which "everyone, as members one of the other, would render mutual service according to the different gifts bestowed on each. This solidarity must be constantly increased until that day on which it will be brought to perfection."[32]

It would seem therefore that *solidarity* is the relationship of mutual service which pervades a brotherly community; the Church being one example of such a community. The community is spoken of in organic terms, as a body. There is a suggestion that the solidarity which exists in the community must always be open to growth.

There are a number of references which would suggest that the Council

---

[28] ibid., § 157. Further on in this paragraph it is suggested that it will not be possible to maintain peace as long as glaring imbalances exist. Solidarity is, therefore, intimately related with the development and maintenance of peace.

[29] ibid., § 190.

[30] SECOND VATICAN ECUMENICAL COUNCIL, *Gaudium et Spes*, in *Proclaiming Justice and Peace: One Hundred Years of Catholic Social Teaching*, Michael WALSH and Brian DAVIES eds., 2nd. edition, (London: CAFOD / Collins, 1991). (Hereafter referred to as *GS*).

[31] SECOND VATICAN ECUMENICAL COUNCIL, *GS*, § 3.

[32] SECOND VATICAN ECUMENICAL COUNCIL, *GS*, § 32.3 & § 32.4.

Fathers tended to think of *solidarity* as something arising inevitably from *interdependence* or, in other words, as a fact of the human condition rather than a moral attitude. "Although the world of today has a very vivid awareness of its unity and of how one man depends on another in needful solidarity, it is most grievously torn into opposing camps by conflicting forces."[33] The Council notes the destructiveness of opposing ideologies, against which the awareness alone of mutual dependence is clearly not an adequate defence. This is a theme which surfaces frequently in the encyclicals of John Paul II as we shall see in due course.

Catholic associations, according to *Gaudium et Spes* contribute much to the development of a "universal outlook," and "help to form an awareness of genuine universal solidarity and responsibility."[34] Here, again, it seems that *solidarity* is seen as a feature of interdependence, albeit one which involves a certain responsibility. The commitment of Christians to service for the common good helps to demonstrate the compatibility of "personal initiative with the solidarity of the whole social organism."[35]

5. Pope Paul VI

Pope Paul VI makes it clear in the social teaching of Pope Paul VI that *solidarity* is not simply a matter of the collaboration of people in the interests of economic progress.

> Dialogue (between cultures) will be fruitful if it shows the participants how to make economic progress and how to achieve spiritual growth as well; if the technicians take the role of teachers and educators; if the training provided is characterised by a concern for spiritual and moral values, so that it ensures human betterment as well as economic growth. Then the bonds of solidarity will endure even when the aid programmes are past and gone. Is it not plain to all that closer ties of this sort will contribute immeasurably to the preservation of world peace.[36]

Here too, Pope Paul reaffirms the fundamental causal relationship between solidarity and peace, already stated by John XXIII. He argues that it is the responsibility of government leaders to draw their communities "into closer ties of solidarity with all men... in order to promote the

---

[33] ibid., § 4.3; also ibid., § 85.

[34] SECOND VATICAN ECUMENICAL COUNCIL, *GS*, § 90.

[35] ibid., § 75.4.

[36] POPE PAUL VI, *Populorum Progressio*, in Michael WALSH and Brian DAVIES, (Eds.), *Proclaiming Justice and peace: One Hundred Years of Catholic Social Teaching*, 2nd. ed., London: CAFOD / Collins, 1991, §73. (Hereafter referred to as *PP*).

development of nations and the preservation of peace."[37]

Speaking of human rights, Paul VI draws attention to the risks inherent in an over-emphasis on equality. "Without a renewed education in solidarity, an over emphasis on equality can give rise to an individualism in which each one claims his own rights without wishing to be answerable for the common good."[38] This warning reflects the comments of both Mounier, and Scheler, that persons are incomparable and unsubstitutable. Solidarity is not to be understood as a statement of mere equality between persons; nor is equality a guarantee of a truly personal relationship.[39]

In international trade, a narrow interpretation of equality constitutes an obstacle to solidarity, because it often ignores the fact that the starting point is one of great disparity between developed and undeveloped nations. In the light of solidarity, equality comes to be understood as equality of opportunity.[40] Conversely, solidarity is the means by which the desire for equality is moderated; becoming a desire for and a commitment to the common good. At the opposite extreme, when there develops an attitude of superiority and a failure to recognise the fundamental equality of dignity between persons and between nations, there arise other "obstacles... to the development of world solidarity: nationalism and racism."[41]

True solidarity is not simply a matter of feelings, because it requires that people take account of the means and ends in which they are called upon to collaborate with others, to ensure that they accord with the "principles of a true humanism."[42] Some people become so caught up in deep feelings of solidarity and emotional identification with others, that they cease to make any judgements of their own.[43]

Pope Paul understands solidarity to be an attitude which is the antithesis of the individualistic attitudes of distrust and selfishness.[44] Nor do social solidarities simply come about as a by-product of individual initia-

---

[37] POPE PAUL VI, *PP*, § 84.

[38] POPE PAUL VI, *Octagesimo Adveniens*, in Michael WALSH and Brian DAVIES, (Eds.), *Proclaiming Justice and Peace: One Hundred Years of Catholic Social Teaching*, 2nd. Ed, London: CAFOD / Collins, 1991, §23. (Hereafter referred to as *OA*).

[39] Cf. Max SCHELER, *Ressentiment*, 121/2; also Emmanuel MOUNIER, *Révolution*, 201/2.

[40] Cf. POPE PAUL VI, *PP*, § 61.

[41] POPE PAUL VI, *PP*, §62.

[42] POPE PAUL VI, *OA*, § 49.

[43] Cf. POPE PAUL VI, *OA*, §50.1.

[44] Cf. POPE PAUL VI, *PP*, § 64.

tives. They have to be worked for as a primary goal of any form of social organisation.

> Nor can he (the Christian) adhere to the liberal ideology which believes it exalts individual freedom by withdrawing it from every limitation, by stimulating through exclusive seeking of interest and power, and by considering social solidarities as more or less automatic consequences of individual initiatives, not as an aim and a major criterion of the value of social organisation.[45]

It becomes clear that social solidarity has to be understood as having a moral import. This is probably the most significant development in the concept of *solidarity*, which we find in the social teaching of Paul VI. As we have seen, however, this interpretation was already implicit in the teaching of Pius XII. Solidarity is a moral stance, or attitude, which is rooted in the fact of our shared humanity. In terms of international development, Paul VI identifies mutual solidarity as "that aid that the richer nations must give to developing nations," as one element in a "threefold obligation," which stems "from the human and supernatural brotherhood of man."[46] He re-affirms the obligatory nature of solidarity when he comments further on that "the duty of promoting human solidarity also falls upon the shoulders of nations."[47]

Paul VI notes that the negative legacy, which sometimes results from colonialism, can be overcome by means of the establishment of new relationships based on free and constructive agreements.

> It is certainly all right to maintain bi-lateral and multi-lateral agreements. Through such agreements, ties of dependence and feelings of jealousy – hold-overs from the era of colonialism – give way to friendly relationships of true solidarity that are based on juridical and political equality.[48]

For Paul VI, evangelisation and solidarity are closely linked. By a Christian "witness which involves presence, sharing, solidarity," irresistible

---

[45] POPE PAUL VI, *OA*, § 26.
[46] POPE PAUL VI, *PP*, § 44. The other two elements are social justice and universal charity.
[47] ibid., § 48.
[48] POPE PAUL VI, *PP*, §52.

questions are evoked in the hearts of those who seek the truth.[49] The Christian message needs to be presented in such a way, in the conditions of modern society, that modern man can find in it "the answer to his questions and the energy for his commitment of human solidarity."[50]

6. The Synod of Bishops

A similar emphasis is to be found in the synodal document *Justice in the World*, which sees the specifically Christian hope of salvation as a sign in which Christians can recognise the broader solidarity which is the "unity of the human family."[51] The challenge for the Church is to "show in its own life greater co-operation between the churches of rich and poor regions through spiritual communion and division of human and natural resources," so that it "may really be the sign of that solidarity which the family of nations desires."[52]

7. Summary of the Concept

In order to arrive at a reasonably accurate understanding of the concept of *solidarity* in the period under examination, it will be helpful to ask four questions, namely a) what causes or contributes to solidarity? b) what are the objectives and goals of solidarity? c) how are these objectives and goals achieved? and d) what are the obstacles to solidarity?

a. It seems clear from various comments of Pius XII that the awareness of mutual necessity can and often does give rise to the expression of *solidarity*. There is no doubt but that *solidarity* is founded on the appropriate balance in society between independence and collaboration. This truth could be said to be the *principle of solidarity*. For both John XXIII and Paul VI solidarity has its roots in human nature, and is promoted or made more evident by the Christian message. There is no hope of *solidarity* without trust. The Second Vatican Council sees the role of the Catholic

---

[49] POPE PAUL VI, *Evangelii Nuntiandi*, in *Proclaiming Justice and Peace: One Hundred Years of Catholic Social Teaching*, eds. Michael WALSH and Brian DAVIES, 2nd. edition, (London: CAFOD / Collins, 1991), §21. (Hereafter referred to as *EN*).

[50] POPE PAUL VI, *PP*, §3.

[51] WORLD SYNOD OF BISHOPS, *Justice in the World*, in *Proclaiming Justice and Peace: One Hundred Years of Catholic Social Teaching*, eds. Michael WALSH and Brian DAVIES, 2nd. edition, (London: CAFOD / Collins, 1991), §55. (Hereafter referred to as *JW*).

[52] ibid., § 59.

associations as important for the growth of *solidarity*.[53]

b. *Solidarity* is seen as having a wide variety of objectives, some of which are socio-economic, others personalist. It is concerned with the resolution of the practical problems of humanity, both on a local and an international level. It acts as a support for the natural social order. Solidarity avoids waste of energy and resources, is committed to the protection of employment, and re-unites the disparate elements of considerable economic potential. On an international level it is concerned with addressing the problems of poverty and migration, as well as the elimination of discrepancies between the resources of nations and the maintenance of world peace. By means of *solidarity*, each person seeks to be useful to all, as one member of a body for all the members, and every Christian is bound to the humblest of his fellows. These are certainly not things that occur automatically simply as a result of the fact of inter-dependence. They require an awareness and a particular attitude towards that mutual need.

c. *Solidarity* achieves its objectives through dialogue, and through agreements based on trust. It promotes personal initiative and responsibility. It is greatly assisted by the renunciation of certain privileges, by the moderation of material demands, by mutual service each according to his own gifts, and by restraint in the use of criticism.

d. Among the factors which limit or damage *solidarity* are the habit of looking at other persons as if they were strangers, and the existence of opposing camps and conflicting forces. Tiredness and uncertainty, jealousy, undue dependence, and unrestrained unilateral criticism, as well as individualism, nationalism, and racism all erode *solidarity* and limit its effectiveness.

How then should we define solidarity as it is presented in the social teaching of the Church up to 1978? We could say that solidarity is the social bond which exists within and between societies and nations, through the awareness of a common human nature and of mutual human necessity. This bond provides the motivation for the realisation of the common good, through the integral resolution of human problems, by means of dialogue, collaboration, aid, and mutual service.

Parent suggests that the concept of *solidarity* was, until very recently, little used and regarded with suspicion in Catholic circles, because of its origins outside the Christian tradition, and indeed in an anti-Christian

---

[53] Cf. SECOND VATICAN ECUMENICAL COUNCIL, *GS*, § 90.

context. He says that the concept of *solidarity* grew up "as a reaction against a Christian Charity which was judged to be incapable of articulating the relationships which would make effective the interdependence which it was sought to promote."[54] *Solidarity* was, therefore, understood as "a refusal to say *communion*," and an attitude to aid which excluded the need to love the recipient.[55] He further argues that what is really at issue is the fear on the part of some that orthopraxis (represented by *solidarity*) would constitute a threat to orthodoxy (represented by *communion*).[56]

Parent may be correct when he says that *solidarity* has tended at times to be regarded with suspicion in some Catholic circles, and he may also be correct in his analysis of the reasons for this. It does seem, however, that the popes from the time of Pius XII onwards were more comfortable with this concept than Parent suggests. This is not really surprising in the case of Pius XII, who had a particular interest in the development of European unity, especially in the post-war years. He would have been likely to encounter the concept of *solidarity* in a positive context, and to have found it readily understood by the constituency to which he was addressing himself, when he spoke of matters relating to European unity, and the role of a new Europe in a wider world.[57] Neither is the openness of John XXIII to a social concept of secular origin all that surprising when we consider his warm welcome for the United Nations Organisation, and for its Universal Declaration of Human Rights, which marked an important watershed in the attitude of the Church to the human rights agenda.[58]

B. FRIENDSHIP

As a philosophical concept, *friendship* has a long history. It was widely discussed among the Greek philosophers, as John Paul II notes.[59] I propose, therefore to examine the concept of *friendship* as it is found in the social teaching of the Church, in the light of its earlier philosophical development.

---

[54] Cf. Rémi PARENT, ibid., 109 & 113.

[55] ibid., 115.

[56] ibid. 116.

[57] Cf. Thomas WOODS, *A European Community of Nations in the Teaching of Pius XII*, Doctoral Thesis presented to the Faculty of Canon Law of the Pontifical Lateran University. (Rome: Lateran University, 1962).

[58] Cf. POPE JOHN XXIII, *PT*, §§ 142-5.

[59] Cf. POPE JOHN PAUL II, *CA*, § 10.

1. The Greek and Roman Philosophers

Aristotle was aware of different points of view as to whether friendship was promoted by likeness between people or by diversity. Some argued that it would be impossible for people to be friends if they didn't have a good deal in common. Others argued, however, that friendship is rooted in the fact that people are different and, therefore, each is in a position to offer something that the other needs or wants. For Aristotle, however, friendship based on self-interest is not genuine and only lasts as long as one person is in a position to offer what the other wants, whether this is a matter of utility or pleasure.[60] Perfect friendship, on the other hand, is based on similitude.

> Perfect friendship is the friendship of men who are good, and alike in virtue; for these wish well alike to each other *qua* good, and they are good in themselves. Now those who wish well to their friends for their sake are most truly friends; for they do this by reason of their own nature and not incidentally; therefore their friendship lasts as long as they are good – and goodness is an enduring thing.[61]

Aristotle goes on to say that this perfect friendship does not exclude usefulness or pleasure, but it does not depend on them either.

This distinction which Aristotle makes between friendship based on similitude and the kinds of friendship based on utility or pleasure is interesting in the context of this study of *solidarity* because it is quite similar to the distinction made by Durkheim and outlined in Chapter One, between the two kinds of solidarity, Mechanical Solidarity (based on similitude) and Organic Solidarity (derived from the division of labour). What is significant is that, for Durkheim, the growing dominance of solidarity based on utility represents a positive development in society, while for Aristotle, the reverse would seem to be the case.

For Cicero, as for Aristotle, true friendship is closely linked to goodness. Friendship is a kind of bond between those who are committed to the good. To this extent, his concept of friendship is somewhat selective and depends on a certain social and moral similitude. "Friendship is nothing other than consensus on all things human and divine, united to devotion and affection; and I know of nothing better, other than wisdom,

---

[60] Cf. ARISTOTLE, *Nicomachean Ethics*, in *The Works of Aristotle*, Vol. 2, translated by W.D. Ross, Great Books of the Western World, ed. Robert Maynard Hutchins, no. 9. (Chicago: Encyclopaedia Brittanica, 1952), VIII, 3, 1156a.
[61] ibid., VIII, 3, 1156b.

which has been given by the immortals to man."[62] Cicero argues further on that "those who admit of a friendship for the sake of interest, destroy the most lovely of the bonds of friendship."[63]

For Epictetus and Seneca, however, friendship is to be found not only among those of a certain social class; it does not depend on noble birth or occupation. Seneca writes that one may sometimes find more easily in a slave the qualities that are indicative of goodness. In his letter to Lucilius, he asks

> Would you not consider that this, whom you call your slave, born of your own progeny, enjoys the same sky, breathes as you do, lives and dies as you do. It would be just as easy for you to see him as a free man, and for him to see you as a slave.[64]

Like Seneca, Epictetus is constrained to accept the fact that, in practice and in law, there is a distinction between slaves and free people, but he argues that according to the law of God we are all equal as brothers.[65] The important characteristic required for friendship is a shared commitment to the good.

> Whoever, then, understands what is good, can also know how to love; but he who cannot distinguish good from bad, and things which are neither good nor bad from both, how can he possess the power of loving? To love, then, is only in the power of the wise.[66]

One further development in the understanding of *friendship* among the stoics is to be found in the thought of Marcus Aurelius. Like the other stoics, he recognises the value of goodness, but he recognises his kinship even with the sinner in a nature that is

> not only of the same blood or seed, but that ... participates in the same intelligence and the same portion of the divinity. I can neither be injured by them, for no one can fix on me what is ugly, not can I be angry with my kinsman, nor hate

---

[62] Marcus Tullius CICERO, *Laelius De Amicitia*, ed. G.B. Bonino, VI, 20. (Turin: Paravia, 1936).

[63] ibid., XIV, 51.

[64] LUCIUS. A. SENECA, *Epistulae ad Lucilium*, Vol. 1. (Pisa: Giardini, 1983).

[65] Cf. EPICTETUS, *Discourses*, translated by George Long, in *Lucretius, Epictetus, Marcus Aurelius*, Great Books of the Western World, ed. Robert Maynard Hutchins, no. 12. (Chicago: Encyclopaedia Brittanica, 1952), I, 13, 1-5.

[66] ibid., II, 22, 3. cf. also ibid., II, 22, 29.

him. For we are made for co-operation, like feet, like hands, like eye-lids, like the rows of the upper and lower teeth. To act against one another then is contrary to nature; and it is acting against one another to be vexed and to turn away.[67]

This is more than simply an expression of sentiment; it has moral consequences. He cannot hate him whom he considers to be his kin.

With Seneca, Epictetus, and Marcus Aurelius, then, friendship seems to be based on a more essential, ontological level of similitude than is the case in the thought of Aristotle or Cicero. It is not that they regard moral good to be unimportant, but rather that they recognise the possibility of a good which is pre-moral.

There appears, then, to be a certain ambiguity in the position of Seneca, Epictetus and Marcus Aurelius. It would seem that if any of them were to choose a friend as such, each would choose a man who was good and wise like himself. However, they also recognise that there is a sense in which friends are not of our choosing; that there exists a moral responsibility of friendship or brotherhood towards all our fellow human beings. This obligation is partly based on similitude – the sharing of the same rational nature, and partly rooted in the acceptance of the diversity of others.

2. St. Thomas Aquinas

St. Thomas explains that, "all existing things, in so far as they exist are good,"[68] and therefore are proper objects of love. Love and friendship, however, are not exactly synonymous. The words for *love* and for *friendship* in most of the Latin based languages are derived from the same root, the Latin verb *amare*. This is not the case in English, where the distinction between the two realities is expressed in the use of two quite distinct words. I would suggest that this distinction is not insignificant.

St. Thomas tells us that friendship is a form of love, which involves a certain capacity for being reciprocated. Irrational creatures are loved only with the love of concupiscence, and not the love of friendship.

> Friendship cannot exist except towards rational creatures, who are capable of returning love, and communicating one with another in the various works of life,

---

[67] MARCUS AURELIUS, *Meditations*, translated by George Long, in *Lucretius, Epictetus, Marcus Aurelius*, Great Books of the Western World, no. 12, ed. Robert Maynard Hutchins. (Chicago: Encyclopaedia Brittanica, 1952), II, 1.

[68] SAINT THOMAS AQUINAS, *Summa Theologiae*, Iae, Q.20, 2. ans. (Hereafter referred to as *ST*).

and who may fare well or ill, according to the changes of fortune and happiness; even as to them is benevolence properly speaking exercised.[69]

Aquinas goes on to explain that: "the movement of love has a two-fold tendency."[70] We love the good which we wish to others, and this is the love of concupiscence. We also love the one to whom we wish the good, and this is the love of friendship. He agrees with Aristotle that, while friendship based on utility or pleasure does have something of the character of friendship, it cannot be described as true friendship.

> When friendship is based on usefulness or pleasure, a man does indeed wish his friend some good: and in this respect the character of friendship is preserved. But since he refers this good further to his own pleasure or use, the result is that friendship of the useful or pleasant, in so far as it is connected with love of concupiscence, loses the character of true friendship.[71]

We can now go on to examine the use of *friendship* in the social teaching of the Church, with a better understanding of its classical philosophical background. In the social teaching between 1891 and 1978, the use of *friendship* is not very extensive. In fact we will need to concern ourselves only with *Rerum Novarum* and *Populorum Progressio*.

3. Pope Leo XIII

In the context of describing the obligations of justice, Leo XIII remarks that the church "seeks persistently for more than justice. She warns men that it is by keeping a more perfect rule that class becomes joined to class in the closest neighbourliness and friendship."[72] It would seem therefore that friendship is the fruit of something greater than simple justice.

Some paragraphs further on, however, Leo XIII implies that friendship is not the deepest bond or relationship open to the human person. For those who obey Christian teaching, "it will be the bond of Christian love rather than of friendship that will unite them."[73] Pride tends to bring about a separation between "the two classes," but an awareness of the life of Christ, "who became poor for our sake," acts as an antidote to this pride, and

---

[69] SAINT THOMAS AQUINAS, *ST*, Iae, Q. 20, 2, ad 3.
[70] SAINT THOMAS AQUINAS, *ST*, Ia IIae, Q. 26, 4, ans.
[71] SAINT THOMAS AQUINAS, *ST*, Ia IIae, 26, 4, ad 3.
[72] POPE LEO XIII, *RN* § 18.
[73] POPE LEO XIII, *RN*, § 21.

facilitates the rapprochement of the two classes "in bonds of friendship."[74]

4. Pope Paul VI

Pope Paul VI argues that when the possession of goods is regarded as the ultimate objective "men harden their hearts, shut out others from their minds and gather together solely for reasons of self-interest rather than out of friendship; dissension and disunity follow soon after."[75] In this way Pope Paul draws a distinction between the relationship based on utility, and that of real friendship. Friendship is referred to in the following paragraph, along with love, as one of the higher values for which man can strive.[76]

In international relations, the bonds that have traditionally joined nations have frequently been bonds of dependence, and these relations have "too often been governed by force." Pope Paul, more than once, uses the concepts of *friendship* and of *solidarity* in the same context, presenting "friendly relationships of true solidarity based on juridical and political equality" as a positive alternative to "ties of dependence and feelings of jealousy – holdovers from the era of colonialism"[77] The arms race has played a major role in the way in which the relationships between nations have developed. Pope Paul says that it is the "task" of delegates to international organisations "to see to it that senseless arms races and dangerous power plays give way to ...a collaboration that is friendly, peace orientated, and divested of self-interest."[78]

While arguing that nations should not allow the axis of domination-dependence to become the foundation on which their relationships are based, he does not ignore that reality of interdependence, nor see it as necessarily conflicting with the demands of true friendship. He quotes an address given on the occasion of his visit to India.

> At Bombay we said "man must meet man, nation must meet nation, as brothers and sisters, as children of God: In this mutual understanding and friendship, in this sacred communion, we must also begin to work together to build the

---

[74] POPE LEO XIII, *RN*, § 20.

[75] POPE PAUL VI, *PP*, § 19.

[76] Cf. POPE PAUL VI, *PP*, § 20.

[77] POPE PAUL VI, *PP*, § 52; cf. also ibid., § 65 in which the Pope looks forward to a new order, facilitated by effective world solidarity, in which "international relationships will be characterised by respect and friendship."

[78] POPE PAUL VI, *PP*, § 84.

common future of the human race."[79]

5. Summary of the Concept

It is immediately clear that *friendship*, as it is understood in the social teaching of the church, does not just come about of its own accord; it has to be worked for. It is the fruit of an attitude that seeks to go beyond the demands of mere justice.[80] Among the things which give rise to friendship are "the deep thought and reflection of wise men in search of a new humanism."[81] This reflection is put into effect in the relations between nations, by means of bi-lateral and multi-lateral agreements, and through the efforts of delegates to international organisations.[82]

When we come to examine the objectives of friendship, we find that the pre-occupations of Leo XIII are different from those of Paul VI, though not un-related. Leo XIII sees friendship as something which will facilitate the coming together of two classes that have hitherto been in conflict.[83] Paul VI is concerned with the elimination of dissension and the development and maintenance of peace between "two worlds," referred to sometimes as the "first world" and the "third world."[84]

The obstacles to *friendship* include pride, which is not unrelated to the desire to dominate and exploit the other (whether an individual or a nation) and self-interest. To this extent there is certainly a continuity between the stoic view of genuine friendship as something which was not based primarily on utility and the view of *friendship* as presented in the social teaching of the Church.

C. SOCIAL CHARITY

According to Pope John Paul II, the concept of *social charity* is particularly associated with Pius XI.[85] However, the concept *charity* without the adjective makes its appearance in a social context, earlier in the social teaching of the church.

---

[79] POPE PAUL VI, *PP*, § 43.
[80] Cf. POPE LEO XIII, *RN*, § 18.
[81] POPE PAUL VI, *PP*, § 20.
[82] Cf. POPE PAUL VI, *PP*, §§ 52 & 84.
[83] Cf. POPE LEO XIII, *RN*, § 20.
[84] Cf. POPE PAUL VI, *PP*, §§ 19, 43, 52, 65 & 84.
[85] Cf. POPE JOHN PAUL II, *SRS*, § 11.

1. Pope Leo XIII

The concept *charity* is used by Pope Leo XIII with specific reference to the healing of the ills of society. He argues that each person and social institution has its own part to play in remedying the evils of society. The role of the clergy is to make

> strenuous efforts to nourish in themselves and to inspire in others the practice of charity, mistress and queen of all the virtues. For indeed it is from a great outpouring of charity that the desired results are principally to be looked for. It is of Christian charity that we speak, the virtue which sums up the whole gospel law. It is this which makes a man ever and entirely ready to sacrifice himself for the good of others. It is this which is man's most effective antidote against worldly pride and immoderate love of self.[86]

2. Pope Pius XI

The encyclical *Quadragesimo Anno* of Pope Pius XI is concerned both with the destructive dominance of the free-market economy and with the spread of socialism. His emphasis on the value of associations of workers, motivated by Christian values, is intended to contribute to the resolution of the problematic relations of labour and capital, in a way which avoids a class conflict. "The unity of the human society cannot be founded on the opposition of classes."[87] Similarly, the Pope argues, neither the free competition of individualist economics, nor the economic dictatorship of socialism are capable of serving as a "true and effective directing principle" for economic life. It is in this context that Pius XI refers to *social charity* as the soul of the social order.

> But it (economic dictatorship) cannot curb itself. Loftier and nobler principles – social justice and social charity – must therefore, be sought whereby this dictatorship may be governed firmly and fully. Hence, the institutions themselves of peoples and, particularly those of all social life, ought to be penetrated with this justice, and it is most necessary that it be truly effective, that is, establish a juridical and social order which will, as it were, give form and shape to all economic life. Social charity, moreover, ought to be as the soul of this order, an order which public authority ought to be ever ready effectively to protect and defend. It will be able to do this the more easily as it rids itself of those burdens which, as We have stated above, are not properly its own.[88]

---

[86] POPE LEO XIII, *RN*, § 45.
[87] POPE PIUS XI, *QA*, § 88.
[88] ibid.

From our point of view this is a helpful passage because it presents *social charity* and *social justice* as co-principles by means of which economic dictatorship may be curbed, while at the same time making a distinction between them. *Social justice* is to establish a new juridical and social order, while *social charity* is to be the soul of that order. It is difficult to avoid the image of body and soul in trying to come to an understanding of what Pius XI means. It would seem that the structure of society can hold together where there is justice alone, but that without *social charity* it has no life principle or inner dynamism.

Pius XI states clearly that it is the role of the public authority to protect and defend the social order, but he implies that, in many cases, this is not being done effectively because the energies of the public authority are engaged in interfering in areas which are not within its proper competence.[89]

The only other point at which Pius XI uses the term *social charity* is when he encourages those who have wandered "far from the truth," to return to the Church and to "stand firm in the ranks of those who ... are striving to restore society according to the mind of the church on the firmly established basis of *social justice* and *social charity*.[90]

While justice without charity is lifeless, charity cannot take the place of justice either, because without justice the social fabric begins to fall apart. Pius XI is critical of the attitude of those who use charity as a means of salving their consciences while living quite comfortably with injustice.

> Quite agreeable, of course, was this state of things to those who thought it in their abundant riches the result of inevitable economic laws and accordingly, as if it were for charity to veil the violation of justice which lawmakers not only tolerated but at times sanctioned, wanted the whole care of supporting the poor commuted to charity alone.[91]

3. Pope John XXIII
Pope John XXIII, like Pius XI, tends to use the two concepts of *justice*

---

[89] Cf. POPE PIUS XI, *QA*, ibid. § 88. This comment can best be understood in the light of Pius XI's earlier presentation of the *Principle of Subsidiarity*, cf., ibid., § 79.

[90] POPE PIUS XI, *QA*, § 126.

[91] POPE PIUS XI, *QA*, § 4. It will be noted that the term *social charity* is only used in a small number of places in the writings of Pius XI. Frequently, the term *charity* is used without qualification but in a social context.

and *charity* together. "All forms of economic enterprise must be governed by the principles of social justice and charity."[92] Similarly, the right of property must be balanced by the principle that "the goods which were created by God for all men, should flow to all alike," and this balancing is the function of "the principles of justice and charity."[93]

Pope John refers, in *Pacem in Terris*, to the need for an appropriate social order which will form the foundation for a true peace. "It is an order that is founded on truth, built up on justice, nurtured and animated by charity, and brought into effect under the auspices of freedom."[94] While he mentions a number of additional constituents of the ideal social order, John XXIII returns to Pius XI's image of a social order established by justice and ensouled by charity.

4. Vatican Council II

The Fathers of the Second Vatican Council comment that in attempting to resolve the problems of the "earthly city" people often find that "the Christian view of things will itself suggest some specific solution in certain circumstances. Yet it happens rather frequently, and legitimately so, that with equal sincerity some of the faithful will disagree with others on a given matter." However, human solutions are not to be confused with the gospel message, and people "should always try to enlighten one another through honest discussion, preserving mutual charity and caring above all for the common good."[95] This "brotherly charity" does more than anything else to reveal God's presence.[96]

5. Pope Paul VI

In a significant passage from Pope Paul VI's encyclical, *Populorum Progressio*, we find *universal charity* referred to in conjunction with *mutual solidarity* and *social justice* as a threefold obligation derived from the "human and supernatural brotherhood of man."[97] *Universal charity* is

---

[92] POPE JOHN XXIII, *MM*, § 39. This is a reference to to the teaching of Pius XI in *QA*, §88. The original Latin text makes it clear that the adjective *social* applies both to *justice* and to *charity*. The relevant expression is "iustitia et caritate, tamquam principibus rei socialis legibus." cf. Pope JOHN XXIII, "Mater et Magistra," *AAS* 56 (1961): 410.

[93] POPE JOHN XXIII, *MM*, § 43.

[94] POPE JOHN XXIII, *PT*, § 167.

[95] SECOND VATICAN ECUMENICAL COUNCIL, *GS*, § 43.2.

[96] Cf. ibid., § 21.4.

[97] POPE PAUL VI, *PP*, § 44.

described as "the effort to build a more human world community, where all can give and receive, and where the progress of some is not bought at the expense of the others."[98] By comparison, *mutual solidarity* is described as "the aid that the richer nations must give to developing nations."[99]

The fact that the source of the obligation, "which concerns first and foremost the wealthier nations," is the brotherhood of man, both human and supernatural, would certainly imply that universal charity is not restricted by the boundaries of nation, class, or creed; and this implication is further strengthened by the very choice of the adjective *universal*.

Further on, referring to the problems encountered by migrants and refugees, Paul VI argues that the "duty of giving foreigners a hospitable reception" is one which is "imposed by human solidarity and by Christian charity."[100]

The apostolic exhortation *Evangelii Nuntiandi* argues that, while the preaching of the Gospel includes human liberation among its objectives, this liberation is doomed unless it is motivated by justice in charity.

> The Church has the firm conviction that all temporal liberation, all political liberation .... carries within itself the germ of its own negation and fails to reach the ideal that it proposes for itself, whenever its profound motives are not those of justice in charity, whenever its zeal lacks a truly spiritual dimension and whenever its final goal is not salvation and happiness in God.[101]

This expression *justice in charity* is, perhaps, a little like the biblical exhortation to "speak the truth in love." The moral goodness of the struggle for justice, and similarly for truth, is determined in part by the motivation of the struggle. In order for liberation to be truly good, it must be conducted in a manner and with an attitude which are compatible with the ultimate end of mankind.

6. Summary of the Concept

It is difficult to arrive at a satisfactory understanding of the concept of *social charity* as used in the social teaching of the church up to 1978, because the use of the concept is so limited. The only way in which this problem can be resolved is to draw in to the analysis, as I have done above,

---

[98] ibid.
[99] ibid.
[100] POPE PAUL VI, *PP*, § 67.
[101] POPE PAUL VI, *EN*, § 35.1.

the use of the concept *charity*, when it is clearly intended to have a social reference.

The most striking thing is the way in which *charity* and *justice*, with or without the adjective *social*, are used together in a way which suggests that they are complementary, but distinct. If we were to examine Durkheim's notion of the more advanced or "organic" social group in the light of the criterion that *charity* is the soul or motivating force of the social order, we might reasonably conclude that, while his *society* is established on a complex structure of justice, it is lacking because of the absence of charity as the primary motivating principle. As we have seen in the previous chapter, this is what lies at the heart of the criticisms of *society* made by both Scheler and Mounier.[102]

The difference between *charity* and *justice* can be understood more easily when we consider the nature of the duty which each involves. As St. Thomas notes, justice is concerned with ensuring that every person receives that to which he is entitled, whether in the relationship between one person and another, or in the appropriate distribution of what is common to all. Because justice demands the proper balance, restitution is a necessary element of justice.[103] There is an obligation to *charity*, but it cannot be expressed in terms of restitution. Firstly, the law of charity is what Pope Pius XI refers to as the "bond of perfection" and this implies that *charity* goes beyond the minimum required by justice.[104] Secondly, the duty of *charity* is such that it is binding on everyone, and not simply on those who have more than they should have, in favour of those who have less. Pope Paul VI defines the obligation of *charity* in terms of building "a more humane world community where all can give and receive."[105]

Looked at in this way, *charity* or *social charity* is the characteristic which safeguards societies against the minimalism to which they would be prone if they were founded on justice alone. It guards against the tendency of societies to deteriorate as a result of the weakness of social bonds based on the motive of self-interest alone. If this is accepted, then it appears that *social charity* has a meaning in the social teaching of the Church, which is similar, if not identical to the meaning of *solidarity* as used by Scheler.

We can say that *social charity* is a virtuous attitude, called forth by the

---

[102] Cf. Chapter 2, 39 and 59.
[103] Cf. SAINT THOMAS AQUINAS, *ST*, IIa IIae, QQ. 61 & 62.
[104] Cf. POPE PIUS XI, *QA*, § 137.
[105] POPE PAUL VI, *PP*, § 44.

human and supernatural brotherhood of man. Its objective is to act as the soul of the social order, assuring true peace. It achieves this objective by a number of practical means, in which it co-operates with and supports the ordinances of social justice. These means include the curbing of economic dictatorship, and the facilitation of an appropriate balance between the rights and obligations of property. Paradoxically, one of the principal obstacles to charity is the complacency with regard to matters of justice of those who "see their abundant riches as the result of inevitable economic laws and accordingly, as if it were for charity to veil the violation of justice which lawmakers not only tolerated but at times sanctioned, wanted the whole care of supporting the poor commuted to charity alone."[106] In other words, what damages charity most is the expectation that it should achieve its objectives without the co-operation of justice.

D. CIVILISATION OF LOVE

The third principle which Pope John Paul II considers to be the same as the principle of *solidarity* is that of the *civilisation of love*. The references to this principle are relatively few, and I have found no evidence to suggest that the concept was ever presented in these terms prior to the pontificate of Pope Paul VI. Michel Schooyans points out that the Second Vatican Council, because of its strong personalist inspiration, placed considerable emphasis on the dignity of the human person, "a dignity such that it is a point of general agreement between believers and non-believers." He then goes on to say: "This teaching is echoed in *Populorum Progressio*. Paul VI emphasises that it is in the name of this dignity that bold and profoundly new transformations must be undertaken, with a view to a *civilisation of love*."[107] It is not, however, in *Populorum Progressio* that Pope Paul VI uses the expression *civilisation of love*, but in his address for the closing of the Holy Year in 1975 and in his Message for the World Day of Peace, 1977.[108]

In the address on the occasion of the ending of the Holy Year, the

---

[106] POPE PIUS XI, *QA*, § 4.

[107] Michel SCHOOYANS, ibid., 51.

[108] Cf. POPE PAUL VI, Address to Mark the Closing of the Holy Year, 25/12/'75, *Insegnamenti di Paolo VI*, XIII (1975): 1564-1568. (Vatican City: Libreria Editrice Vaticana, 1976); cf. also idem, Message for the World Day of Peace 1977, in *Insegnamenti di Paolo VI* XIV (1977): 1021-1028. (Vatican City: Libreria Editrice Vaticana, 1978). (*Insegnamenti di Paolo VI* is hereafter referred to as *IP6*).

Pope's comments take the form of a prayer to God who has "embraced every man, yes, everyone needful of understanding, of help, of comfort, of sacrifice; even if unknown to us personally, even if troublesome or hostile, but marked with the incomparable dignity of a brother."[109] He predicts that

> the wisdom of fraternal love ... will burst forth with a new fruitfulness, with victorious felicity, with regenerative sociality. Neither hatred, nor contention, nor avarice shall be its dialectic, but love, love which generates love, the love of man for man, not for any short-term or equivocal interest, or in the form of any bitter or poorly tolerated condescendence, but for love of you, you O Christ, found in the suffering and the need of every one of our fellows....The civilisation of love will prevail in the anguish of implacable social struggles, and will offer to the world the dreamt of transfiguration of a finally Christian humanity.[110]

It is clear from the above passage that Pope Paul sees the new flowering of fraternal love as a product of the reality and the awareness of human dignity, which in turn is rooted in God's uncalculating love. The *civilisation of love* is not founded primarily on self-interest, and it is not just a temporary arrangement for as long as it suits the needs of the individual.

There is implicit in the reference to "the anguish of implacable social struggles," Paul VI's promotion of the *civilisation of love* as an alternative to the "class struggle" which is seen as inevitable in the Marxist ideology. To this extent the *civilisation of love*, without being in any sense a *third way*, is seen to transcend the limitations both of the individualist and the socialist ideologies.

In the same Peace Day address, Pope Paul explains that, while peace "seems to have become the equivalent and perfective expression of civilisation,"[111] it is not something which comes about of its own accord, or which is ever fully achieved or secure. Referring once again to the *civilisation of love*, he says:

> Peace is a vertex which presupposes an interior and complex support structure; it is like a flexible body which must be supported by a strong skeleton. It is a construction which owes its stability and its excellence to the carrying power of causes and conditions, which it often lacks, and which even when they are

---

[109] Pope PAUL VI, Address to Mark the Closing of the Holy Year, 25/12/'75, *IP6* XIII (1975): 1566.

[110] ibid., 1567.

[111] Pope Paul VI, Address for World Peace Day, 1977, *IP6* XIV (1976): 1021.

operative, do not always fulfil the function assigned to them, so that the summit of the pyramid of Peace might be high, and that it might be stable on its base.[112]

As with the principle of *social charity*, we see here also a clear acceptance of the need for social structures, but also a recognition of the fact that these structures are frequently deficient. The Pope points out that international agreements on human rights and fundamental liberties are the "documents of our civil progress. They are the epic of peace in so far as they are the shield of life." However these agreements, intended to strengthen the framework of the social "skeleton," serve only to indict civilisation as a "derisive and violated reality, if they remain no more than dead letters."[113]

The reference to a "strong skeleton" prompts a comparison with the image used by Pope Pius XI in which *social charity* acts as the soul of the social order. The "strong skeleton" of civilisation is only able to sustain and extend peace, if it is a civilisation ensouled by love. The challenge for humanity, then, is to achieve an "equation between true peace and the dignity of life" upon which may be erected "a new cornice on the horizon of our civilisation of life and peace, the civilisation – once again we say it – of love."[114]

Pope Paul concludes his Message for the World Day of Peace by commenting that "there remains an unresolved question; how to realise such a programme of civilisation? How to truly twin life and peace. ... What is needed," he says, "is the help of the God of peace."[115]

From the above analysis, it would seem that, for Pope Paul VI, while the *civilisation of love* is not a social type, in the sense of a capitalist, socialist, or tribal society, it does represent a very definite character of social organisation, i.e., a community motivated by love. What gives rise to the *civilisation of love* is the awareness of the essential and universal dignity of the human person as one who is embraced by God. The realisation of the *civilisation of love* requires the help of the God of peace. The ultimate objective of the *civilisation of love* is the extension and maintenance of peace, and the overcoming of implacable social struggles. This objective is achieved by means of reinforcing and rendering more

---

[112] POPE PAUL VI, Address for World Peace Day, 1977, ibid., 1023.
[113] POPE PAUL VI, Address for World Peace Day, 1977, ibid., 1027.
[114] POPE PAUL VI, Address for World Peace Day, 1977, ibid., 1028.
[115] ibid.

effective the social support structure which leads to peace.

We come now to the three other concepts mentioned above which, while not actually identified with *solidarity* by Pope John Paul II, may nonetheless shed some light on our understanding of *solidarity*. It will not be necessary to go into quite as much detail in analysing them, as in the case of those already dealt with above. For this reason, without sub-dividing the treatment into separate sections for the magisterium of each of the Popes, I intend to explore, where applicable, each of these concepts in terms of what gives rise to it, what its objectives are, how it achieves these objectives, and what constitute the primary obstacles to the fulfilment of these objectives.

E. COMMON GOOD

The concept of the *common good* is widely discussed by St. Thomas in the *Summa Theologiae*, especially in those sections dealing with government and with the virtue of justice. The *common good* is related to the individual good in a dialectic manner. Each person is concerned with his own good and is naturally inclined to resist anyone who seeks to take that good away from him. The end towards which one person's activity is oriented is his own good, and not particularly the good of others.[116]

Citing Aristotle, however, St. Thomas remarks that human persons are naturally social and that life together in society requires that someone should take responsibility for the *common good*.

> For many, as such, seek many things, whereas one attends only to one. Wherefore the Philosopher says, in the beginning of the *Politics*, that wherever many things are directed to one, we shall always find one at the head directing them.[117]

He distinguishes between two models of leadership. The first is a leadership of domination in which one person imposes his will on another in a master / slave relationship. The second model is found where one person directs another for the other's own good or for the *common good*.[118] For St. Thomas, the whole basis of the *common good* is the common, ultimate end of mankind.[119]

---

[116] Cf. SAINT THOMAS AQUINAS, *ST*, Ia, Q.96, 4 ans.; also II IIae, Q.58, 9 ad 3.

[117] SAINT THOMAS AQUINAS, *ST*, Ia, Q.96, 4 ans.

[118] Cf. ibid.

[119] Cf. SAINT THOMAS AQUINAS, *ST*, Ia IIae, Q. 90, 2, ad 2.

Just as intermediary ends are subject to the ultimate end, so the individual good of each person is subject to the common good, and that of each smaller group is subject to the good of the whole community.[120] The *common good* is not something totally vague because it is always related to the concrete conditions in which individual people live and to the individual ends that they have.[121] Yet the *common good* is not merely the sum of the individual goods of the members of any society. There is not merely a difference of quantity but also a qualitative difference between the concepts of *individual good* and *common good.*

> The common good of the realm and the particular good of the individual differ not only in respect of the many and the few, but also under a formal aspect. For the aspect of the common good differs from the aspect of the individual good, even as the aspect of whole differs from that of part.[122]

The achievement of the *common good* is in the interest of all the members of a community, and so it is also the responsibility of all the people. This responsibility, however, is exercised on behalf of the people by those who hold public office.[123] The *common good*, therefore, is the fruit of legal justice which, according to St. Thomas, is in a better position than particular justice to be impartial and to consider the deepest needs of each and every member of the community.[124]

Accordingly, St. Thomas says that the sole function of law is to promote the *common good* and those virtues which pertain to it. All laws must be oriented towards this end. While it is frequently argued that laws should be changed in order to keep pace with social conditions, St. Thomas cautions that only the advantage of the *common good* is an adequate justification for changing laws, since the *common good* is the principal reason for their existence.[125]

---

[120] Cf. SAINT THOMAS AQUINAS, *ST*, Ia IIae, Q.90, 3, ad 3.

[121] Cf. SAINT THOMAS AQUINAS, *ST*, Ia IIae, Q.90, 2, ad 1 & ad 2.

[122] SAINT THOMAS AQUINAS, *ST*, IIa IIae, Q58, 7, ad 2.

[123] Cf. SAINT THOMAS AQUINAS, *ST*, Ia IIae, Q90, 4 ans. Also Ia, Q.96, 4 ans.; and II IIae, Q.40, 1 ans.

[124] Cf. SAINT THOMAS AQUINAS, *ST*, IIa IIae, Q.58, 9, ad 3. St. Thomas notes that the *common good* is related to the *universal good* as justice is related to charity; cf. ibid., IIa IIae, Q.58, 6 ans. This may help to clarify the relationship of justice and charity as discussed above.

[125] Cf. SAINT THOMAS AQUINAS, *ST*, Ia IIae., Q. 90, 2, sed contra.; Ia IIae, Q. 96, 3 ans.; Ia IIae, Q.97, 2 ans.

Among the obstacles to the achievement of the *common good*, is
sedition within the state, which arises from the tendency to individualism
and selfish interest. In the case of sedition, St. Thomas comments, it
becomes particularly important for all the members of the community to
rally to the defence of the *common good* in support of the rulers.[126]

All of the popes since Leo XIII develop the concept of the *common
good* to some extent in their social teaching, though it is particularly
associated with the encyclicals of Pope John XXIII. Schooyans remarks:

> Up to Paul VI, reflection on the common good progressively extended its scope,
> beginning with the consideration of particular goods: the goods of persons, of
> families, of intermediate groups, of nations, and arriving finally to consider the
> whole of humanity.[127]

The fathers of the Second Vatican Council offer a number of definitions of the *common good* in the course of *Gaudium et Spes*. "The common
good... is the sum of those conditions of social life which allow social
groups and their individual members relatively thorough and ready access
to their own fulfilment."[128] "The common good embraces the sum of those
conditions of the social life whereby men, families and associations more
adequately and readily may attain their own perfection."[129]

It becomes immediately obvious from these definitions that the
common good is closely linked to the good of individual persons and
intermediate groups of persons. This point is repeatedly emphasised in the
social teaching of the Popes. "We have already said that the state has no
authority to swallow up either the individual or the family. To the extent
that the common good is not endangered or any person hurt, justice
requires full freedom of action for both."[130]

Aubert remarks that it is important to take account of the reasons for
the caution of Leo XIII on this matter.

> While wishing to react in the name of scholastic tradition, focussed on the
> common good, against an individualist view of society and property, he was

---

[126] Cf. SAINT THOMAS AQUINAS, *ST*, IIa IIae, Q.42, 2 ans.

[127] Michel SCHOOYANS, ibid., 39.

[128] SECOND VATICAN ECUMENICAL COUNCIL, *GS*, § 26.

[129] ibid., § 74.

[130] POPE LEO XIII, *RN*, § 29; cf. also POPE PIUS XI *QA*, § 25; Pope PIUS XII *Radio
Message to mark the Fiftieth Anniversary of Rerum Novarum*, 1/6/'41, *AAS* 33 (1941) 221/2;
and *PT* §§ 56 & 139.

careful to avoid giving any support to the totalitarian tendencies which the
doctrinaire socialism of his time frequently presented.[131]

The responsibility for the achievement of the *common good* is primarily that of the state. "By virtue of its office the state ought to care for
the common good."[132] "Its whole *raison d'etre* is the realisation of the
common good in the temporal order."[133] It is noted that, due to the
increasing complexity of relations between nations, consideration needs to
be given to the establishment of international structures to assure the
universal common good.

> Today the universal common good presents us with problems which are world-
> wide in their dimensions; problems, therefore which cannot be solved except by
> a public authority with power, organisation and means co-extensive with these
> problems, and with a world-wide sphere of activity. Consequently the moral
> order itself demands the establishment of some such general form of public
> authority.[134]

While the attainment and preservation of the *common good* is primarily
the responsibility of the state, every individual member and group in
society has a part to play, and this part cannot be arrogated to itself by the
state. The classical statement of this Principle of Subsidiarity is made by
Pope Pius XI, when he says:

> Just as it is gravely wrong to take from individuals what they can accomplish by
> their own initiative and industry and give it to the community , so also is it an
> injustice and at the same time a grave evil and disturbance of right order to assign
> to a greater and higher association what lesser and subordinate organisations can
> do.[135]

Pope Pius XI set out to promote the activity of professional and
workers' organisations as an important factor in the promotion of the

---

[131] Roger AUBERT, "L'Encyclique *Rerum Novarum*: Point d'Aboutissement d'une
Lente Maturation," *De* Rerum Novarum *à* Centesimus Annus. (Vatican City: Pontifical
Council for Justice and Peace, 1991) 23.

[132] POPE LEO XIII, *RN*, § 26.

[133] POPE JOHN XXIII, *MM*, § 20; cf. also ibid., §§ 37, & 151; idem, *PT* §§ 54 & 136;
SECOND VATICAN ECUMENICAL COUNCIL, *GS* § 73.3; and POPE PIUS XI, *OA*,
§46.1.

[134] POPE JOHN XXIII, *PT*, §137; Cf. also SECOND VATICAN ECUMENICAL
COUNCIL, *GS*, § 84, and POPE PIUS XI, *OA*, § 44.

[135] POPE PIUS XI, *QA*, § 79.

common good of a country. Pope Paul VI commented that the training and development facilitated by such organisations "do much to cultivate in them an awareness of the common good and its demands upon all."[136] The importance of this active participation of individuals and intermediary groups in the promotion of the common good is repeated frequently throughout the social magisterium.[137]

As a "sum" of social conditions whereby people may attain self-fulfilment, the *common good* is not brought about by any one cause, but by many. These include:

a) "the maintenance of peace and order" which is "of as much importance to the public as to private good."[138]

b) the "employment of the greatest possible number of workers."[139]

c) care in the exercise of distributive justice, with special reference to wages and prices,[140] and the needs of disadvantaged groups.[141]

d) the guaranteeing of personal rights in "a state juridical system which conforms to the principles of justice and rightness."[142]

The concept of the common good recognises the existence of a hierarchy of values, in so far as some goods are more fundamental to the human person than others. "The common good is something which affects the needs of the whole man, body and soul. ... (Rulers) must respect the hierarchy of values, and aim at achieving the spiritual as well as the material prosperity of their subjects."[143]

It is also possible to identify a number of factors which tend to prevent the development of the *common good*. These include:

a) government "solely or mainly by means of threats and intimidation,

---

[136] POPE PAUL VI, *PP*, § 38; cf. also POPE PIUS XI, *QA*, §85.

[137] Cf. POPE JOHN XXIII, *MM*, §§ 44, 65, & 117; also idem, *PT*, § 100; and POPE PIUS XI, *OA*, § 46.1.

[138] POPE LEO XIII, *RN*, §29.

[139] POPE JOHN XXIII, *MM*, §79; cf. also POPE PIUS XI, *QA*, §74.

[140] Cf. POPE LEO XIII, *RN*, § 27; also POPE PIUS XI, *QA*, § 58; and POPE JOHN XXIII, *MM*, §§ 71 & 112.

[141] Cf. POPE JOHN XXIII, *MM*, §§ 133-135.

[142] POPE JOHN XXIII, *PT* §70; cf. also ibid., § 60. Among these rights are specifically mentioned the right to participate in government cf. ibid., § 74, and the right to exercise a free vote, together with the corresponding obligation, cf. *GS* § 75.

[143] POPE JOHN XXIII, *PT*, § 57; cf. also SECOND VATICAN ECUMENICAL COUNCIL, *GS*, § 60, which emphasises the importance of providing "a sufficient quantity of cultural benefits, especially of those which constitute the so-called basic culture."

or promises of reward."[144]

    b) failure to take the human person into account at all times.[145]

    c) employment practices which scorn the dignity of workers.[146]

    d) the enslavement of the state to the greed of men.[147]

    e) "the diversion of the exercise of authority from the service of the common good to the interests of one or another faction or of the rulers themselves."[148]

    f) the holding back of unproductive resources.[149]

We have seen the reservations expressed by Scheler and Mounier about the tendency in modern society to speak of the equality of persons. Pope Paul VI reflects the same concern when he comments that "without a renewed education in solidarity, an over-emphasis on equality can give rise to an individualism in which each one claims his own rights without wishing to be answerable for the common good."[150]

The *common good* looks beyond the temporal order. The needs and the circumstances of the temporal order are constantly changing, but the anchor which gives a certain continuity to the *common good* is the fact that it "finds its ultimate meaning in the Eternal Law,"[151] and its tendency towards God who is the "supreme and inexhaustible good."[152]

In conclusion, we can say that the *common good*, which is rooted in the nature of the human person, is the ultimate human good in the temporal order. Socio-moral attitudes such as *solidarity*, the inspiration for which is significantly contributed by the *common good* are, in themselves, intermediate goods and constitutive elements of the *common good*.

---

[144] POPE JOHN XXIII, *PT*, § 48.

[145] Cf. POPE JOHN XXIII, § 55.

[146] Cf. POPE PIUS XI, *QA*, § 101.

[147] Cf. POPE PIUS XI, *QA*, § 109.

[148] SECOND VATICAN ECUMENICAL COUNCIL, *GS*, § 73.3; cf. also ibid., § 75.4.

[149] Cf. SECOND VATICAN ECUMENICAL COUNCIL, *GS*, § 65.2. While the requirements of the common good do not conflict with the right to property, the public authorities may determine the use of private property in the interests of the common good, cf. POPE LEO XIII, *RN*, § 35; POPE PIUS XI, *QA*, § 49; SECOND VATICAN ECUMENICAL COUNCIL, *GS*, § 71.3, & POPE PAUL VI, *PP*, § 24. When required by the needs of the common good, private property may be expropriated for public use, but only with appropriate compensation, cf. SECOND VATICAN ECUMENICAL COUNCIL, *GS*, § 71.5 & POPE PAUL VI, *PP*, § 24.

[150] POPE PAUL VI, *OA*, § 23.

[151] SECOND VATICAN ECUMENICAL COUNCIL, *GS*, § 78.

[152] POPE PIUS XI, *QA*, § 43.

F. MYSTICAL BODY

For some time before Pope Pius XII wrote his encyclical letter *Mystici Corporis Christi*, the concept of the mystical body had been developed in Christian theology as a means of expressing the social cohesion of the Church and its intimate links with the person of Jesus Christ.[153] Already in the teaching of Pope Pius XI, we have seen that one of the factors which creates the co-operation necessary for the common good is that "the members of society deeply feel themselves members of one great family and children of the same heavenly Father; nay that they are one body in Christ, but severally members one of another."[154]

It is clear to all who have eyes to see that the Church is a society or social organisation of some kind. It has its own juridical structures which facilitate its cohesion. Just like any other social body, however, it can only be understood when we discover the source and the objective of its social cohesion. Pope Pius XII rejects the rationalism and naturalism which fails to see anything in the Church beyond a purely juridical or social entity.

> On the one hand the error of rationalism persists, rejecting as absurd anything which transcends the powers of the human mind, side by side with the kindred false doctrine of naturalism which, in the Church of Christ sees nothing, and refuses to see anything, apart from purely juridical and social ties.[155]

The central point that Pius XII makes is that the Church is not simply an invisible, spiritual entity, but a "perfect social body," in which all the members are united by a common aspiration in seeking a common end.[156] Over and above the juridical ties which it has, in common with any other society with a common end in view, the Church has a "further principle of unity arising from those three virtues which knit us most closely with God:

---

[153] Cf. e.g, Emile MERSCH, *Le Corps Mystique du Christ: Etudes de Theologie Historique*, with a preface by Fr. J. Lebreton. (Paris: Desclée, 1936). Mersch argues that the concept exists implicitly in the Synoptic gospels and in the Acts of the Apostles. He notes it's first explicit use in the First Letter to the Corinthians, Ch. 12: 12 (cf. Emile MERSCH, ibid., 381), and he traces its development in the writings of the Fathers of the Church, in the Scholastic period, and up to the present century.

[154] POPE PIUS XI, *QA*, §137. This passage refers back to the Letter of St. Paul to the Romans, Ch. 12.

[155] POPE PIUS XII, *Mystici Corporis Christi*. (London: Catholic Truth Society, 1943). (Hereafter referred to as *MCC*).

[156] POPE PIUS XII, *MCC*, §62.

Christian faith, hope and charity."[157]

The *Body of Christ* is characterised by charity. There is a direct proportion between the union of the members with God, who is the source of cohesion of the *Body of Christ*, and their union with each other in Charity.[158] In this, the *Body of Christ* is similar to the *personal communities* of Scheler and Mounier, and those envisaged in the social teaching of the Church, held together by the bonds of *solidarity, friendship* and *social charity*.

Another similarity between the *Body of Christ* and some of the concepts we have examined is the idea that, in the *Body of Christ* each of the members "retains his own personality."

> In the mystical Body the cohesive force, intimate though it is, unites the members with one another in such a way that each of them wholly retains his own personality. ... In any living physical body the sole final purpose for which each and every individual member exists is the benefit of the whole organism, whereas any social structure of human beings has for its ultimate purpose, in the order of utilitarian finality, the good of each and every member, inasmuch as they are persons.[159]

One aspect of this retention of one's own personality is the liberty of conscience of the individual person.[160]

As is the case with every society, there are conditions for membership of the Body of Christ. The Church is a society restricted, not by geographical boundaries or political allegiance, but by the sharing of a common Baptism into a common faith.

> Only those are to be accounted really members of the Church who have been regenerated in the waters of Baptism and profess the true faith, and have not cut themselves off from the structure of the body by their own unhappy act or been severed therefrom for very grave crimes, by the legitimate authority.[161]

Pope Pius XII states very clearly, however, that the obligations of

---

[157] POPE PIUS XII, *MCC*, § 70.

[158] Cf. POPE PIUS XII, *MCC* §§ 49 & 73.

[159] POPE PIUS XII, *MCC*, §59. This is an important statement. It implies that an organic image of solidarity, such as Durkheim proposes, is inadequate to take account of the personal reality of human society. It also complements Mounier's comment that, while the individual is at the service of society, the needs of society are always subject to the needs of the person.

[160] Cf. POPE PIUS XII, *MCC*, § 86.

[161] POPE PIUS XII, *MCC*, § 21.

Charity, emanating from the *Body of Christ* are not to be seen as exclusive.

> It is true that Christ has only one Bride, the Church; yet the love of the divine Bridegroom is so universal that in His Bride he embraces without exception every member of the human race. ... A true love of the Church therefore requires not only that in the Body itself we should be members one of another and mutually careful one for another, each rejoicing in another member's glory and suffering in his sorrow; but also that in other human beings not yet united with us in the Body of the Church we should see brethren of Christ according to the flesh, called with us to the same eternal salvation.[162]

Here Pius XII seems to foreshadow the concept of *solidarity*, rooted in the common humanity of all persons, which was to be developed in the social teaching of the Church after his own time.

It is suggested in *Populorum Progressio* that the relationship of the members within the *Body of Christ* gives a sharper focus to the desire of all people to

> establish closer ties of brotherhood....This struggle towards a more human way of life certainly calls for hard work and imposes difficult sacrifices. But even adversity, when endured for the sake of one's brothers, and out of love for them, can contribute greatly to human progress. The Christian knows full well that, when he unites himself with the expiatory sacrifice of the divine saviour, he helps greatly to build up the Body of Christ, to assemble the people of God into the fullness of Christ.[163]

This willingness on the part of the individual person to make sacrifices for the sake of the community is very much a part of some of the other concepts which we have examined, especially that of the *common good*.

In conclusion, we can say that the *Body of Christ*, like the *Civilisation of Love* is more concrete than a moral attitude or principle of social organisation. What we have seen above is also sufficient for us to recognise that, as a social type, the Church / *Body of Christ* is unique in that it is firmly rooted in the person of Christ as its source and its end, acting visibly in the body through a visible head, the Vicar of Christ.[164] It is a society in the world which looks beyond the world for its meaning and its final end.

---

[162] POPE PIUS XII, *MCC*, § 95; cf. also POPE JOHN XXIII, *MM*, § 159.
[163] POPE PAUL VI, *PP*, § 79.
[164] Cf. POPE PIUS XII, *MCC*, § 38.

G. COMMUNION

We come, now, to the last of the concepts which I intend to consider in this chapter, namely the concept of *communion*. We have already seen how Mounier uses *communion* to describe the most perfect interpersonal relationship in society. The concept is commonly used in the social teaching of the Church from the Second Vatican Council onwards. In the period under examination in this chapter, it is not, however, as clearly developed as *solidarity* or the *common good* in terms of its source, its objectives, and its means of achieving them. We are told that the companionship of male and female "produces the primary form of interpersonal communion. For by his innermost nature man is a social being, and unless he relates himself to others he can neither live, nor develop his potential."[165] This brief comment offers us two parameters at least for a definition of *communion*; its source in the creation of rational beings who are equal but different, and its objective in the development of the human potential of each person who participates in the *communion*. The ultimate development of the human potential of the person is *communion* with God, and it is in this "vocation" that we find "the basic source of human dignity."[166]

In one passage from *Gaudium et Spes*, we find a striking correspondence with the later development of the concept of *solidarity*. We are told that *interdependence* which is related to technical progress does not exhaust the human capacity for relationship. *Communion* at the level of interpersonal relationships is qualitatively different and reflects more closely the truly human potential of the person for dialogue.

> One of the salient features of the modern world is the growing interdependence of men one on the other, a development promoted chiefly by modern technical advances. Nevertheless brotherly dialogue among men does not reach its perfection on the level of technical progress, but on the deeper level of interpersonal relationships. These demand a mutual respect for the full spiritual dignity of the person. Christian revelation contributes greatly to the promotion of this communion between persons.[167]

Interdependence itself is morally neutral and, as a phenomenon, it is not exclusive to human persons. *Communion*, on the contrary, is a moral

---

[165] SECOND VATICAN ECUMENICAL COUNCIL, *GS*, § 12.3.
[166] SECOND VATICAN ECUMENICAL COUNCIL, *GS*, § 19.
[167] SECOND VATICAN ECUMENICAL COUNCIL, *GS*, § 23.

response to *interdependence* and, as such, is to be found only on the higher level of personal relationships.

One of the means by which *communion* contributes to the development of the person is the family, which is described as "a kind of school of humanity." The family effectively fulfils this role through the "kindly communion of minds and the joint deliberation of spouses."[168]

Communion, like *solidarity* is not something aspired to by individual persons alone. It is also a way in which the relationships between nations may be directed. The synodal document *Justice in the World* speaks of the bishops being gathered "in communion with all who believe in Christ and with the entire human family."[169] The document goes on to suggest that the Church, through its own internal communion should be a "sign of that *solidarity* which the whole family of nations desires."[170] The universal mission of the Church makes it appropriate that she should "enter into communion with the various civilisations, to their enrichment and the enrichment of the Church herself."[171] Pope Paul VI, recalling his comments at Bombay, links *communion* and *friendship*, adverting to the sacredness of the vocation to interpersonal dialogue.

> At Bombay we said "Man must meet man, nation must meet nation, as brothers and sisters, as children of God: In this mutual understanding and friendship, in this sacred communion, we must also begin to work together to build the common future of the human race."[172]

Other references to *communion* in the social teaching of the Church focus largely on the internal *communion* which is the Church's witness in the world to the dignity of the person and his vocation to *communion* with God. The Church is the "visible sign of the encounter with God."[173] The practical expression of this *communion* is to be found in the pastoral relationship between bishops or pastors and people,[174] the communion of the clergy "which has its source in the Sacrament of orders,"[175] the

---

[168] SECOND VATICAN ECUMENICAL COUNCIL, *GS*, § 52.
[169] WORLD SYNOD OF BISHOPS, *JW*, § 1.
[170] WORLD SYNOD OF BISHOPS, *JW*, § 59.
[171] SECOND VATICAN ECUMENICAL COUNCIL, *GS*, § 58.2.
[172] POPE PAUL VI, *PP*, § 43.
[173] POPE PAUL VI, *EN*, § 28.
[174] Cf. POPE PAUL VI, *OA*, § 4; also idem, *EN* §§ 58 & 60.
[175] POPE PAUL VI, *EN*, § 68.3.

relationship of co-operation between the churches,[176] and the church's "lively solicitude for the Christians who are not in full communion with her."[177]

In conclusion, we have in the concept of *communion*, a mode of interpersonal relationship, the immediate objective of which is the enrichment of all those who participate in it, and the final objective of which is the growth of relationship with God. *Communion* is facilitated by various means, including the educational role of the family, the witness of the Church, and the revelation of God himself.

H. CONCLUSIONS

The conclusions to this chapter are best presented in the form of the three problems with which we began, namely:

a. To establish the meaning of *solidarity* as it is used in the social teaching of the Church between 1891 and 1978.

b. To establish whether and why it is appropriate to say that the principle of *solidarity* is the same as the principles of *friendship, social charity,* and the *civilisation of love*.

c. To establish whether anything can be learnt about *solidarity* by examining concepts such as the *common good*, the *body of Christ*, and *communion*.

As far as *solidarity* itself is concerned, I have suggested that, in its use in the body of material which I have considered, it may be defined as the social bond which exists within and between societies and nations, through the awareness of a common human nature and of mutual human necessity. This bond provides the motivation for the realisation of the common good, through the integral resolution of human problems, by means of dialogue, collaboration, aid, and mutual service.

Solidarity presupposes an "other," whether an individual person or a community of persons, with whom I am engaged in relationship. The question arises as to whether or not *solidarity* depends on the response of that other. If solidarity is an attitude it would seem that I can be in solidarity with someone who is not in solidarity with me. If, however, it is a bond, then it implies at least a certain minimum of reciprocity. Pope Paul VI refers to the obligation of "mutual solidarity."[178] This would seem to

---

[176] Cf. WORLD SYNOD OF BISHOPS, *JW*, § 59; also POPE PAUL VI, *EN*, § 64.2.
[177] POPE PAUL VI, *EN*, § 54.2.
[178] POPE PAUL VI, *PP*, § 44.

imply that mutuality is not an essential element of the definition of solidarity. Nonetheless, the element of reciprocity is undoubtedly important for the social effectiveness of *solidarity*.

The way in which *friendship* is contrasted with *Christian love* may offer some help in clarifying the meaning of *solidarity*.[179] It seems that the concepts mentioned by Pope John Paul II in *Centesimus Annus* as being the same as *solidarity* are those which are not specifically Christian, but which have a rather more universal application. They tend to be contrasted with the more specifically Christian ones, as *friendship* is contrasted here with *Christian love*. We have seen that the terms *Christian charity* and *social charity* are sometimes used in a way that suggests a distinction between them. Likewise the expression *Christian solidarity* is sometimes used, but more frequently *solidarity* is used on its own in a manner that would suggest that it is a concept reaching beyond Christianity.

What we have seen in the concept of *social charity* is that while it goes hand in hand with *social justice*, it seems to reach beyond the limits of what is merely just. This it has in common with the attitude of *solidarity*. Leo XIII explains that the joining of class to class in the "closest neighbourliness and friendship" is made possible, not by justice alone, but by "keeping a more perfect rule," i.e., the rule of charity.[180] Here we have a link between *charity* and *friendship*, which would suggest that *charity* is in some sense prior to *friendship*

Elsewhere we have a point of comparison between *universal charity* and *mutual solidarity*. *Universal charity* is described as "the effort to build a more humane world community, where all can give and receive, and where the progress of some is not bought at the expense of others." *Mutual solidarity*, on the other hand is described as "the aid which the richer nations must give to the developing nations."[181] If we take "aid" to mean practical development assistance, then *solidarity* appears to be more narrowly defined, and perhaps more a matter of praxis than *charity*. The problem is that this is not reflected in some of the other references to *solidarity* which we have examined.

While the *civilisation of love* is undeniably similar to *social charity*, *friendship*, or *solidarity*, in many of its characteristics it seems that the concept *civilisation of love* is more concrete or material than the others. It

---

[179] Cf. POPE LEO XIII, *RN*, § 21.
[180] POPE LEO XIII, *RN*, §18.
[181] POPE PAUL VI, *PP*, § 44.

is less an attitude or a principle and more a social entity, albeit a rather unique one. The comparison might more helpfully be made between *love* and the other three concepts mentioned above, in which case the *civilisation of love* would be the concrete manifestation of that love in the ordering of society.

A second significant difference that I find between the *civilisation of love* and the other three concepts is that it is more specifically and overtly spiritual than any of the other three, as they appear in the social teaching of the Church, at least up to 1978.

The *common good* is not a mode of relationship as are *solidarity, friendship*, and *social charity*. It is more correctly thought of as the fruit of such a relationship, and to this extent seems to have more in common with the *civilisation of love*. There is undoubtedly a close link between the *common good* and *solidarity*, but it appears to be one of finality rather than one of identity. The need to promote the *common good* is born of man's nature, his personal desire for the good, and his natural impulse to seek that good in society with others.[182] The outcome of this natural desire to seek the *common good* is that the *common good* itself becomes, as it were, a final cause of authentically human social cohesion.

> Because order, as St. Thomas well explains, is unity arising from the harmonious arrangement of many objects, a true, genuine social order demands that the various members of a society be united together by some strong bond. This unifying force is present not only in the producing of goods or the rendering of services ... but also in that common good, to achieve which all Industries and Professions together ought, each to the best of its ability, to cooperate amicably.[183]

The specifically Christian dimension of the *Body of Christ* concept sets it apart from some of the other concepts which we have studied to date. It should be noted, however, that the *personal community* of Scheler tends towards the notion of the perfect social group being realised only in union with God. The *collective person* of Mounier is even more specifically Christian in its conception. It is not, therefore, the spiritual dimension *per se*, but its specific Christological formation, that makes the *Body of Christ* unique as a description of the ecclesial society.

---

[182] Cf. POPE JOHN XXIII, *PT* §§ 55 & 132.
[183] POPE PIUS XI, *QA*, § 84; cf. also SECOND VATICAN ECUMENICAL COUNCIL, *GS*, §§ 68.1 & 75.4.

Communion clearly has much in common with *solidarity* and *friendship*, but, like the *Body of Christ* it would appear to be a more specifically theological or ecclesial concept, at least in the way it is used within the social teaching of the Church up to 1978. It would seem to be significant that we do not come across any development of this concept in the encyclicals which deal with the more concrete social issues, e.g., the condition of workers, the rise of socialism, and the search for world peace. This would tend to support the view of Parent, that the real tension between *solidarity* and *communion* is the tension between orthopraxis and orthodoxy.

In conclusion, I would argue that *solidarity*, in the social teaching of the church from 1891 to 1978, is to be understood primarily as a social relationship based on the moral implications of a shared humanity, and that it is sufficiently close in meaning to *friendship* and *social charity* for it to be said that these three are the same. As has been mentioned previously, the social teaching of the Church, in the period under examination, was engaged in a gradual movement from the particular to the universal. Slight variations in the common sense meaning of these terms probably contribute to *friendship* being more appropriate for use at the level of the particular, and *solidarity* where a more universal application is intended, with *social charity* somewhere in the middle of the range.

There are also, however, slight shifts and nuances of meaning in each of these concepts, even at times within the usage of the same Pope. For example, *solidarity* is more like *friendship* when it is used in a way which implies reciprocity, but more like *social charity* when it doesn't carry that implication. This fluctuation results in a weakening of the sense of equivalence, not unlike the way in which some monetary currencies rise and fall within an agreed band in the European Monetary System. To continue the analogy, the important thing is to be able to recognise when one of these terms is used in such a way as to give it a meaning which is completely outside the "band of equivalence." As I have suggested, it appears that the concept *civilisation of love* does not sit as easily within the band as do the other concepts named by John Paul as equivalents of solidarity.

It would also be well to remember that, when Pope John Paul II makes his comparison in *Centesimus Annus* between *solidarity, friendship, social charity*, and *the civilisation of love*, he compares them as principles.[184] In many passages, it is not very clear whether these terms are used to refer to precise principles or to abstract concepts, or what difference this might make to their being perceived as equivalents.

---

[184] Cf. POPE JOHN PAUL II, *CA*, § 11.

Chapter Four
SOLIDARITY IN THE
THOUGHT OF KAROL WOJTYLA

Before entering into our examination of the thought of Karol Wojtyla, one important difficulty must be acknowledged and the manner of responding to it outlined. The writings of Wojtyla were originally published in Polish and, until recently, few of them were available in translation. One of his major works *Osoba i Czyn* was published in English in 1979 under the title *The Acting Person*.[1] It has been argued that, in her supervision of the English edition, Anna-Teresa Tymieniecka edited the text in such a way that the fundamentally Thomistic position of Wojtyla is less evident, and the phenomenological influence more emphasised.[2] Indeed, something of the translator's excessive freedom with the text can be suspected even in the translation of the title, which would be more accurately rendered in English as *Person and Act*.

It is clear, however, that Wojtyla only intended to make use of the phenomenological method to supplement what could be learnt about the person through the application of the principles of Thomistic metaphysics. Wojtyla distances himself from the "fundamental tenet of idealistic thought that *esse* equals *percipi*."[3] He argues elsewhere, in a way which is totally consistent with St. Thomas, that we cannot bypass the "ultimate ontological foundation" of the person as a source of action. "If the *something* did not exist, then it could not be the origin and the subject of the dynamism which proceeds from its being."[4]

Wojtyla is, however, inclined to the view that the dynamic aspect of being, and of the Person in particular, while not in any sense denied, is not

---

[1] Karol WOJTYLA, "The Acting Person," *Analecta Husserliana*, (The Yearbook of Phenomenological Research), 10 (1979). (Dordrecht: D. Reidel, 1979). (Hereafter referred to as *Acting Person*). *The Acting Person* was originally published as *Osoba i Czyn*. (Cracow: Polski Towarzystwo Teologiczne, 1969).

[2] Cf. Georges KALINOWSKI, "La Pensée Philosophique de Karol Wojtyla et de la Faculté de Philosophie de l'Université de Lublin," *Aletheia*, 1988: 201.

[3] Karol WOJTYLA, *Acting Person*, 46; cf. also note 21 which appears at the end of this sentence, and in which Wojtyla includes Husserl among those with whom he disagrees.

[4] Karol WOJTYLA, *Acting Person*, 72/3.

given its full weight in the thought of St. Thomas.[5] The phenomenological method, however, because it takes lived experience as its starting point, seemed to be particularly suitable as a means for revealing the human personal dynamism.

In this chapter I will be depending to a large extent on *The Acting Person*. For the sake of accuracy, however, I will subject this use to the authentication both of the unedited version of the English translation, found as an appendix to the work, and of the Italian edition, which is based on the second and definitive English edition, which itself has not been published to date.[6] I will also be drawing on other works of Wojtyla, which will act as a kind of cross-check. Finally, there seems to be an acceptance among the colleagues of Wojtyla that Josef Seifert, while depending on the English translation, has succeeded in grasping accurately the essence of Wojtyla's original thought in *Osoba i Czyn*, so I will make use of his presentation of *The Acting Person*.[7]

In the phenomenological method of Wojtyla, the approach to the person is made through an analysis of the experience of personal action. The validity of this approach is explained by Wojtyla in some of his writings using the terminology of theory and praxis. Praxis follows from theory (*operari sequiter esse*), especially on the ethical level, but Wojtyla points out that, from the perspective of epistemology, it is the praxis which reveals the theory, and therefore theory (person) is approached through praxis (action).[8]

A close investigation of personal action reveals the complex interaction of the many elements which constitute the acting person and his relationship to the world around him. Wojtyla argues from the experience

---

[5] Cf. Karol WOJTYLA, *Acting Person*, 27/8. Definitions of person in Scholastic philosophy tend to be quiditive. The possibility is discussed by C. P. O'Donovan, that St. Thomas, in discussing created nature, did not always exploit the real distinction between essence and existence, with the result that he sometimes appears to call something a subsistent because of its substantial form, whereas in fact it would be a subsistent because of its possession of substantial *esse* which, within this perspective is inseparable from form; cf. C.P. O'DONOVAN, *Person as Subsistent in the early Teaching of St. Thomas Aquinas*, Ph.D. Dissertation. (Rome: Pontifical Gregorian University, 1967), 75.

[6] Karol WOJTYLA, *Persona e Atto*. (Vatican City: Libreria Editrice Vaticana, 1982).

[7] Josef SEIFERT, "Karol Cardinal Wojtyla and the Cracow/Lublin School of Philosophy," *Aletheia*, 1981: 130-199; cf. Tadeusz STYCZEN, "Reply to Kalinowski: By way of an Addendum to the Addenda," *Aletheia*, 1988: 218.

[8] Cf. Karol WOJTYLA, "Teoria-Prassi: Un Tema Umano e Cristiano," *Incontri Culturali*, 10 (1977): 33/4. (Hereafter referred to as *Teoria-Prassi*).

of action that, while all personal acts are intentional (i.e., oriented by the person towards objects), the primary object and value of every act, properly speaking, is the person himself and his own self-fulfilment. This point, to which we shall return, is of fundamental importance to the thought of Wojtyla, and specifically to the understanding of *solidarity*.

While it is theoretically possible to consider the person and his acts in isolation, the reality is that persons exist alongside and frequently act together with other persons. This raises the question as to the precise nature of existing and acting together which best promotes the integrity of every person. It is in this context that Wojtyla introduces the concept of *solidarity*.

Before attempting to establish the meaning of *solidarity* in the thought of Wojtyla, it will be necessary to come to a clearer understanding of what he means by *person*, and of the challenges to the integrity of the person which arise from the social or communal dimension of the human reality. The need for these clarifications will contribute significantly to the structure of this chapter.

A. THE STRUCTURE OF THE PERSON IN THE ACTION

Prof. Alfred Wilder op., in the course of an analysis of two articles by Wojtyla, published prior to *The Acting Person*, identified three basic notions in which Wojtyla characterises "the personal humanity of our subjectivity."[9] These three notions are, consciousness, self-possession, and self-fulfilment.[10] The same three basic characteristics proper to the human person can also be identified, though discussed in greater depth, in *The Acting Person*.

1. The Experience of The Person in the Act

The first characteristic of the person given in experience is experience itself, or consciousness. It must be acknowledged that to be conscious as opposed to unconscious is a condition not limited exclusively to persons. All animals can be said to be conscious in this sense. The consciousness

---

[9] Alfred WILDER op, "Community of Persons in the Thought of Karol Wojtyla," *Angelicum*, 56 (1979), 22. One of the articles referred to is "Osoba: podmiot i wspolnota," (to a private translation of which Wilder had access). It was subsequently published as "The Person: Subject and Community", *The Review of Metaphysics*, 33 (1979/80). The other article is "Participation and Alienation," *Analecta Husserliana*, 6 (1976).

[10] Cf. Alfred WILDER, ibid., 222/3.

which is proper to the person, however, is quite diversified and complex, and is revealed in action.

The knowledge we have of the person is, according to Wojtyla, dependent on our experience of man. One of the fascinating things about this experience is its diversity. No one man encompasses the whole of human experience, and so my experience of other men complements my experience of myself, rather than duplicating it in every case. Yet the experience I can have of myself extends well beyond the limits of the experience I can have of any other man. I can never be the subject of another person's experience; I can never have numerically the same experience as he has. It is in an exterior sense, and with reference to my self-experience, that I come to realise that the other is a subject like me. Nonetheless, out of this diversity of experience comes a very definite unity in our understanding of what a person is; a unity which incorporates elements of interiority and of exteriority.[11]

The knowledge of oneself precisely as person is the basis on which it is possible to understand and accept the personal reality of others. This self-knowledge is not consciousness, but rather it is the fruit of consciousness, and it is most readily accessible to us in action.

> Our position is that action serves as a particular moment of apprehending – that is, of experiencing – the person. This experience is, of course, inherently connected with a strictly defined understanding, which consists ... in an intellectual apprehension grounded on the fact that man acts in its innumerable recurrences.[12]

Wojtyla makes the classical distinction between *actus humanus voluntarius* and *actus hominis*, a distinction which is rendered in English as between, on the one hand, *man-acts*, and on the other hand, what merely *happens-in-man*. As regards what merely happens in man, a person may or may not be conscious of it. This fact has its own significance to which Wojtyla adverts in his discussion of the dynamism and potentiality of the psyche and the soma. The primary consideration at this stage, however, is

---

[11] Cf. Karol WOJTYLA, *Acting Person*, 14. Seifert comments that Wojtyla, by recognising that the other person is in some sense given to us as an object of our experience, places himself in opposition to Scheler; cf. Josef SEIFERT, ibid., 136.

[12] Karol WOJTYLA, *Acting Person*, 10.

the man-act or human action, which of its very nature is conscious.[13] Wojtyla argues that there is a two-fold dimension to the kind of consciousness which is given in personal action. In the first place it is a conscious acting, and in the second place it is a consciousness in which the person experiences himself as a subject of action. The first, or "reflective," function of consciousness is the mirroring "of everything that constitutes the object of cognition and knowledge – and especially the object of self-understanding and self-knowledge."[14] There is undoubtedly a certain passivity about this function of consciousness.

The second function of consciousness is what facilitates the focussing of attention on the subject of the action. This Wojtyla calls the "reflexive" function, because it recalls consciousness, as it were, from its intentional object, and gives the human subject to it, as its object instead.[15] It is through this reflexive function of consciousness that self-knowledge is gained. Seifert explains the reflexive function of consciousness as follows:

> Consciousness has also the task of letting us experience these acts and actions "from within" as our own actions. While they are a fully objective reality, they are given to the subject not only "from without" in some fashion as that *of* which the subject is aware, but they are also consciously experienced "from within" as our very own being and acting.[16]

The experience of one's own subjectivity is a feature both of human actions and of what happens in man. In the reflexive action of consciousness, however, the acting person becomes aware of himself not only as subject (i.e., the one in whom the experience is happening), but also as actor (i.e., the one who is the cause of what is happening). He discovers his

---

[13] Following the lead of J. Seifert, I will use the substantive *act* to refer to the whole range of human acts, including knowledge which is not strictly voluntary. I will distinguish the specifically voluntary human act by referring to it as *action*.

[14] Karol WOJTYLA, *Acting Person*, 41. This reflective function of the consciousness is something that happens in man. He is aware of himself as the subject of reflective consciousness, but not as the *actor*.

[15] Karol WOJTYLA, *Acting Person*, 44. As Wilder notes, it is important to be sensitive to the ambiguities which arise when we use terms like *subject* and *object*. cf. Alfred WILDER, ibid., 217. It is clear, for instance, that when Wojtyla speaks of the conscious subject of action, consciousness itself is not the subject in question, but there is a subject who is conscious. Likewise, when he refers to the subject being given to itself as object, he does mean to imply that the subject becomes objectified in the sense of being de-personalised.

[16] Josef SEIFERT, ibid., 153/4.

own efficacy. While efficacy is a term which could be applied to non-human causality also, Seifert points out that it is used by Wojtyla as a *terminus technicus*, to describe the experience that a person has that a particular act is of his own making.[17]

All occurrences in which man is involved as subject, whether they are actions or simply things that happen in man, are understood by Wojtyla in terms of the traditional theory of Act and Potency.[18] The importance of the experience of efficacy in the specifically personal act is that it is through his own efficacy that the potentiality of the person is brought to act. The experience of efficacy links the person immediately with his action, and is closely linked with the experience of responsibility. "We attribute the act to this self as its conscious author. In such agency there appears the factor of will and therefore of liberty and hence that of moral responsibility. This brings us to what is essential in man's subjectivity."[19]

> For all the distinction that we make between the subject of the experience and the actor who acts, it is impossible to deny that he who acts is simultaneously the one in whom something or other happens.

A hallmark of Descartes' view is his splitting of the human being into an extended substance (the body) and a thinking substance (the soul), which are related to one another in a parallel way and do not form an undivided whole, one substantial *compositum humanum*[20]

In reality, however, it is not consciousness which is the subject, but some really existing subject who is conscious. The person is given to himself in action as a concrete existing being. According to St. Thomas: "Consciousness and self-consciousness are something derivative, a kind of fruit of the rational nature that subsists in the person, a nature crystallised in a unitary, rational, and free being, and not something subsistent in

---

[17] Cf. Josef SEIFERT, ibid., 159.

[18] Wojtyla notes that, in this sense, there is an active dimension even to those occurrences which we think of as primarily passive – the occurrences of consciousness which merely happen – in that they proceed from potency to act. Cf. Karol WOJTYLA, *Acting Person*, 65.

[19] Karol WOJTYLA, "The Person: Subject and Community," *The Review of Metaphysics*, 33 (1979/80): 280. (Hereafter referred to as *Subject*).

[20] Karol WOJTYLA, "Thomistic Personalism" in *Person and Community: Selected Essays*, translated by Theresa Sandok OSM, Catholic Thought From Lublin, Vol. 4. (New York: Peter Lang, 1993), 169.

themselves."[21]

Wojtyla speaks of St. Thomas' view of the person as an objectivistic view. According to him, St. Thomas, while always recognising that a person is a distinct subject of existence and activity, presents and analyses the person in an objective way. This, he says, is unhelpful, when it comes to addressing the issues with which modern philosophy and psychology are particularly concerned.

> He shows us the particular faculties, both spiritual and sensory, thanks to which the whole of human consciousness and self-consciousness...takes shape, but that is also where he stops. Thus St. Thomas gives us an excellent view of the objective existence and activity of the person, but it would be difficult to speak in his view of the lived experience of the person.[22]

A part of what is reflected in consciousness is the collection of emotions and feelings that happen in man. The reflective element of consciousness always seems to be capable of reflecting these, no matter how intense they become. At times, however, it seems that the reflexive element is no longer able to grasp the significance of these experiences which are presented to it. This can be either because of the intensity of the feelings and emotions involved, or because of a weakness in the reflexive capacity. This is what Wojtyla refers to as the emotionalisation of consciousness i.e., when experience oppresses understanding. The meanings of particular feelings fade from consciousness, even though the feelings themselves remain. "This is practically tantamount to a breakdown in self-knowledge; for consciousness, without ceasing to mirror the emotive distances just as they come, loses its controlling, that is to say, its objective, attitude toward them."[23]

If there are times when the emotive element of man wreaks havoc in human consciousness, there is also the converse problem of whole aspects of what is happening in man being lost to consciousness. This applies particularly to the somatic potentiality of man, but also to aspects of human emotivity which are banished from consciouness. It is in the sub-conscious that objects are kept from experience in a kind of sub-experience. This raises a question about the dynamism that expels or represses these objects

---

[21] Karol WOJTYLA, ibid., 170; cf. also idem, *Acting Person*, 72; and idem, *Person and Community*, 278.

[22] Karol WOJTYLA, "Thomistic Personalism," 170/1.

[23] Karol WOJTYLA, *Acting Person*, 53.

from experience, which is clearly related in some way to the will. The absence of certain experiences from the consciousness has the result that our actions are not always exactly what we think they are. This has implications for personal freedom, because freedom depends on truth.

There is however another dynamism proper to the sub-conscious, but always within the same subject, which constantly seeks to raise this material to the surface of consciousness. As far as Wojtyla is concerned, this struggle to liberate the moments trapped in the subconscious is one of the essential tasks of morality and education.[24]

We have briefly considered the first of the basic notions that characterises our personal humanity, namely that a person is given as a being who grasps himself as the subject and effective actor at the origin of all his actions, and is capable of experiencing in his freedom, a sense of responsibility in relation to his actions.

2. The Person as Self-Possessing

Every voluntary action is, of its nature, intentional. In other words, it is directed towards some object of the will. The will which is manifested in action is not, however, exclusively directed towards intentional objects.[25] In a very real sense the person is himself the primary object of his own action; he is self-possessing.

> The person is, owing to self-determination, an object for himself, in a peculiar way being the immanent target upon which man's exercise of all his powers concentrates, in so far as it is he whose determination is at stake. He is in this sense, the primary object or the nearest object of his action.[26]

This is so precisely because the person experiences himself, and no one else, as the actor who is at the origin of his own actions. His will is an expression of who he is and is primarily engaged in the bringing to act of his own potency. It can be truly said, therefore, that the person, through the actions that he performs, and through his choice of intentional objects, determines who he becomes.

---

[24] Cf. Karol WOJTYLA, *Acting Person*, 95.

[25] Wojtyla uses the expression *intentional objects* to refer to objects in the world outside the personal subject, which become the focus of the person's exercise of will. Cf. Karol WOJTYLA, *Acting Person*, 108.

[26] Karol WOJTYLA, *Acting Person*, 108.

Quite clearly there is no question of the person determining himself essentially because, as Wojtyla reminds us more than once, action follows being.[27] Because of its emphasis on approaching the person through his actions, the phenomenological method has a unique contribution to make to the understanding of the dynamic aspect of being, and specifically of the person. The first act of every person is the act of being itself, but this act is in turn a potency to further or conjugate act by means of which the person determines himself accidentally, through the exercise of his own freedom.[28]

Closely related to the concept of self-determination, Wojtyla finds that the person is also self-governing. Seifert remarks that "this capacity of self-governance is incommunicable and is one reason for the absolute incommunicability of the person, for the uniqueness that solely a person possesses."[29] This comment is significant in that it is reminiscent of Scheler's statement that the member of the person-community is unrepresentable. The incommunicability of the person, as Wojtyla understands it, will obviously be significant when we come to consider his concept of solidarity.

It is in the exercise of the freedom of his will, or self-determination, that the person transcends himself in the action.[30] Transcendence is a somewhat ambiguous term. For Kant, it refers to what is *a priori* and therefore "beyond" in the sense that it is outside the scope of empirical experience. When Wojtyla uses the term transcendence he uses it in a double sense. Man transcends himself in knowledge by possessing objects which are outside himself, and this is what Wojtyla refers to as horizontal transcendence. When Wojtyla refers to the transcendence of the person in the action, however, he means that the person, as it were, steps beyond the boundaries of his fixed nature. This transcendence is what Wojtyla calls vertical transcendence, because it involves the person's possession of

---

[27] Cf. Karol WOJTYLA, *Subject*, 275.

[28] Cf. Karol WOJTYLA, *Acting Person*, 73. This is one situation in which the there is an obvious error of translation/edition in the English, because the text actually reads "coming into existence ... may be seen as the first act of every being." The Italian translation is more faithful to the principle of St. Thomas to which Wojtyla refers, and reads "l'esistenza, secondo san Tomasso, è il primo atto di ogni essere." Cf. Karol WOJTYLA, *Persona e Atto*, 99.

[29] Josef SEIFERT, ibid., 163. From the context, it can be taken that Seifert is referring here to human or finite persons.

[30] Cf. Karol WOJTYLA, *Acting Person*, 111.

himself as object.[31] It is worth noting that, elsewhere, Wojtyla uses a different terminology to refer to the same reality. He says that "human action according to St. Thomas has simultaneously a transcendent and an immanent profile."[32] The *immanent profile* in this case corresponds to the reality of vertical transcendence.

It may be helpful at this point to outline briefly Wojtyla's understanding of *nature* and its relationship to *person*. He suggests that there are two possible ways in which nature can be understood. In the first place it can be considered as some specific "property of a specific subject" or, considered abstractly, "the specific trait common to all human beings by the very fact of their being humans."[33] In this sense nature refers to "everything that is going to be born or is contained in the fact itself of birth as its possible consequence:"[34] On the other hand, according to Wojtyla, it would seem on the basis of phenomenological reduction, that the concept of nature has to be understood in a narrower sense "to include the dynamism which is directly and solely the consequence of birth itself; the dynamism that is exclusively inborn or innate," or in other words that which is pre-determined in man.[35] In that case, nature would refer to the dynamism of man's activation, as opposed to the dynamism of his action which would be the domain of the specifically personal. The question is, therefore, whether we interpret *person* and *nature* to be in some sense antagonistic, perhaps after the manner of Scheler's *spirit* and *life*. Wojtyla argues that, while there is undoubtedly a complexity evident in man, there is also a fundamental unity. Even in what happens in man, where he does not experience himself as the actor, he still experiences himself as the subject of what is happening.

> The total experience, which gives both a simple and fundamental perception of the human being ... supplies the evidence for the unity and the identity of the man subject. This is accompanied by the synthesis, on the ground of the one and the same ontological support, of acting and happening that takes place in man, the synthesis of actions and activations, of efficacy and subjectiveness.[36]

---

[31] Cf. Josef SEIFERT, ibid., 166.
[32] Karol WOJTYLA, *Teoria-Prassi*, 36.
[33] Karol WOJTYLA, *Acting Person*, 77.
[34] Karol WOJTYLA, *Acting Person*, 76.
[35] Karol WOJTYLA, *Acting Person*, 78.
[36] Karol WOJTYLA, *Acting Person*, 79.

This conclusion is directly related to Wojtyla's understanding of the human person as a being who is both transcendent and integrated in his actions. He expresses his dissatisfaction with the scholastic doctrine that the will is a "rational appetite,"[37] because this seems to make the will nothing more than "some immanent striving which simply proceeds from the inner principles of a nature and which only *happens* in man (and thus *appetitus* is the opposite of free self-determination)."[38] Wojtyla, on the other hand, is anxious to present the will as the free expression of the personal dynamism of man.

3. The Person as Self-Fulfilling

For Wojtyla, "the real transcendence of man in freedom cannot be severed from his response to the good in the sense of a being which is intrinsically precious."[39] It is this free response, the interior content of the act, that constitutes moral value.[40]

The process by which values are presented to the will is referred to, by Wojtyla, as *motivation*, and he cautions his reader against confusing motives with emotions. "Essentially, motives only stimulate the will, but do not arouse emotions."[41] The motives serve to elicit the response of the will to a value or values by presenting these to the will.

> The greater the good the greater becomes its power to attract the will and thus also the person. The crucial factor in determining the maturity and the perfection of the person is his consent to be attracted by positive authentic values, his unreserved consent to be drawn in and absorbed by them. But this makes it all the more necessary to stress that all the forms and degrees of such absorbtion or engagement of the will are made personal by the moment of decision.[42]

Truth plays a dual role in the response of the will to values. Before any act of decision can take place, there must first be a cognitive act in which the object is made present to the will and recognised for what it is. Thus we have a judgement of ontological truth that is practical.[43] Here, once again, we detect the so-called "horizontal" aspect of the person's self-

---

[37] Cf. e.g., SAINT THOMAS AQUINAS, *ST*, I IIae, Q.18, Art.2., ans.
[38] Josef SEIFERT, ibid., 170.
[39] Josef SEIFERT, ibid., 168.
[40] Cf. Karol WOJTYLA, *Valutazioni*, 127.
[41] Karol WOJTYLA, *Acting Person*, 129.
[42] Karol WOJTYLA, *Acting Person*, 127.
[43] Cf. Karol WOJTYLA, *Acting Person*, 140/1.

transcendence.

The fact that the will is motivated towards one or more values does not in any sense mean that the will is no longer free. The freedom of the will is assured by the fact that its relation to truth is deeper than its relation to the objects of volition.[44] As an aspect of the exercise of self-determination and self-governance, the will refers to the truth the object or objects presented to it in cognition.

> Choice as well as decision making ... is performed in reference to the truth of the object recognised as a positive good. Thus in both there is presupposed the cognitive experience of truth; for the cognitive experience to which the deliberation of the will takes recourse is not merely constitutive of objects of cognition but is first and foremost evaluating them with respect to that truth about the object which shows it as a positive or negative good."[45]

The act of simple decision involves the commitment of the will to the pursuit of one particular object, or to its rejection following the reference to truth on the axiological level. The act of choice is somewhat more complex because it presupposes that the will is motivated by a number of objects, all of which are perceived to be values, but some of which may compete against each other, or even be mutually contradictory. In this case, the act of decision pre-supposes choice, but, one way or the other, it is decision that constitutes the personal character of the action.[46]

It is in the context of this act of decision that we discover again the vertical aspect of the transcendence of the person in the action. If we bear in mind the fundamental principle of Act and Potency, we see that every action in some sense completes the person, even as it also actuates some potential in the intentional objects to which the will is committed. Person and action are not two separate and self-sufficient entities, but rather "a single deeply cohesive reality."[47]

In so far as the person determines himself in all his actions he becomes an object for himself, not in the intentional sense as in the case of something that is desired, but in the sense that he is the first to sustain the effects of his own action.[48]

---

[44] Cf. Karol WOJTYLA, *Acting Person*, 138.

[45] Karol WOJTYLA, *Acting Person*, 141.

[46] Cf. Karol WOJTYLA, *Acting Person*, 129/131.

[47] Karol WOJTYLA, *Acting Person*, 149.

[48] Cf. Karol WOJTYLA, *Acting Person*, 108.

Wojtyla explains that the twin structure of man's willing and acting "serves as the basis of morality – or of moral value as an existential reality – and it is owing to it that morality as a modality of conduct participates in the innerness of man and achieves a measure of durability in him."[49] In other words, it is only because of the structures of self-determination and self-fulfilment that man's willing of objects external to himself has any lasting personal significance. When he does good a person becomes good, and when he does evil he becomes evil. Wojtyla makes a distinction at this point between the existential order and the axiological order.

> Existentially every action is some kind of fulfilment of the person. Axiologically however, this fulfilment is reached only through the good, while moral evil leads ...to non-fulfilment. This approach appears somewhat convergent with the view that all evil, including moral evil, is a defect.[50]

By contrast, in Scheler's system, moral growth does not consist so much in a change in the orientation of the will, but rather a change in the content of the experience of good and evil, what Wojtyla calls the *ideal axiological essence*, or *ethos*.[51]

This brings us to the whole question of conscience. According to Wojtyla, it is an error to think of conscience as something purely cognitive. Undoubtedly the self-fulfilment of the person in action depends on the recognition of the truth which is a cognitive act, but it depends equally on the surrender of the will to the truth. This is the context in which the most vital function of the conscience is exercised, namely the development of the sense of duty or obligation.

> The function of conscience consists in distinguishing the element of moral good in the action and in releasing and forming a sense of duty with respect to this good. The sense of duty is the experiential form of the reference to ...the moral truth, to which the freedom of the person is subordinate.[52]

Conscience is an action rather than an experience. Wojtyla says that "the obligation which man experiences in conscience is manifested immediately to the efficacy of his person, to the duty to be the one who

---

[49] Karol WOJTYLA, *Acting Person*, 151.
[50] Karol WOJTYLA, *Acting Person*, 153.
[51] Cf. Karol WOJTYLA, *Valutazioni*, 81.
[52] Karol WOJTYLA, *Acting Person*, 156.

carries out a certain action, or not to be such a one."⁵³

The experience of duty follows from the experience of truth. In some situations the truth appears self-evident, while in other situations the evidence has to be carefully checked and verified by conscience. Wojtyla makes a distinction between the concepts of *right* and *wrong*, which he considers to be subjective, on the one hand, and objective concepts of *true* and *false* on the other. To say that something is right is to state that I experience it as true and as a norm which I ought to obey. *Right* and *wrong* are fit and adequate terms when attributed to norms, but Wojtyla enters a caveat, arguing that this subjective statement concerning the experience of truth sometimes tends to obscure the fact that truth itself, as a value, is objective. When the concomitance of the existential and the axiological is lost to view, the basis of morality becomes purely subjectivist.

> The conscience is no lawmaker; it does not itself create norms; rather it discovers them, as it were, in the objective order of morality and law. The opinion that man's individual conscience could itself establish this order distorts the correct proportions in the relations between the person and the society or community and – on a different level – between the human creature and the creator.⁵⁴

The notion of obligation or responsibility brings with it the notion of someone to whom a person is responsible. This is where we see again the implications of the way in which the human subject is given to himself in experience as the object also of his actions. The acting person is responsible for the realisation of values which he recognises to be good, but first of all among these values to be realised is the person himself. The fact that an action is performed by a person and that the person is fulfilled in his action is what is referred to as the personalistic value of the action, and it takes precedence over all the others. Without prejudice to the participation of the person in society or community, which we shall shortly discuss, it is clear for Wojtyla that "the first and fundamental responsibility that arises in acting, on the basis of self-determination and self-dependence is the responsibility for the subject, for the moral worth of the ego who is the agent performing the action."⁵⁵

---

⁵³ Karol WOJTYLA, *Valutazioni*, 155.
⁵⁴ Karol WOJTYLA, *Valutazioni*, 165. Here Wojtyla disagrees fundamentally with Kant.
⁵⁵ Karol WOJTYLA, *Valutazioni*, 171.

4. The Integration of the Person in the Act

Wojtyla's understanding of the transcendence of the person is not to be interpreted in the sense that the ego, as it were, leaves the man behind. There is no meaning to self-knowledge, self-possession, self-determination, or self-fulfilment without reference to the one who is known, possessed, determined, and fulfilled.[56] The transcendence of the person in the action, in freedom and truth, is a question of maximising the actuation of human potentiality in a way which is specifically appropriate to persons. This is possible only because of the identity and the appropriate relation which prevails between the various elements that constitute the person as a single dynamic ontological whole.

This identity and appropriate relation is what Wojtyla refers to as integration. Without it, he maintains, transcendence would be in a void. There are two distinct, though related, foci in which we experience the integration of the person in the action. These are the potentiality and dynamism of the *soma* and of the *psyche* respectively. The *psyche* and the *soma* each has its own proper dynamic, but they come together and complement each other in the action, and receive in action a new meaning and significance which is specifically personal.[57] Events which are purely somatic and those which are purely psychic belong to the category of things that happen in man. In action not only are these psychic and somatic events subordinated to the control of the will, but the psycho-physical dynamisms "play an active role in self-determination, this is, in making the human person's freedom emerge."[58]

In his treatment of the love of man and woman, Wojtyla explains that a relationship based exclusively on a response to sensations or even to sentiments connected with another person lacks integration because it ignores the whole truth about the other, and thus makes true freedom of choice and action impossible. He recognises, however, the very real value of these sensations and sentiments, as parts of the whole, in facilitating the commitment of the will.[59]

---

[56] Cf. Karol WOJTYLA, *Valutazioni*, 190.
[57] Cf. Karol WOJTYLA, *Acting Person*, 197.
[58] Karol WOJTYLA, *Acting Person*, 199.
[59] Cf. Karol WOJTYLA, *Love and Responsibility* (London: Collins, 1981), 114ff. (Hereafter referred to as *Love*).

The first aspect of integration which Wojtyla examines is the experience of the dependence of the psychical on, and its conditioning by, the somatic. The body is the means and it dictates the manner in which the person can externalise himself. In action "the objectification of the body becomes an integral element in the objectification of the whole personal subject, to whom the body belongs."[60]

Wojtyla notes, however, that the body seems to have a certain subjectivity of its own in that some things happen which are not the result of the efficacy of the person. These are aspects of the specifically somatic or *reactive* dynamism of the body. Obviously, if this reactivity is not directed in some sense by the person to whom the body belongs, there arises a conflict, or an experience of dis-integration. "The integrity of the man-person consists therefore in the normal, indeed in the possibly perfect matching of somatic subjectivity with the efficacious and transcendent subjectivity of the person."[61]

The integration of the person on the somatic level is the function of various bodily skills, some of which are so commonplace that they are scarcely even noticed. By means of skill or proficiency the somatic dynamism is not overcome, but brought under the direction of the will, and this is the proper understanding of integration.[62]

The notion of a reactive dynamism raises the question of instinct. Wojtyla takes two examples, the instinct for self-preservation and the instinct for sex and reproduction. The notion of the integration of the person in the action would suggest that instincts, while rooted in the somatic, are not exclusively somatic, but rather are open to the control and direction of the psyche.[63]

The integration of the person in the action is seen from a different perspective in the case of the psychic dynamism. The term *psyche* "refers to that which makes man an integral being, indeed, to that which determines the integrity of his components without itself being of a bodily or somatic nature."[64] The significant distinction between the emotions of the psyche and the reactions of the body, is that the emotions transcend the capacity of the body in quality and in essence. Just as the body responds to

---

[60] Karol WOJTYLA, *Acting Person*, 206.
[61] Karol WOJTYLA, *Acting Person*, 212.
[62] Cf. Karol WOJTYLA, *Acting Person*, 213/4.
[63] Cf. Karol WOJTYLA, *Acting Person*, 215/6.
[64] Karol WOJTYLA, *Acting Person*, 221.

motor-stimuli, so the consciousness is exposed to and responds to affective stimuli coming from material objects which give rise to sensations and feelings.

> For instance the feeling of bodily pain makes the inward workings of one's own body come within the scope of consciousness. ...These sensations reveal to every man not a separate subjectivity of the body but the somatic structure of the whole subject that he is, of the whole ego. They reveal to what extent he is a body, to what extent his soma participates in his existence and his acting.[65]

The relationship of feeling to the body does not, however, make feeling a purely bodily or somatic response. Wojtyla points out that while I can be conscious of a feeling, I can not feel a consciousness.[66] This realisation, while it establishes a precedence of consciousness, also indicates that it is precisely feeling which bridges the gap between the body and consciousness. A closer examination of the psychic dynamism reveals the experience of feelings which are not rooted in the body at all, even though it is equally true that these feelings could not be experienced outside of the body. These include aesthetic, religious, and moral feelings, which provide the "evidence that the emotive element in him (man) somehow corresponds to what is spiritual and not merely sensual."[67] As Seifert remarks:

> Integration is such a powerful principle of unification that it allows a certain over-stepping of the dividing line between what merely happens in man and human action. The meaning of such an integration and lifting-up of non-free acts into the domain of freedom is best seen in the way in which freedom can appropriate certain spiritual emotions.[68]

While feelings are always intentionally directed, it is not the case, according to Wojtyla, that the only possible access to values is through feeling. Neither is it a valid position to advocate the rejection of sensations or emotions so as to allow man to act solely according to reason, as Kant did. In either case disintegration would result owing to the separation of

---

[65] Karol WOJTYLA, *Acting Person*, 229. In other words, while the body has a subjectivity of its own, this subjectivity is not separate from that of the personal subject as a whole. Certain aspects of it may, however, be outside the consciousness of that personal subject.

[66] Cf. Karol WOJTYLA, *Acting Person*, 230.

[67] Karol WOJTYLA, *Acting Person*, 231.

[68] Josef SEIFERT, ibid., 177.

action from experience.[69]

Wojtyla speaks of what he describes as emotional stirrings which occur in man and which are accompanied by some kind of somatic response, so that psyche and soma act, as it were, in concert; e.g., in the case of a response to beauty, or in the case of remorse. Emotional stirrings arise and then fade away, unless they become fixed in what we may call an affective state.

> An affective state is spoken of most appropriately only when an emotion has become fixed, though to what extent an emotion once fixed still remains but a stirring is another matter. What we call an affective state, however, seems very often to have already departed from its original emotive core ...and has since been taken over by the will.[70]

The whole thrust of Wojtyla's argument in relation to the psyche is to point out that here, as in the case of the soma, there is a close interplay between what happens in man and the actions which he performs as a result of his own efficacy. There is a certain tension involved in this interplay because man often has "the most vivid awareness that it is not he who is acting but that something is happening in him... In this connection we see that ...situations of deeply stirring emotions and passion present a special task for him to cope with."[71]

The integration of the person in the action on the level of his psychic dynamism is once again the function a special kind of skill or proficiency which operates to relieve the tension between spontaneous emotivity and personal efficacy. The essential feature of integration, however, is that this moral proficiency or virtue as it can rightly be called, does not suppress the emotions, just as the motor skills do not suppress the bodily reactions.

> It lies in the nature of proficiencies to aim at subordinating the spontaneous emotivity of the subjective ego to its self-determination. They thus tend to subordinate subjectivity to the transcendent efficacy of the person. Their way to achieve this end, however, is to make the best use of emotive energy and not to suppress it.[72]

---

[69] Cf. Karol WOJTYLA *Fondamenti*, 81; cf. also Karol WOJTYLA, *Acting Person*, 233 & 243.

[70] Karol WOJTYLA, *Acting Person*, 241.

[71] Karol WOJTYLA, *Acting Person*, 243.

[72] Karol WOJTYLA, *Acting Person*, 252/3.

As Seifert remarks elsewhere, integration is not merely a matter of our "gaining a formal dominion over ourselves and our bodies. ...Our free decisions ought to be based on the truth about being."[73] Integration on the psychic level is a process which begins later and which lasts until the end of man's life. As the process of integration progresses there develops a greater correspondence between the active and the affective dimensions in man with "the result that the will – guided by the light of reason – learns how by spontaneous reference to emotion ...to choose and to adopt the real good."[74]

I have treated the integration of the person in the action under its own separate heading for reasons of clarity only. Integration is, in the final analysis, just as dependent on freedom and truth as transcendence is. Furthermore, as will be evident from the above exposition, the integration specifically of the person demands the transcendence of the person, just as his transcendence is meaningless except in the light of his integration.

B. COMMUNITY:
A CHALLENGE TO THE INTEGRITY OF THE PERSON

The Acting Person is not about the person in relation to society and community. Yet Wojtyla regards it as important to consider briefly the issue of intersubjectivity. The final Chapter of *The Acting Person* is of considerable importance for the purposes of this study because, although Wojtyla deals with society and community elsewhere, this would seem to be the only place in which he develops the concept of solidarity in his philosophical, as opposed to his papal writing. The chapter entitled "Intersubjectivity by Participation" will, therefore, form the nucleus of our analysis of his concept of solidarity, because it is in the light of this chapter that Wojtyla's other writings on society and community will have to be examined.

We have established so far that the human person, as experienced in his specifically personal action, is self-knowing, self-determining and self-fulfilling, and that these characteristics reflect his transcendence and his integration as a dynamic ontological unity. We have seen the essential part that both freedom and truth have to play in the action, and therefore in the dynamic existence of the person. The task that arises for us at this stage is

---

[73] Josef SEIFERT, ibid., 175.
[74] Karol WOJTYLA, *Acting Person*, 253.

to establish whether and how it is possible for the person to enter into co-existence and co-action with other persons, in such a way as to retain and perhaps even enhance these essential personal characteristics. Wojtyla poses the challenge in the following terms: "What is the significance of the fact of acting with others for the personalistic value of the action?"[75]

1. Participation

In *The Acting Person, solidarity,* as an aspect both of the person and of the community, is discussed in the context of *participation,* so it is with this reality that we must take up our analysis. It is not only frequent and usual, "but indeed of universal occurrence" that persons act together with others.[76] A plurality of persons may exist in close contact with each other, and work alongside each other on the same project. Even allowing that each of them is self-possessing and self-fulfilling and that, therefore, there is a personalistic quality to their acting, this fact of itself does not give to their existing or their action that quality that makes it truly co-existence and co-action.[77] Just as action presupposes the experience of oneself as subject, co-action necessarily involves some sense of the other as subject, without any loss of the experience of one's own subjectivity. Since action is the dynamic manifestation of the person, what is said of action in this regard applies also to existence which, as we have seen, is the first act of the person.

The notion of existing or acting together with others implies some kind of adaptation of the person to relations with others. This adaptation is what Wojtyla calls participation. It is the subjective moment of the person's membership of the community of acting.[78] Wojtyla identifies two kinds of inter-personal relations, which he refers to as *I–You* relations and *We* relations. As Wilder points out, Wojtyla is not concerned with relations of the *I–he, I–she, I–they,* or even *I–you (plural)* type, precisely because these relations do not imply mutual awareness.[79] The two relation types on which Wojtyla does focus his attention represent two fundamental dimensions of community, one of which emphasises what is personal in man and the other

---

[75] BUTTIGLIONE, Rocco, *Il Pensiero di Karol Wojtyla* (Milan: Jaca Book, 1982), 197.

[76] Karol WOJTYLA, *Acting Person,* 263.

[77] Cf. Karol WOJTYLA, *Acting Person,* 279.

[78] Cf. Karol WOJTYLA, *Acting Person,* 270. & 279.

[79] Cf. Alfred WILDER, ibid., 227.

of which emphasises what is social or communal. The fact that there are these two kinds of relations leads to the conclusion that there are also two profiles of participation.[80] The choice of the word *profile* is not without significance, as we shall see, because we are not speaking of two different realities, but of two aspects of one and the same reality.

The first profile of participation is the one which is discovered in the *I–you* relation. It is not possible strictly speaking to have an experience of the subjectivity of another person. Our experience of another man, however, allows us to know that, while he is *you* in my consciousness he is also another *I*, a subject like myself, though not identical with me. In this way I can experience the other as a person, even if I cannot enter into the experience of his subjectivity. "When I experience him as a person, I am coming the closest to that which constitutes his self as the only and unique reality of a human being."[81]

The experience of the other as a person allows the further experience of myself as *you* in relation to his *I*. Thus the experience of the other has a reference back to myself. As Wojtyla puts it, the *I* is constituted in the *you*.[82] The result is that, in the moment of participation in an *I–you* relation the reality of man's personal subjectivity is revealed both with reference to myself and with reference to the other. According to Wojtyla: "This moment does not yet constitute community; its significance is rather in its more complete experience of one's self or *I* by testing it to some extent in the light of the other *I*."[83]

While it is only when two people become for each other reciprocally *I* and *you* that we actually have the full specificity of the community, Wojtyla explains that there is nevertheless a real experience of the inter-personal pattern even when the experience is only mono-directional. Accordingly, "it is precisely participation and nothing else that, in the case of a fully reciprocal relation *I–you*, is the essential constitutive of community."[84] This means that the first condition for any participation in

---

[80] Cf. Karol WOJTYLA, *Subject*, 305.

[81] Karol WOJTYLA, "Participation et Alienation," *Analecta Husserliana*, 6 (1977), 66. (Hereafter referred to as *Participation*).

[82] Cf. Karol WOJTYLA, *Subject*, 291. Wilder notes that there is no question in Wojtyla as there is in Scheler as to whether or not it is the *we* of the group or the *I* of individual personal distinction which first appears in the consciousness. For Wojtyla it is the *I* that first comes to light, cf. Alfred WILDER, ibid., 228.

[83] Karol WOJTYLA, *Subject*, 293.

[84] Karol WOJTYLA, *Subject*, 294.

the humanity of another is that I begin with myself as a personal subject. Participation "is conceived first as the property of the person which is expressed in the capacity to stamp as personal one's own existence and action, when existing and acting with many people."[85]

If participation is to be something authentically personal, it must reflect the active dimension of the person. Man must not simply be revealed as subject in the relation *I–You*; "he should be accepted and confirmed. Such an acceptance and confirmation is the moral and ethical expression of the sense of the interpersonal community."[86] There is thus associated with the notion of participation, an experience of responsibility or obligation with specific reference to the person as value. This corresponds to the person's responsibility for self-fulfilment in freedom and truth, with the added dimension that now I am responsible, not just with respect to the good that is myself, but also with respect to the good that is the other. The principal dimension of inter-human community, according to Wojtyla, is both metaphysical and normative, and it "may be reduced to treating and actually experiencing *the other one* as one's own self."[87] It is only when this transcendent value of the person is mutually and consistently confirmed that we can speak of a "communion of persons."[88]

The dynamic involved in the *we* relationship is quite different. It involves a plurality of persons experiencing themselves as a definite *we*. Wojtyla is not concerned here with society so much as with the social dimension of community.[89] Wilder explains the distinction between the personal and the social dimensions of community in terms of the experience of relation that is involved. "When a person is revealed as *you*, I stand facing him. When persons are revealed as *we*, I stand with them."[90]

The reality of social community is grasped and understood through some action; an action which is in common. Wojtyla explains that this

---

[85] Karol WOJTYLA, *Subject*, 288.

[86] Karol WOJTYLA, *Subject*, 296.

[87] Karol WOJTYLA, *Subject*, 295. The other remains other, but is experienced in a way which allows him to be recognised as *another self like me*. The element of will involved in participation is a point of contact between Wojtyla and Kant. Because the other *I* is to be treated as myself – i.e., as an end rather than a means, Wojtyla comments that his thesis is possibly confirmed by Kant's second formulation of the Categorical Imperative; cf. Karol WOJTYLA, *Participation*, 68.

[88] Karol WOJTYLA, *Subject*, 297.

[89] Cf. Karol WOJTYLA, *Subject*, 298.

[90] Alfred WILDER, ibid., 231.

means more than just a multiplicity of actions. "*In common* means that action, and together with it the existence of those many *I*'s ...is in relation to some value. This therefore deserves the name of common good."[91] In other words, in the *we* profile of participation, the person experiences primarily the duty or responsibility of realising the good of the community as a whole. In this case, as Wojtyla remarks, the *I*'s are constituted by the *we*, just as in the former case, each *I* was constituted by the corresponding *you*. Through the common good, the human *I* finds itself more fully and fundamentally precisely in the human *we*.[92] Wojtyla notes that the human social reality indicated by *we* is akin to the reality analysed by Aristotle under the notion of *friendship*.[93]

It is accurate, though somewhat incomplete, to think of the common good as being the same as the good of the community. This understanding is open to the possibility of a one-sided interpretation. Recognising the truth in the context of the common good involves recognising the integral link between the good of the community and the good of each person who participates in it.[94] Wojtyla says:

> It is impossible to define the common good without simultaneously taking into account the subjective moment, that is, the moment of acting in relation to persons. When we consider this moment we see that the common good does not consist solely in the goal of the common acting performed by a community or group; indeed it also, or even primarily, consists in that which conditions and somehow initiates in the persons acting together, their participation, and thereby develops and shapes in them a subjective community of acting.[95]

The relation to the common good, just like the decision to pursue one's own good or the good of the other, "should also be founded on the relation to truth and to 'true' or 'honest' good, for only then does the right standard of the common good appear."[96]

In the various relations of the *we* type, the *I*'s who form the society

---

[91] Karol WOJTYLA, *Participation*, 298.

[92] Cf. Karol WOJTYLA, *Subject*, 299/300.

[93] Cf. Karol WOJTYLA, *Participation*, 68.

[94] Here it seems that Wojtyla is trying to avoid any possibility that the *common good* might be interpreted in a way which allowed the good of the collectivity to dominate over the good of the persons of which it is formed.

[95] Karol Wojtyla, *Acting Person*, 281.

[96] Karol WOJTYLA; *Acting Person*, 300.

"have a disposition, not only to think of themselves in the category *we*, but to realise what is essential for the *we*, and therefore for the social community."[97] This disposition is what characterises the second profile of participation, that of participation in society.

As mentioned earlier, we have considered two profiles of participation rather than two realities. The *I–You* and the *We* communities

> must mutually penetrate and condition each other in the experience and shaping of community life. Man in his full genuineness as a person whose personal identity is revealed by *I–You* relations which possess the profile of a community of persons, is and must be constantly inscribed into the true sense of the common good."[98]

It is a fact that not all personal communities are socialised or structured. This is not necessarily a problem either on the practical or on the axiological level. The reverse, however, is a problem. When a society loses its communal dimension it begins to lose sight of the inviolable dimension of the persons which make it up.[99]

Wilder notes that Wojtyla has a more positive view of society than that of Scheler. This is not because Wojtyla was blind to the possibility of society becoming depersonalised, but rather because he was open to the possibility of the personal dimension remaining at the root of the *we* relationship, and conditioning the "standing and working with others in pursuit of the common good, which is the determining mark of a society."[100] Wojtyla doesn't assume that a society is a defective community; rather he takes it as quite normal that a community should be socialised. Society in effect is experienced as social community, because *I* and *you* experience ourselves as *we*.[101] Both profiles of participation would be expressed in the social community. Participation, guided by the principle of subsidiarity, would be exercised with a view both to personal fulfilment and to the realisation of the common good.[102]

Nonetheless achievement of the common good is fraught with diffi-

---

[97] Karol WOJTYLA, *Subject*, 302.
[98] Karol WOJTYLA, *Subject*, 305.
[99] Cf. Alfred WILDER, ibid., 236.
[100] Alfred WILDER, ibid., 232.
[101] Cf. Karol WOJTYLA, *Subject*, 305.
[102] Cf. Karol WOJTYLA, *Subject*, 303.

culty because all sorts of deviations are found even in the smallest community. The common good is not realised automatically, without a struggle. In a comment, which reflects his own experience as much as anything else, Wojtyla describes the nature of the struggle and affirms its value.

> The measure of effort put into the realisation of the common good, the measure of individual sacrifices, including exile, prison, and death, has and continues to witness to the magnitude of that good, to its superiority. These situations, especially the extreme ones, convince us of the truth that the common good is in itself a condition of the individual good of the particular members of the community.[103]

Accidental human groupings often emerge from interpersonal relations, and they rarely live up to the dignity of the human subjectivities involved in them. It is precisely because it is not automatic that the work of forming human community impinges upon us as a serious duty.[104]

2. Alienation

The antithesis of participation is alienation, which is the driving of a wedge between the person and his action on the one hand, and what is perceived to be the common good on the other. Man is at the centre of both Marxist theory and personalist thought, and both are aware of the reality of human alienation. Each, however, perceives it differently. Given its denial of man's transcendence, Marxism rejects the reality of any kind of alienation other than that which is fundamentally economic. While recognising the importance of man's links with nature and the world of things, Christian personalism sees this relationship as secondary to man's encounter with his fellow man and with God. For this reason "if man's relation with nature is in disorder, the way to reconciliation is not primarily through changes in the economic situation but rather through the interior transformation of human freedom."[105] For Wojtyla, therefore, just as participation is essentially a personal reality, so the roots of alienation are always to be found in man's relation with his fellow man.[106] "Alienation is nothing else but the contradiction of participation, the weakening or simply

---

[103] Karol WOJTYLA, *Subject*, 301.
[104] Cf. Alfred WILDER, ibid., 234.
[105] Pavel LATUSEK, *Incontro tra il Personalismo e il Marxismo in Polonia*, ibid., 67.
[106] Cf. Karol WOJTYLA, *Participation* 72; also idem, *Subject*, 305 ff.

the annihilation of the possibility to experience another human being as the other *I*."[107]

Wojtyla identifies two principal causes of alienation, namely individualism and totalism (or collectivism). Individualism is the refusal of the individual person to consider any good other than his own. The individualist sees acting together with others as limiting rather than fulfilling. For him the only reason for forming a community would be to protect the individual from the others.[108] Totalism, while it is the opposite of individualism, paradoxically has its foundations in the acceptance of the basic principle of individualism, i.e., that the good of the individual is in conflict with the good of society. Totalism therefore imposes the good of society against the good of the individual person.

> The good thus advocated by totalism can never correspond to the wishes of the individual, to the good he is capable of choosing independently and freely according to the principles of participation; it is always a good that is incompatible with and a limitation upon the individual. Consequently the common good frequently presupposes the use of coercion.[109]

The philosophical basis for the totalist view, on the other hand, is that the individual man can only be understood in the context of society and can, therefore, only take his norms from society, so that the coincidence of individual and common interests is only a matter of time.[110] Needless to say, in this vision of things, the concept of the person as self-possessing, self-determining and self-fulfilling is excluded. Thus it becomes clear that the reality and experience of the person's alienation in society, when it is something that happens in man, can become a contributory factor in the disintegration of the person. When, on the other hand, alienation is the result of the person's own action, it would seem that it can be regarded as a symptom of some defect in his personal integration.

It would seem that, while a community is certainly damaged by the refusal of one or more persons to contribute to the common good, the damage to the common good is far greater when every person in the community is denied the exercise of his freedom and his initiative, as

---

[107] Karol WOJTYLA, *Participation*, 69.
[108] Cf. Karol WOJTYLA, *Acting Person*, 274.
[109] Karol WOJTYLA, *Acting Person*, ibid., 274.
[110] Cf. Alfred UTZ, *Entre le Neo-Liberalisme et le Neo-Marxisme*, ibid., 162/3.

occurs when totalism is the prevailing attitude. For most of his adult life Wojtyla had first hand experience of the workings of totalism, first under a fascist system and subsequently under a communist system. As Buttiglione comments, however, it would be mistaken to simply identify individualism with Western Capitalism, or to identify totalism with Marxist socialism because, as far as Wojtyla is concerned, both individualism and totalism are human attitudes rather than political or social structures.[111]

C. SOLIDARITY:
A SYNTHESIS OF COMMUNALISM AND PERSONALISM

We have seen how the extremes of individualism and totalism tend to limit, or even to exclude, participation. These extremes are generally associated with social systems. What is more fundamental, however, is to consider the personal attitudes which characterise the manner of being and acting of the person in societies and communities, because it is ultimately the attitudes of persons that determine the nature of social and communal structures. It will be important to note that Wojtyla does not consider any social grouping to be more than a quasi-subject. For him, "Being and acting together with others does not constitute a new subject of acting but only introduces new relations among the persons who are the real and actual subjects of acting."[112] The quasi-subjectivity of the community by contrast with the subjectivity of the person is affirmed also in the context of the relationship of two people who are deeply in love.

The deeper and riper their union is, the more surely a man and a woman feel that they form a single subject of action. This feeling, however, does nothing to alter the objective fact that they are in reality two different beings, and two different subjects of action.[113]

Even the most extreme forms of individualism and totalism are incapable of fully extinguishing the natural desire for participation and the revulsion against the experience of alienation. In even the best of human communities, on the other hand, there are difficulties involved in realising the two profiles of participation in their appropriate balance, i.e., in a way which both respects the personalistic value of the action and fosters the good of the community as a whole. The success of this enterprise is largely dependent, according to Wojtyla, on the presence of two authentic human

---

[111] Cf. Rocco BUTTIGLIONE, *Il Pensiero di Karol Wojtyla*, ibid., 200.
[112] Karol WOJTYLA, *Acting Person*, 277.
[113] Karol WOJTYLA, *Love*, 147.

attitudes, and the absence of two corresponding nonauthentic attitudes. Buttiglione describes these attitudes, identified by Wojtyla, as "habits of behaviour with respect to the common good."[114] The authentic attitudes are *solidarity* and *opposition*,[115] while the nonauthentic ones are *conformism* and *non-involvement*.[116] It is, perhaps, significant that each of the other attitudes would appear to be defined in some sense with reference to *solidarity*, which seems, therefore, to be a key to understanding the whole question of the appropriate being and acting of the person along with others.

Wojtyla introduces solidarity as an "attitude" and explains that it is "the natural consequence of the fact that human beings live and act together."[117] It would seem important to clarify how he intends his reader to understand the term *natural* in this case. It is possible that he uses the term to imply that solidarity is innate or pre-determined in man, belonging to the dynamism of activation, rather than describe it as *personal* in which case it would belong to the dynamism of man's action, implying an act of the will.[118] The context would suggest, however, that Wojtyla understands *natural* – at least in this case – in its broader, more personal sense, meaning a property or trait which is possible only as a consequence of having been born human. This interpretation would allow us to understand solidarity as an expression of the transcendence and integration of the person.

1. Solidarity, Participation, and the Common Good

The personal character of solidarity would seem to be confirmed by Wojtyla's contention that solidarity is "the attitude of a community in which the common good properly conditions and initiates participation, and participation in turn properly serves the common good, fosters it and furthers its realisation."[119] Referring, in his commentary on the Second

---

[114] Rocco BUTTIGLIONE, ibid., 201.

[115] Cf. Karol WOJTYLA, *Acting Person*, 283/4.

[116] Cf. Karol WOJTYTLA, *Acting Person*, 288. In the literal English translation, of *Osoba i Czyn*, the latter is referred to as *avoidance* rather than *non-involvement*. cf. ibid., 345; the corresponding term in the Italian text is *scansarsi*, cf. Karol Wojtyla, *Persona e Atto*, 324.

[117] Karol WOJTYLA, *Acting Person*, 284.

[118] Cf. Karol WOJTYLA, *Acting Person*, 76ff.

[119] Karol WOJTYLA, *Acting Person*, 285. In the Italian edition of *Osoba y Czyn*, the term *fondamento* is used, in place of *atteggiamento* in this sentence, cf. Karol WOJTYLA, *Persona e Atto*, 321.

Vatican Council, to a passage from *Gaudium et Spes* (The Pastoral Constitution on the Church in the Modern World), Wojtyla says: "The words quoted synthesise in a certain sense the significance and the value of the attitude of human identity and authentic solidarity, which consists in the correct orientation of the freedom of the individual towards the common good."[120] It is clear from the above statements that solidarity is understood as being directed towards the attainment of a good; in this case the common good. It is not, therefore, to be understood as something that merely happens in man.

What does Wojtyla mean when he says that solidarity is the "attitude of a community?" In so far as a community is not a subject, but only a quasi-subject, it only makes sense to speak of the "attitude of a community" if it is understood as the holding in common, or together, of personal attitudes by a plurality of persons, in respect of one or more other persons.

It would seem that there is a bi-directional aspect to solidarity. As well as being the attitude of the community towards its members in which participation is promoted and oriented towards the common good, solidarity also "means a constant readiness to accept and to realise one's share in the community because of one's membership within that particular community."[121]

In "The Person: Subject and Community," Wojtyla does not use the term *solidarity*, but he does refer to the "disposition" which personal subjects have in various types of social community "not only to think of themselves in the category *we*, but to realise what is essential for the *we*, and therefore for the social community."[122] This disposition or readiness corresponds with that dimension or movement of solidarity which is the attitude of the one with respect to the many.

Irrespective of whether solidarity is experienced as the attitude which the many have in common, or the attitude of one person with respect to the many, it seems clear that it is fundamentally the same attitude. It seeks to bring about the appropriate balance between the two profiles of participation, which we may refer to as the personalistic profile and the

---

[120] Karol WOJTYLA, *Alle Fonti del Rinnovamento* (Vatican City: Libreria Editrice Vaticana, 1981), 259. The reference is to *GS*, §31.

[121] Karol WOJTYLA, *Acting Person*, 285.

[122] Karol WOJTYLA, *Subject*, 302. It is worth noting that in the Italian translation of *Osoba i Czyn* the term *readiness*, to describe solidarity is rendered as *disposizione*, cf. Karol WOJTYLA, *Persona e Atto*, 321.

social profile. It is always the function of solidarity to promote the common good through the correct orientation of participation, and by so doing to promote also the good of the individual personal subject.

This dual objective of solidarity explains why Wojtyla is concerned that the person, while being always ready to play his part, is always careful not to infringe upon the obligations and duties of others, and yet again is willing, when the incapacity or inadequacy of the other makes it necessary for the common good, to go beyond the limits of his own normal responsibility. It is clear that I can not fulfil myself as a person without playing my part. This is, as it were, the communal dimension of the transcendence of the person. If I exceed my own part, however, I limit the part that you can play and this "is intrinsically contrary to participation and the essence of the community."[123] Here we see the implications of solidarity in the service of the *I–You* profile of participation.

Wojtyla recognises, however, that there are situations in social and individual life that make it necessary for one person to take over part of the duties and obligations of another. He does not indicate what these situations are, but they must surely include situations such as illness, imprisonment, destitution, and exile in which one person is no longer in a position to fulfil his responsibilities either toward the community, or toward certain other members of the community. Wojtyla says:

> In such a situation, to keep strictly to one's own share would mean, in fact, lack of solidarity. Such a possibility indicates that in the attitude of solidarity, the reference to the common good must always remain alive: it must dominate to the extent that it allows one to know when it is necessary to take over more than one's usual share in acting and responsibility.[124]

Here we see the implications of solidarity in the service of the *we*, or social, profile of participation.

From the perspective of the attitude of solidarity, therefore, the person who is a community member is thought of simultaneously as irreplaceable in himself and complementary to every other member. To recognise this is to acknowledge the flexibility and complexity of the attitude of solidarity, and it is one of the reasons why it is sometimes difficult to be precise about its meaning.

---

[123] Karol WOJTYLA, *Acting Person*, 285.
[124] Karol WOJTYLA, *Acting Person*, 285.

2. Neighbour: The Solidarity of all Humanity

Solidarity, as we have seen, implies membership of a community. Frequently one person will be a member of many communities, each of which has as its object the realisation of its own particular common good. Just as the common good of each community is simply a particular and limited expression of the universal common good, so membership and participation in a particular social community is but a limited expression of membership in the community of all humanity or, as Wojtyla puts it, participation "in the very humanness of others."[125]

Wojtyla distinguishes between the person understood as *member of a community*, and the person understood as *neighbour* which has a more universal reference. He says:

> The content of the notion of *neighbour* differs essentially from what is contained in the notion *member of community*....Participation itself means something else when it refers to a member of a community than when it refers to a neighbour.[126]

In so far as participation means something different in each case, this gives rise to the question as to what difference this may make to our understanding of solidarity. One important difference between the particular community and the human race is the conditions of membership. Membership of a particular community may be an accident of birth or a conscious option. To a greater or lesser degree membership of particular communities can be revoked and the corresponding responsibilities abrogated, though obviously the more closely the community is bound to the nature of the person e.g., the family, the more irrevocable membership becomes. In the case of the human race, however, membership is synonymous with the existence of the person, and is a condition of all his acting. As Wojtyla says:

> Membership of any community presupposes the fact that men are neighbours, but it neither constitutes nor may abolish this fact. People are, or become, members of different communities; in these communities they either establish close relations or they remain strangers – the latter reflects a lack of communal spirit – but they are all neighbours and never cease to be neighbours.[127]

---

[125] Karol WOJTYLA, *Acting Person*, 294.
[126] Karol WOJTYLA, *Acting Person*, 292.
[127] Karol WOJTYLA, *Acting Person*, 293.

Participation in the humanity of every man does not imply a different kind of solidarity. Rather it calls for a deepening and an extension of solidarity and, most important of all, it reveals the true foundation of solidarity as ontological rather than simply emotional. Wojtyla, while recognising that the particular community reflects more concretely the relationship referred to in the notion of *neighbour*, adverts to the fact that the particular community "also limits and, in some respects, removes to a more distant plane or even overshadows the broader concept of neighbour."[128] There is a constant challenge to broaden the scope and the exercise of solidarity. Elsewhere, Wojtyla says:

> The phrases quoted demonstrate how Vatican II understands the scope of human solidarity, which it considers a sacred thing. One arrives at this solidarity, understood in a global sense, taking as a starting point, so to speak, those more restricted human circles in which people are solidary among themselves.[129]

It would appear that the fact of shared humanity and its implications are more readily experienced on the level of the particular community of which a person is a member than they are in the universal reference system of the *neighbour*. As a result, alienation can still occur when solidarity is mis-conceived as something purely emotional or conditional. Wojtyla remarks:

> Man's alienation from other men stems from a disregard for, or a neglect of, that depth of participation which is indicated in the term neighbour and by the neglect of the interrelations and intersubordinations of men in their humanness expressed by this term, which indicates the most fundamental principle of any real community.[130]

Wojtyla's use of the concept of neighbour has a resonance with the terminology of Latin-American liberation theology. Jon Sobrino makes much the same point as Wojtyla when he comments that what we see first is not always first in the order of reality. He argues that the root of solidarity is in the objective fact that "each of us is socially a part of all

---

[128] Karol WOJTYLA, *Acting Person*, 293.
[129] Karol WOJTYLA, *Alle Fonti del Rinnovamento*, 256; cf. SECOND VATICAN ECUMENICAL COUNCIL, *GS*, §30.
[130] Karol WOJTYLA, *Acting Person*, 297.

humankind."[131]

Wojtyla acknowledges that "it is natural for us to be closer with our family or our compatriots than with the members of other families or other nations."[132] While this closeness or natural attraction may assist the orientation of participation to the common good or, in other words, solidarity, it does not constitute it. It is in the universal reference to the person as *neighbour* that we discover the essentially ontological rootedness of solidarity. The value involved in solidarity is not the feeling of closeness, but the human person, and every human person, irrespective of whether or not he gives rise to an experience of closeness.

This distinction would seem to reflect the difference between the Schelerian and the Wojtylian understandings of the nature of moral value. For Scheler, as we have seen, moral value can not be pursued as an immediate object of personal action, because moral value is the experience of goodness, and to actively seek this experience would be pharisaical. It would appear to follow that the community ought not to actively pursue the common good as a moral value. For this reason, it is difficult to avoid the conclusion that, for Scheler, solidarity can only ever be something that *happens* in man. For Wojtyla, on the other hand, moral value is something that a person decides to realise, and this means that his concept of solidarity must inevitably be tied to the exercise of the will in action to realise the common good. This is probably what Wojtyla means when he says:

> This relation to the common good, which unites many subjects into one *we*, should also be founded on the relation to truth and to true or honest good, for only then does the right standard of the common good appear. In its essence the common good is the good of many; in its fullest dimension it is the good of all.[133]

The role of solidarity in facilitating participation and orienting it to the common good, would appear to be not unlike the role of a skill or proficiency in the integration of the person. As we have already seen, the integration of the person involves the development of somatic skills by means of which the will harnesses and controls the dynamism of the body, and of psychic skills or proficiencies by means of which the will asserts itself in relation to the dynamism of the psyche.[134] There is also

---

[131] Jon SOBRINO, "Bearing with One Another in Faith," in *Theology of Christian Solidarity.* (New York: Orbis, 1985), 8.
[132] Karol WOJTYLA, *Acting Person*, 292.
[133] Karol WOJTYLA, *Subject*, 300.

undoubtedly a form of dynamism which makes itself felt in the social context. (The expression *group dynamic* is in common usage). The struggle to establish and maintain one's own freedom and, at the same time, to exist and act together with others is a key element in this social dynamism. The integration of the person and his transcendence in society or community requires the exercise of some skill, or proficiency if it is to be consistently successful.

It is possible to envisage solidarity simply as the attitude of the will on the basis of which a particular decision is taken and an action performed which represents the proper orientation of participation to the common good. In that sense one person might be described as being "in solidarity" with another person or persons. It would seem, however, that the fullest expression of solidarity is only to be seen when it has developed into a kind of skill or proficiency, so that it has become an aspect of the person's will and of his action in every situation. Adapting the words of Wojtyla, we could say that, always referring to the truth, the will learns to spontaneously choose the true common good and to reject what is opposed to it.[135] In this process the will harnesses the feeling of closeness but is not determined by it.

For St. Thomas, an acquired moral virtue could be described as a habit of the mind, by which we live righteously, of which no one can make bad use.[136] Wojtyla does not directly refer to solidarity as a virtue in *The Acting Person*, but it certainly appears to have the characteristics of an acquired simple moral virtue. Firstly it is concerned with action as the perfection of the personal potentiality for participation. This is in keeping with the understanding of virtue as the perfection of a power.[137] Secondly, it is oriented towards the personalistic value of the action rather than simply the completion of a particular task.[138] In the third place, it is also concerned not merely with the development of a capacity but with the right use of that capacity, i.e., in acting together with others. According to St. Thomas a moral virtue is a habit which confers not only aptness to act, but also the right use of that aptness. To that extent it is a proficiency in the proper exercise of the will. "The subject of a habit which is called a virtue simply,

[134] Cf. Karol WOJTYLA, *Acting Person*, 213/4 & 252/3.
[135] Cf. Karol WOJTYLA, *Acting Person*, 253.
[136] Cf. SAINT THOMAS AQUINAS, *ST*, Ia IIae, Q.55, 4, ans.
[137] Cf. SAINT THOMAS AQUINAS, *ST*, Ia IIae, Q.55, 1, ans.
[138] Cf. Karol WOJTYLA, *Acting Person*, 265 & 279.

can only be the will, or some power in so far as it is moved by the will."[139] Finally, as Wojtyla mentions, solidarity has the characteristic of constancy. "Solidarity means a constant readiness to accept and to realise one's share in the community."[140]

3. Solidarity, Opposition, and Dialogue

The second authentic attitude identified by Wojtyla is the attitude of *opposition*. Opposition can be understood in a variety of ways, some of which are constructive and some of which are destructive, but the attitude to which Wojtyla is referring is one that is consistent with solidarity and is fully committed to the common good. It represents, therefore, not opposition to the common good or, indeed, opposition to other persons as such, but opposition with regard to the manner in which participation is oriented to the common good.[141]

The attitude of opposition would appear to be a manifestation of the reality that the transcendence of the person, and therefore his self-fulfilment, depends not only on freedom but also on truth.[142] The person who engages in constructive opposition subjects his participation in the community to the reference to truth. In this way he ensures that his participation will not take a form which conflicts either with the common good, or with the true good of any person in the community, including himself. The close relationship that exists between the two authentic attitudes can, therefore, be easily seen; solidarity is the attitude that ensures appropriate participation, and opposition is the attitude that excludes inappropriate participation. For Wojtyla, opposition arises from solidarity and serves it, and the facilitation of opposition is the task of every human community.

In order for opposition to be constructive, the structure, and beyond it the system of communities of a given society must be such as to allow the opposition that emerges from the soil of solidarity not only to express itself within the framework

---

[139] SAINT THOMAS AQUINAS, *ST*, Ia IIae, Q.56, 3, ans.
[140] Karol WOJTYLA, *Acting Person*, 285. In explaining what he means by virtue, Wojtyla says: "Virtue is effectiveness, and indeed constant effectiveness. If it were only occasionally effective it would not be sufficient for we should only be able to say that a given man had succeeded in controlling an impulse, whereas virtue must guarantee that he will certainly control it; cf. Karol WOJTYLA, *Love*, 169.
[141] Cf. Karol WOJTYLA, *Acting Person*, 286.
[142] Cf. Karol WOJTYLA, *Subject*, 287.

of the given community but also to operate for its benefit.[143]

I would suggest that constructive opposition is the communal equivalent of that struggle which Wojtyla identifies in the individual person between the dynamism of the will and the dynamism of the sub-conscious, the former seeking to expel certain objects from experience, and the latter seeking to raise them to the surface.[144]

In so far as opposition is an aspect of the participation of the person in the community, which is oriented towards the common good, it must be ensured that opposition itself does not become a cause of alienation. Rather, it must in some way invite the participation of others. This would appear to be the significance of Wojtyla's situating of dialogue as a mechanism whereby opposition is made to serve solidarity, and solidarity is strengthened by dialogue. Indeed, it would seem that, just as opposition is a product of the person's reference of his participation to truth, so dialogue itself is the process whereby the community refers opposition to the judgement of truth.

The subordination of action to truth is the essential element of discernment, without which both solidarity and opposition tend to become corrupted, solidarity becoming no more than empty conformism, and opposition leading to complete withdrawal from the pursuit of the common good.

> Indeed the lack of discernment may very easily distort the attitude of solidarity as well as that of opposition, changing either of them in concrete situations into non-authentic attitudes deprived of their true personalistic value. The touchstone for discernment is the dynamic subordination of action to truth.[145]

4. Solidarity and Conformism

Wojtyla explains that the non-authentic attitude of conformism is constituted, not simply by the fact of being and acting in conformity with others, but by the fact that this conformity is purely external in nature and does not reflect truthfully the transcendent will of the person who conforms. According to Wojtyla: "Conformism evidences not only an intrinsic lack of solidarity but simultaneously an attitude of evading oppo-

---

[143] Karol WOJTYLA, *Acting Person*, 286/7.
[144] Cf. Karol WOJTYLA, *Acting Person*, 95.
[145] Karol WOJTYLA, *Acting Person*, 288.

sition."[146]

When the acts of a person are governed by conformism, what happens in effect is the creation of a rift between the person and community, while it appears that the person is all the while acting together with others. Wojtyla argues that what appear to be the actions of the person become, in effect, nothing more than activations which are happening in him as a result of his complete subordination to the will of the others in the community. "Conformism consists primarily in an attitude of compliance or resignation, in a specific form of passivity that makes the man-person to be but the subject of what happens instead of being the actor or agent responsible for building his own attitudes and his own commitment in the community."[147] The end result is that the person himself remains unfulfilled in spite of his apparently positive participation and, for want of a properly oriented participation, the common good is impoverished. It can be seen, therefore, how clearly conformism conflicts with the stated role of solidarity.

5. Solidarity and Non-Involvement

The significant difference between non-involvement (or avoidance) on the one hand, and conformism, on the other, is that non-involvement refuses to engage in a pretence of participation. On a certain level, then, it could be argued that, with reference to truth, non-involvement is more authentic than conformism. At times, Wojtyla notes, this attitude is adopted specifically in order to make a point in relation to the common good. "Non-involvement then becomes a kind of substitute or compensatory attitude for those who find solidarity too difficult and who do not believe in the sense of opposition."[148] The problem, as Wojtyla point out, is that non-involvement represents a failure to pursue participation which "is a fundamental good of a community."[149] Where this attitude prevails, the common good is not realised as it might be through solidary opposition and, because the common good is not realised, the fulfilment of the person is also denied or limited. It becomes clear, therefore, that non-involvement is not consistent with solidarity.

Wojtyla acknowledges that, under certain conditions, participation of

---

[146] Karol WOJTYLA, *Acting Person*, 289.
[147] Karol WOJTYLA, *Acting Person*, 289.
[148] Karol WOJTYLA, *Acting Person*, 291.
[149] Ibid.

any kind may appear to be impossible or futile. While this may appear to justify non-involvement from the perspective of the person who withdraws, it does not render the situation authentic. The personalistic good may be safe-guarded, but the common good still loses out. "If the members of a community see the only solution to their personal problems in withdrawal from the communal life, this is a sure sign that the common good in this community is conceived of erroneously."[150]

6. Conclusions

At this point we are in a position to draw together into a more coherent definition the various elements of Wojtyla's concept of solidarity. We can say that solidarity is the authentic attitude governing the action of a person or of a community of persons, whereby participation is initiated and oriented to the realisation of the common good. Solidarity is rooted in the metaphysical reality of a shared human nature, and interprets the common good of particular communities in the light of the universal common good of humanity. In seeking to realise the common good in a way which is more authentic or truthful, solidarity frequently gives rise to the complementary attitude of opposition, which in turn gives rise to the need for truthful dialogue. When the attitude of solidarity consistently directs the will towards the realisation of the common good, it becomes habitual, taking on the characteristics of a virtue, and enabling the will to spontaneously direct participation to the common good. It can be seen from the above that the efficient cause of solidarity is the acting person or the acting community, and its final cause is the common good.

a. Solidarity and Similar Concepts. In the previous chapter, I noted that, in his encyclical letter *Centesimus Annus*, Pope John Paul II, has identified the principle of *solidarity* with those of *friendship* and *social charity*. I also suggested that both *communion* and *common good* have some definite connection with *solidarity*. Before concluding this chapter, it will be important to establish briefly the extent to which the relationship between these various concepts is to be found in the philosophical thought of Karol Wojtyla, in his earlier or pre-papal period.

The concept of *friendship* is treated, not in *The Acting Person*, but in *Love and Responsibility* A comparison between the two concepts is quite

---

[150] Karol WOJTYLA, *Acting Person*, 291.

revealing. Wojtyla makes a distinction between sympathy and friendship. Sympathy, he says "is love at a purely emotional stage, at which no decision of the will, no act of choice, as yet plays its proper part."[151] By contrast,

> in friendship the will is actively involved itself. For this reason friendship truly takes possession of the whole human being, it is something which he chooses to do, it implies a decisive choice of another person, an other *I*, as the object of affection.[152]

Wojtyla argues that, while sympathy is not friendship, it has an important role to play in initiating and sustaining friendship. The problem is that people are frequently content with the experience of sympathy and make no effort to form it into friendship.[153] This reflects Wojtyla's belief, already discussed, that the experiences which happen in man must be integrated through a free act of the will.

I would suggest that, for Wojtyla, the experience of closeness is to solidarity, as the experience of sympathy is to friendship. In either case, the experience is helpful and worthy of the person, but the person is only integrated in solidarity or in friendship when his will chooses as its object another person or persons. What, then, is the difference between solidarity and friendship? A final answer to this question may be premature at this stage, but it would appear that, while friendship is normally thought of as something that is formed between a plurality of persons (i.e., at least two) without any particular formality, solidarity would frequently appear to express the formation of a similar bond of self-giving within the framework of some kind of social structure, though not any one structure to the exclusion of all others.

When Wojtyla speaks of love in *Love and Responsibility*, he is referring particularly to the relationship of reciprocal self-giving that is the foundation of marriage. In this context we are presented once again with the same kind of distinction that we have seen in the case of both solidarity and friendship. Neither sense impression nor sentiment, both of which arise from the same intuition, have the characteristics of true love. While the former, in isolation, considers the other person only as a means of pleasure,

---

[151] Karol WOJTYLA, *Love*, 89.
[152] Karol WOJTYLA, *Love*, 91.
[153] Cf. Karol WOJTYLA, *Love*, 91/2.

162 *Karol Wojtyla*

the latter, on its own, creates for itself an idealisation of the *other* which is not in harmony with the truth.[154] For Wojtyla,

> Love in the full sense of the word...is an authentic commitment of the free will of one person (the subject) resulting from the truth about another person (the object)....In the moral order there can be no question of slurring over or neglecting the *sexual* values to which the senses and emotions react. Our concern is simply to bind these values tightly to the value of the person, since love is directed not towards the *body* alone, nor yet towards *a human being of the other sex*, but precisely towards a person.[155]

Once again, then, we find that it is only when both the action and the experience are taken into account, and when the experience is brought under the guiding force of action in freedom and truth, that the person is integrated. It is clear, in the context, that the love of which Wojtyla is speaking is *agape* or *caritas*, not excluding – but certainly not exclusively – *eros*.[156] There seems therefore to be a close correspondence between love (charity) and solidarity, in that the sensation and the sentiment of love are to love itself, as the sentiment of closeness is to solidarity. As in the case of friendship, the difference would seem to be that, while love does not necessarily imply the context of social organisation, this would seem to be implied in the case of solidarity. This would explain why John Paul II would later speak of *solidarity* as being the same reality as *social charity*.

We have seen earlier in this chapter that the concept of solidarity is very closely related to that of the *common good*, in that solidarity orients participation towards the realisation of the common good. Looked at from a different perspective, the common good, being the end of acting together with others, can be looked upon as the final cause of solidarity. Wojtyla argues that "the common good has to be conceived of dynamically and not statically...it must liberate and support the attitude of solidarity."[157] It would seem reasonable, on the basis of this, to say that the more universal and spiritual the concept of the common good, the more capable it should be of evoking solidarity. The difficulty, inevitably, is that the common good tends to be perceived more narrowly and in more material terms.

Lastly, the question arises as to what relationship, if any, Wojtyla

[154] Cf. Karol WOJTYLA, *Love*, 110-112.
[155] Karol WOJTYLA, *Love*, 123.
[156] Cf. Karol WOJTYLA, *Love*, 98.
[157] Karol WOJTYLA, *Acting Person*, 287.

posits between solidarity and *communion*. Wojtyla speaks of communion in the context of the *I–You* relation. Communion comes into being when two or more persons experience and treat one another as personal subjects. According to Wojtyla, this communion possesses a normative meaning.[158] Furthermore, he says: "By virtue of interpersonal communion, there arises the mutual responsibility of the person for the person."[159] If we think of action, and therefore solidarity, as something that arises from responsibility, then it would seem that, in some sense, communion precedes solidarity. On the other hand, communion could never be expressed or known except in the act of solidarity. If we accept Wojtyla's interpretation of the person and his action, in terms of theory and praxis, this relation between communion and solidarity might be taken as an example of theory preceding praxis ontologically and ethically, while praxis precedes theory in the field of epistemology.[160]

    b. The Originality of Wojtyla's Concept of Solidarity. The thought of Wojtyla in *The Acting Person* relies heavily on the heritage of St. Thomas Aquinas. The strict relationship in St. Thomas between human action, the will, and the intellect is of particular significance, since Wojtyla chooses to approach the understanding of the person through the experience of personal action.[161] As we have noted, however, Wojtyla was less than happy with the traditional understanding of the will as appetite, which tended to obscure the dynamic aspect of the person. As I have already mentioned, O'Donovan suggests that, while St. Thomas was aware of the real distinction between essence and existence, he did not assert or exploit this distinction as much as he might have.[162] This would explain why the existential or dynamic aspect of the person might appear to take a secondary place in his thought. It was partly because of it's capacity to high-light the dynamic aspect of the person in action that Wojtyla was originally attracted by the phenomenological method of Scheler.

---

[158] Cf. Karol WOJTYLA, *Subject*, 295/6.

[159] Karol WOJTYLA, *Subject*, 297.

[160] Cf Karol WOJTYLA, *Teoria-Prassi*, 34.

[161] Cf. Saint THOMAS AQUINAS, *ST*, Ia IIae, Q.19, art. 3-7. St. Thomas makes it clear in these articles that there is a formal dimension in ethics without which the objective dimension loses its truly objective character.

[162] Cf. C.P. O'DONOVAN, *Person as Subsistent According to the Early Teaching of St. Thomas Aquinas*, ibid., 75.

There are many striking differences, however, between Wojtyla's thought and that of Scheler, and these contribute to a significant difference in their concepts of solidarity. At the heart of all the differences is the understanding of person and action and the role of the will and of the intellect in personal action.

At first sight, Scheler's notion of subordination seems to be quite similar to Wojtyla's understanding of the integration of the person. In Scheler's case, however, what is brought together and placed in the appropriate relation are the spiritual and the vital values, all of which are ultimately known only on the level of experience. While integration, for Wojtyla, incorporates the reflexive as well as the reflective elements of human consciousness, it would appear that it never goes beyond the reflective level in the case of Scheler. Harvanek points out that "Wojtyla's inclusion of truth in his analysis of action is not found, at least with the same emphasis, in Scheler."[163]

An important point of divergence between Scheler and Wojtyla would seem to be the question of responsibility or duty. Both Wojtyla and Scheler are concerned with the realisation of values, but, as we have seen, this means something different for each of them. For Scheler, good and evil are something to be measured in the light of one's own values.[164] Duty is a source of the negative character of moral experience, and is, therefore, something to be excluded. Wojtyla argues repeatedly that Scheler's exclusion of the notion of duty from his ethics is in conflict with the very concept of ethics. This exclusion of duty, as we have seen, is related to the exclusion of the will from its central place in the realisation of moral value, and the restriction of the field of morality to the realm of lived experience.[165]

When we place side by side with this ethics of emotion, Scheler's view of the community of persons as a subject in its own right, it becomes easier to understand the roots of Scheler's concept of collective guilt. It seems to be a wave of feeling in the collective consciousness, and can be collective only because it does not enter the realm of truth and freedom. Wojtyla, on the other hand, for two related reasons, could not accept a principle of

---

[163] Robert F. HARVANEK, "The Philosophical Foundations of the Thought of John Paul II," in *The Thought of Pope John Paul II*, ed. John Mc. Dermott (Rome: Gregorian University Press, 1993), 13.

[164] Cf. Karol WOJTYLA, *Valutazioni*, 150.

[165] Cf. Karol WOJTYLA, *Valutazioni*, 164-6.

collective responsibility or collective guilt. Firstly, he does not accept that any social grouping has anything more than a quasi-subjectivity. The person only retains his integrity and his transcendence when he retains the responsibility for his own actions. Secondly, for Wojtyla, the experience of responsibility or duty is reflexive as well as reflective. It is related to the person's experience of himself as the actor, rather than simply as someone to whom something is happening.

Acting together with others, therefore, while it implies acting in common, must be seen, not as one action done by a plurality of people, but as a plurality of personal acts, directed towards a common end, i.e., the common good. This direction of personal acts towards the common good is the essence of solidarity, and it points up the dynamic or voluntary aspect of solidarity, something which is not to be found in the thought of Scheler.

There are many points of agreement between the thought of Wojtyla and that of Mounier. An important point of convergence is the experience which each of them had of the rise and fall of Fascism, followed by the rise of Marxist communism in Europe. In the thought of each of them there is to be found the evidence of the real personal experience of structural individualism and totalism.

Both Wojtyla and Mounier place considerable emphasis on the integrity of the person as a being composed of body and spirit, and each asserts the mutual dependence of body and spirit. Wojtyla's wider interpretation of the concept of *nature* resonates with Mounier's preference for the concept of *human condition*, which conveys a sense of freedom and potentiality.[166] Both men are, in other words, concerned with the person as a dynamic being rather than a static essence.

This concern with the person as dynamic leads to a number of other points of agreement in the thought of Wojtyla and Mounier. Each of them, as we have seen, emphasises the reflexive aspect of personal consciousness, and the role of truth and freedom in the context of a system of values. Mounier, like Wojtyla, has a very concrete understanding of how action completes the person, through the realisation of values.[167]

On the communal level, Wojtyla and Mounier share an understanding of alienation as something which has to do with relations between persons. In this context, they are both critical of the Marxist concept of alienation

---

[166] Cf. Candide MOIX, ibid., 126/7.
[167] Cf. Emmanuel MOUNIER, *Personnalisme*, 105-9.

which sees it as having to do with the relations between persons and things.

There are some interesting points of divergence between Wojtyla and Mounier. Mounier, to a certain extent at least, seems to subscribe to the idea of the collective person as if the community were in some sense a subject in its own right. This may have something to do with his tendency to use the language of being and existence somewhat loosely at times.

The most important point of divergence, from our point of view, is that Mounier only uses the term *solidarity* when the reality to which he is referring is negative or unsatisfactory. He speaks of the Marxist concept of the *solidarity of things*, the Sartrian image of a *solidarity of cavemen*, and refers to the contribution of one person's failure to another person's negative response as a *solidarity of adversaries*. By contrast, Mounier uses the terms *communion* and *love* when he is describing the characteristics of a personalist community. One possible explanation for Mounier's apparently negative use of *solidarity* is to be found in the fact that, as Parent tells us, this term had its origins in a non-Christian and even, at times, an anti-Christian context. It was often used in a way which implied a failure of Christian charity, and demanded action rather than words. For this reason *solidarity* came to be understood as a term which fell short, or lacked the spiritual depth, of charity or communion.[168] Parent, therefore, recognises in the apparent tension between *communion* and *solidarity*, the more fundamental tension between orthodoxy and orthopraxis. Could it be that Mounier, like other Catholics of his time, was uneasy with *solidarity* because he felt it overemphasised praxis at the expense of theory (*communion*)? It must be admitted that such an attitude would appear to be out of character with Mounier.

Parent argues that the really important issue is not the dialectic or tension between orthodoxy and orthopraxy, but rather the tension between two aspects of orthodoxy, namely *communion* together and *taking sides* with others. It is, in his view, the role and the meaning of solidarity as praxis to hold these in tension.[169] Another way of putting this would be to say that the orthopraxis of solidarity incorporates two different ways of *being together with others*, the first of which, *communion*, corresponds to the relation *we*, and the second of which, *taking-sides*, corresponds with a relation of *I–You* (when *you* is understood precisely as the *other*).

---

[168] Cf. Rémi PARENT, "Solidarité, Communion, Parti-Pris," ibid., 113/4.
[169] Cf. Rémi PARENT, ibid., 122.

What is the significance of Wojtyla's use of *solidarity* in a more positive sense than Mounier uses it? It does not represent a simple preference for *solidarity* over *communion*, because Wojtyla uses both terms. It is certainly quite clear from his writings that Wojtyla sees no conflict between theory and praxis, though there is a certain tension between them. The person is always the subject, the actor who is responsible for his own action. It is primarily through his action that the person is known, that he possesses, determines, and fulfils himself. Likewise, in community, the praxis is only authentic when it respects the theory.

From the context, it would seem credible that Wojtyla uses the term *solidarity* to express the kind of praxis which is able to hold people together in communion, while at the same time taking sides with those who are at risk of alienation, always accepting the implied need for constructive opposition that goes along with taking sides.

Chapter Five
WOJTYLA AS POPE JOHN PAUL II: FURTHER DEVELOPMENT OF THE CONCEPT OF SOLIDARITY

Karol Wojtyla was elected Pope in 1978 and took the name John Paul II. Already, in Kracow, his work as a philosopher had been carried out in conjunction with the exercise of his ministry as a bishop. It is my contention that, with his election as Pope, he did not cease to be a philosopher, but rather his philosophical work acquired a new and rather unique context. This context is both international and multi-national, pastoral and administrative, spiritual and social. The purpose of this chapter is to examine how the concept of *solidarity* fared in this new context, and this will involve tracing the continuity between the thought of Wojtyla and the teaching of John Paul II, as well as identifying whatever development might have taken place in, and perhaps because of, the new context in which he found himself working.

Before entering into the discussion of *solidarity* in the addresses and writings of John Paul II, I think it is important to acknowledge the problem of authorship, which inevitably arises in the case of a public figure of international importance. To what extent can it be said that Karol Wojtyla is the author of the addresses and writings of Pope John Paul II? At present there is very little public knowledge as to the extent to which first drafts are prepared, or final drafts corrected by the Pope himself. Rumours abound as to who may or may not have had a hand in the writing of an encyclical, or the preparation of an address given on a pastoral visit. An exception would appear to be the encyclical *Redemptor Hominis*. Writing in 1995, Pope John Paul says:

> You will remember that my first encyclical on the Redeemer of man ...appeared a few months after my election on October 16, 1978. This means that I was actually carrying its contents *within* me. I only had to "copy" from memory and experience what I had already been living on the threshold of the papacy.[1]

---

[1] POPE JOHN PAUL II, *Crossing the Threshold of Hope*, ed., Vittorio Missori, (London: Jonathan Cape, 1994), 48.

It seems reasonable, however, to say that Karol Wojtyla is probably not the sole author, in the more restricted sense, of most of the addresses that Pope John Paul delivers, or of the letters and documents published in his name.

The concept of authorship may, however, be understood less restrictively, without doing violence to the basic concept that a certain person is responsible for the origination, development, or promotion of a particular concept or idea.[2] It is widely recognised, for example, that much of the material contained in the bible was not actually written by the person who is generally accepted as the author.[3] The case of papal addresses and writings is somewhat different, but the principle is the same. In keeping with the intention of presenting the thought of Karol Wojtyla / John Paul II, rather than that of his *curia*, I will not be using documents issued by the various Pontifical Councils and Congregations of the Vatican in this chapter, but will restrict myself to using documents issued in the pope's own name, and addresses which he has personally delivered.

In the case of Pope John Paul II it is possible to identify a particularly philosophical and anthropological approach which is not present in the writings of previous popes. It is also possible, I believe, to recognise a consistency and a continuity between Wojtyla and John Paul II in the manner in which many key concepts are used.[4] John Conley also identifies clear traces of the phenomenological method of Wojtyla in the documents of John Paul II.[5] This would suggest that, to whatever extent he is not the author in the more restrictive sense, Wojtyla's thought is nonetheless being faithfully represented. As indicated above, there is, therefore, no difficulty in acknowledging that Karol Wojtyla is in a real sense the author of the

---

[2] Cf. *Webster's Dictionary of the English Language*, (New York: Webster's Press, 1977), s.v. "author"; also *Concise Oxford Dictionary of Current English*, 7th. edition, (Oxford: Oxford University Press, 1982), s.v. "author."

[3] Cf. Raymond E. BROWN and James C. TURRO "Canonicity," §§87-9, *Jerome Biblical Commentary*, Vol. 2, (Englewood Cliffs, New Jersey: Prentice Hall, 1968), 531/2.

[4] A striking example of this continuity would be the pope's handling of concepts such as *truth* and *freedom*, cf. KAROL WOJTYLA, *Acting Person*, 158-175, and POPE JOHN PAUL II, *VS*, § 61; cf. also the concept *neighbour* cf. KAROL WOJTYLA, *Acting Person*, 297, and POPE JOHN PAUL II, *SRS*, § 39.

[5] Cf. JOHN J. CONLEY, "The Philosophical Foundations of the Thought of John Paul II: A Response," in *The Thought of Pope John Paul II*, ed., John M. Mc. Dermott, (Rome: Gregorian University Press, 1993), 23-26.

addresses and writings of Pope John Paul II.[6]

In the course of this Chapter, I intend to begin by examining interdependence as the condition of solidarity, or the context in which it is to be found. I will then go on to consider the addresses and writings of John Paul II, in the light of the same four questions posed in Chapter Three, i.e., a) what causes or contributes to solidarity? b) what are the objectives and goals of solidarity? c) how are these objectives and goals achieved? and, d) what are the obstacles to solidarity? It should then be possible to formulate a definition of solidarity as it is found in the teaching of John Paul II, and to compare this definition with others elaborated in the course of the earlier chapters.

A. SOLIDARITY: CONDITIONS AND CONTEXT

As we have already seen in the previous chapter, Wojtyla discusses the concept of solidarity in the final chapter of his work, *The Acting Person*, a chapter entitled "Intersubjectivity by Participation." The issue of participation, and of solidarity as the attitude which facilitates it, arises out of the fact that the person is not an isolated subject in a world of objects, but rather a subject among subjects. It should not be surprising, therefore, that the concept of *interdependence* also plays a central role in the papal writing of John Paul II on solidarity.

1. The Reality of Interdependence

The fact that people are mutually dependent is something that can be readily observed. In the course of a homily during his 1987 visit to Chile, John Paul II emphasised the fundamental bond established between all people by reason of a common human nature.

> Dear brothers and sisters..... The bonds which unite men are more and of greater importance than those which can separate them. Many centuries ago, my predecessor, Pope Saint Leo the Great said: "Under the name of neighbour we must consider not only those who are joined to us by bonds of friendship or family ties, but also all men with whom we share a common nature."[7]

---

[6] I will continue to distinguish between material written prior to 1978 and that written since 1978, by referring to the author of the former as Karol Wojtyla, and that of the latter as John Paul II. This is not to imply any philosophical rift between the two, but simply for the sake of greater clarity.

[7] POPE JOHN PAUL II, Homily at Punta Arenas, Chile, 4/4/'87, § 6, *IGP2* X-1 (1987): 1039.

Human work is one concrete expression of interdependence, and in a world in which "work is carried out within a dense framework of interdependences, which in many ways condition its possibilities and its development," this reality of interdependence is becoming more apparent.[8]

The growth of regional economies and even of a global economy actually create new relationships of interdependence, and make the network of interdependence more complex. It is no longer merely a question of the interdependence of persons, but the interdependence of communities, nations, and even continents. "It is a fact that each country is or will be in need of the others, because mutual interdependence on the economic, political, and cultural levels is becoming ever more unavoidable."[9] The question of human work is also a key aspect of this global interdependence, because "the problems of work have for some time taken on a relevance such that they transcend local, regional, national and international geographical boundaries."[10] More efficient communication and travel contribute to this greater awareness of interdependence.[11]

Two factors in particular remain to be mentioned which increasingly present themselves as expressions of the reality of human interdependence. Among the urgent challenges which face many nations, and which, in some sense affect all nations, are the defence of the environment and the problem of external debt.[12] The resources of the earth, though abundant, are finite. The essential elements of the environment impinge on the lives of every person, through the air we breathe, the food we eat, and the water we drink. Dependence on the environment is a vital component of interdependence.[13]

Similarly, external debt is a significant factor in interdependence. Some

---

[8] POPE JOHN PAUL II, Address to Representatives of the Association of Catholic Workers, 6/12/'86, § 2, *IGP2* IX-2 (1986): 1855/6.

[9] POPE JOHN PAUL II, Address to the Ambassador of Venezuela, 15/12/'90, *AAS* 83 (1991): 730; cf. idem, Address to Workers, Taranto, Italy, 28/10/'89, § 6, *AAS* 82 (1990): 580.

[10] POPE JOHN PAUL II, Address to Lancia Workers, Ivrea, Italy, 19/3/'90, § 4, *IGP2* XIII-1 (1990): 703.

[11] Cf. POPE JOHN PAUL II, Address to a Plenary Session of the Council of Europe, Strasbourg, 8/10/'88, § 11, *AAS* 81 (1989): 683.

[12] Cf. POPE JOHN PAUL II, Address to the Ambassador of Brazil, 2/4/'90, *AAS* 82 (1990): 1989.

[13] Cf. POPE JOHN PAUL II, Address to the Diplomatic Corps, N'Djamena, Chad, 1/2/'90, § 3, *AAS* 82 (1990): 824; also idem, Address to the Ambassador of South Korea, Vatican, 30/3/90, *AAS* 82 (1990): 984.

nations have borrowed money which they cannot repay without undermining their economies. Nations which have lent money have little hope of recovering it if the economies of the debtor nations are destroyed. The debt question has a particular relevance for the internal relations of debtor nations also, as those who bear the burden of repayment are often not those who have benefited from the increased spending, funded by borrowing. The pope says: "An ethical judgement should be brought to bear on the international debt in order to demonstrate the responsibilities of all the parties concerned and the profound international interdependence of the progress of humanity."[14]

Finally, it is implicit in the notion of interdependence, that dependence is a mutual relationship, even though this mutuality is not always recognised. The rich also depend on the poor; the strong on the weak. This is a factor upon which John Paul II frequently focuses his attention in speaking about solidarity. Truth leads us to recognise "the dignity, equality, and fraternal solidarity of all human beings, and it prompts us to reject every form of discrimination."[15] The equality of all human persons is the foundation of human dignity, and of the right to participate in development.[16] According to the Pope, "the essential character" of effective solidarity "is to be perceived in the radical equality of all men and women," and this has major implications in relation to the kind of politics in which we engage.[17]

It is, however, worth recalling the reservations which both Mounier and Scheler had about predicating equality of human persons. Equality is a concept which expresses quantity, and as such it is appropriate when speaking of strict justice. When we are dealing with the human person, however, we are not dealing with something which can be quantified. In the case of the person, it can rightly be argued that strict justice is injury (*summa iustitia injuria*). Any authentic response to the human person must

---

[14] POPE JOHN PAUL II, Address to the Diplomatic Corps, Buenos Aires, Argentina, 6/4/'87, § 3, *HSSP*, 226.

[15] POPE JOHN PAUL II, Address at the Raj Ghat Monument, Delhi, India, 1/2/'86, § 2, *AAS* 78 (1986): 738.

[16] Cf. POPE JOHN PAUL II, Address to Members of the Union of Catholic Jurists of Italy, 10/12/'88, § 4, *AAS* 81 (1989): 764; also idem, Address to Intellectual and Commercial leaders, Santa Cruz, Bolivia, 12/5/'88, § 9, *IGP2* XI-2 (1988): 1347.

[17] POPE JOHN PAUL II, Message for World Peace Day, 1987, 8/12/'86, § 4, *AAS* 79 (1987): 49; cf. also idem, Message for World Communications Day, 24/1/'88, § 3, *AAS* 80 (1988): 1360.

ultimately reach beyond the merely quantitative to the qualitative level, which is proportioned to love rather than to strict justice. In this context it is worth noting, therefore, that John Paul II sees equality as something which must be transcended if there is to be a genuine solidarity. "Beyond the reciprocity of rights and strict justice in equality of treatment, we must arrive at a common solidarity in the face of the great stakes of humanity."[18]

We must now move on to consider the relationship between interdependence and solidarity, which is a constant theme in the thought of John Paul II. A careful examination of the pope's teaching reveals that he does not always present this relationship in quite the same terms. In some places he speaks of interdependence as a moral category which requires solidarity. Elsewhere he speaks of interdependence being transformed into solidarity, or again of the awareness of interdependence giving rise to solidarity.

2. Interdependence as a Moral Category

Interdependence as a reality is an aspect of the human condition. Of itself it is morally neutral for the simple reason that interdependence is not a matter of choice. It can be seen, however, as an opportunity. Pope John Paul argues that interdependence must be recognised as a "moral category."[19] On a number of occasions he refers to the need to recognise interdependence as a moral principle, because of its impact on the lives of people. "The interdependence which these days characterises and conditions the lives of individuals and peoples must be a moral principle which leads to the firm and persevering determination in favour of the common good, always avoiding the temptation to dominate the weak."[20] To say that something is a moral principle is to say that it must always be a guiding influence in our decisions about what is good.

What all this means in effect is that interdependence is a foundation on which human rights are established. The fact that the concept of human rights is one which is constantly evolving is, at least in part, a reflection of the fact that new forms of interdependence are constantly manifesting

---

[18] POPE JOHN PAUL II, Address to the Diplomatic Corps, Vatican, 12/1/'85, *HSSP*, 99/100.
   [19] POPE JOHN PAUL II, Address to the Diplomatic Corps, Dar es Salaam, Tanzania, 1/9/'90, § 3, *AAS* 83 (1991): 211.
   [20] Pope JOHN PAUL II, Address to the Ambassador of Argentina, 30/11/'89, *AAS* 82 (1990): 689.

themselves. Interdependence, while it is not in itself a moral value, cannot be divorced from morality because it constitutes a permanent challenge to people to act in a way which contributes to the common good. To use the language of *The Acting Person*, our awareness of interdependence must not simply be reflective; it must also be reflexive.[21]

Probably the most significant presentation of interdependence as a moral category, requiring the response of solidarity, is to be found in the encyclical letter *Sollicitudo Rei Socialis*.

> It is above all a question of interdependence, sensed as a system determining relationships in the contemporary world, in its economic, cultural, political and religious elements, and accepted as a moral category. When interdependence becomes recognised in this way, the correct response as a moral and social attitude, as a virtue, is solidarity.[22]

Addressing the people of Detroit, the pope acknowledges the tendency to protect one's own interests, in the face of interdependence, and argues that this tendency must be balanced by a sense of solidarity.

> Dear friends: America is a very powerful country. The amount and quality of your achievements are staggering. By virtue of your unique position, as citizens of this nation, you are placed before a choice and you must choose. You may choose to close in on yourselves, to enjoy the fruits of your own form of progress and to try to forget about the rest of the world. Or, as you become more and more aware of your gifts and your capacity to serve, you may choose to live up to the responsibilities that your own history and accomplishments place on your shoulders. By choosing this latter course, you acknowledge interdependence, and opt for solidarity.[23]

This passage would seem to present the response to interdependence as something which, logically at least, takes place in two stages. Firstly there must be the acknowledgement of *de facto* interdependence, which does not by definition lead to the choice of what is good. Secondly there is the option for a good response, namely solidarity, rather than an evil one.

John Paul II's constant reference to solidarity as a duty, corresponds to his recognition of interdependence as a moral category. Duties derive from rights. "The reality of work creates a union of all in an activity which has

---

[21] Cf. Karol WOJTYLA, *Acting Person*, 44.
[22] POPE JOHN PAUL, *SRS*, §38.
[23] POPE JOHN PAUL II, Address to the People of Detroit, 19/9/'87, §§ 8/9, *IGP2* X-3 (1987): 672/3.

one single significance," and this gives rise to a "duty of solidarity," which the pope describes as an "experience of the first order."[24] Solidarity is a duty which finds its roots in interdependence,[25] and conscience.[26] For Christians "solidarity is a moral duty stemming from the spiritual union of all human beings who share a common origin, a common dignity, and a common destiny.[27]

3. The Transformation of Interdependence into Solidarity

It is clear that Pope John Paul does not consider interdependence as something negative, but rather as a challenge which has very positive potential. Interdependence is not something which must be replaced, but rather something which must be transformed. "The conviction is growing of a radical interdependence and consequently of the need for a solidarity which will take up interdependence and transfer it to the moral plane."[28] Donal Dorr remarks that "these words are a key to understanding the word *solidarity* in the specific technical meaning the pope is giving to it: solidarity is the correct moral response to the fact of interdependence."[29]

The pope adverts to the tendency towards individualism which is the futile attempt to escape from the reality of interdependence.[30] This tendency often leads to the replacement of social solidarity by "coercive structures and bureaucratic mechanisms."[31] He points out that "interdependence can be experienced as coercion, or alternatively welcomed and accepted as a moral duty. When it is interpreted in this second way,

---

[24] POPE JOHN PAUL II, Address to Lancia Workers, Ivrea, Italy, 19/3/'90, § 3, *IGP2* XIII-1 (1990): 701.

[25] Cf. POPE JOHN PAUL II, Address to Citizens at Castel San Giovanni, Italy, 5/6/'88 *IGP2*, XI-2 (1988): 1812.

[26] Cf. POPE JOHN PAUL II, Letter to the Islamic World concerning the Lebanese People, 7/9/'89, § 5, *AAS* 82 (1990): 82/3; also idem, Address to Participants in a Congress organised by the Bishops' Commission of the European Community, 11/10/'91, § 6, *IGP2* XIV-2 (1991): 805.

[27] POPE JOHN PAUL II, Address to the People of Detroit, U.S.A., 19/9/'87, § 6, *IGP2* X-3 (1987): 668/9.

[28] POPE JOHN PAUL II, *SRS*, § 26.

[29] Donal DORR, "Solidarity and Integral Human Development," in *The Logic of Solidarity*, eds., Gregory Baum and Robert Ellsberg, (New York: Orbis, 1989), 148.

[30] Cf. POPE JOHN PAUL II, Address to Youth, Antananariva, Madagascar, 29/4/'89, § 2 *IGP2*, XII-1 (1989): 982.

[31] POPE JOHN PAUL II, Address to Participants in a Convention on *Rerum Novarum*, 15/5/'91, § 6, *AAS* 84 (1992): 149.

interdependence is transformed into a value: the value of solidarity."[32]

The pope maintains that "interdependence must be transformed into the value of solidarity *based on the principle that the goods of creation are meant for all.*"[33] This principle implicitly embraces various elements of interdependence: equality, mutual need, common human nature, shared environment etc. The pope is in effect applying a version of the classical *is–ought* argument to the reality of interdependence.

As the scope of this work is philosophical, it would not be appropriate here to enter into theological speculation. It would be impossible, however, to offer an adequate treatment of the theme without referring, at least in passing, to the theological dimension of interdependence and of solidarity in the thought of John Paul II. The pope argues that "God has created our basic interdependence and called us to solidarity with all."[34] He argues, for example, that it is part of the plan of divine providence that "the goods of creation are meant for all," and that the other person is to be seen as "our neighbour...to be made a sharer, on a par with ourselves, in the banquet of life, to which all are equally invited by God."[35] He sees the poverty of Jesus Christ as an affirmation of the human dignity and fundamental equality of the poor.[36] Given the foundational role which John Paul II attributes to God in the condition of human interdependence, it is to be expected that God will also have a place among the causes of solidarity, and among its goals.

B. THE CAUSES OF SOLIDARITY

We must move on now to consider how interdependence is transformed into solidarity. What are the causes of solidarity?

1. Awareness and Truth

Pope John Paul frequently states that the *awareness* of interdepen-

---

[32] POPE JOHN PAUL II, "Address to the Citizens, Castel San Giovanni, Italy," 5/6/'88, *IGP2* XI-2 (1988): 1812; cf. idem, "Address to Workers," Verona, Italy, 17/4/'88, § 3, *IGP2* XI-1 (1988): 938.

[33] POPE JOHN PAUL II, *SRS*, § 39; cf. also idem, Address to Participants in aStudy Week of the Pontifical Academy of Sciences, 27/10/'89, § 4, *IGP2* XII-2 (1989): 1048; idem, Address at the Airport, Praia, Cape Verde, 25/1/'90, § 7, *IGP2* XIII-1 (1990): 183; and idem, Address at the Airport, Guinea-Bissau, 27/1/'90, § 7, *IGP2* XIII-1 (1990): 224/5.

[34] POPE JOHN PAUL II, Address to the People of Detroit, U.S.A., 19/9/'87, § 6, *IGP2* X-3 (1987): 668/9.

[35] POPE JOHN PAUL, *SRS*, § 39.

[36] Cf. POPE JOHN PAUL II, *VS*, § 100.

dence gives rise to solidarity. Addressing the workers at ATAC, the Rome bus company, he says: "Solidarity is also a moral virtue, given rise to by the consciousness of the co-natural interdependence which joins every human being to his fellows in the various components of his existence."[37] In the course of an address to the ambassador of Zimbabwe, the pope once again refers to the important contribution made by the awareness of interdependence, and places it side by side with the awareness of the unity of the human family.

> A deeper awareness of the unity of the whole human family and of the radical interdependence of all peoples is gradually fostering a widespread conviction that only genuine solidarity, understood as a moral category determining human relations can effectively safeguard the dignity and rights of individuals, and therefore build peace within societies and between nations.[38]

The awareness of interdependence is to be understood not merely as awareness of the fact, but also as acceptance of the moral implications of interdependence. It is a practical and not merely a theoretical awareness. This is stated in a number of places, but perhaps most explicitly with reference to the Church. "Solidarity is the expression of the Church's life and of her dynamism in Christ. Such solidarity involves a *practical* awareness of the great network of interdependence that exists among God's people."[39] The awareness of interdependence is related to "an openness to the problems of others."[40] In a slight variation on the theme, the Pope comments that interdependence contributes to the awareness of brotherhood, which is the basis for living in solidarity.

> One must teach, inculcate, and live that solidarity which is rooted in an awareness of the brotherhood of all the members of the human family. Today one can see a growth in that awareness, brought about by the interdependence of individuals

---

[37] POPE JOHN PAUL II, Address to ATAC Transport Workers, Rome, 19/3/'88, § 6, *AAS* 80 (1988): 1337.

[38] POPE JOHN PAUL II, Address to the Ambassador of Zimbabwe, Vatican, 17/1/'91, *IGP2* XIV-1 (1991): 124; cf. also idem, "Address to the Ambassador of Santa Lucia," Vatican, 28/10/'91, *AAS* 84 (1992): 960/1.

[39] POPE JOHN PAUL II, Address to U.S. Bishops on *Ad Limina* visit, Vatican, 9/9/'88, § 2, *AAS* 81 (1989): 177.

[40] Cf. POPE JOHN PAUL II, Address to the Diplomatic Corps, Vatican, 11/1/'86, § 2, *AAS* 78 (1986): 642.

and of peoples throughout the whole world.[41]

Recognition of the fact of interdependence is, at least notionally, distinct from the acceptance of its implications. It would seem, therefore, that, we must take account of an interim stage in the process that transforms interdependence into solidarity; a stage which follows the recognition of *de facto* interdependence, and precedes the actual option for what leads to the common good. This stage would be a form of reflection on the alternative choices that are presented by interdependence. It would involve the reference of these choices to moral truth, in the manner outlined by Wojtyla in chapter four of *The Acting Person*. "The sense of duty is the experiential form of the reference to (or dependence on) the moral truth, to which the freedom of the person is subordinate."[42] Conscience, as it were, distinguishes the moral good in a particular attitude towards others, i.e., solidarity, and releases a sense of duty in its regard.

The causal relationship between truth and solidarity is explicitly stated by John Paul II on a number of occasions. In his message for World Peace Day 1987, he says "The spirit of solidarity...finds its roots in truth and has need of the truth in order to develop."[43] Solidarity, when it is rooted in truth, becomes "the firm basis for a new world order."[44] Truth about the human person, and about the socio-economic factors that impinge upon his existence is the only basis on which solidarity can be established. In an address to the Italian bishops, Pope John Paul refers to "the emergence of new and insidious forms of poverty" and "the spread of sicknesses which find fertile soil in lifestyles which deny the truth of the person. In this context," he says: "There is a risk that solidarity is more stated than lived."[45]

In the thought of John Paul II, this truth about the person, while it can be arrived at by means of human reason, finds its ultimate confirmation in

---

[41] POPE JOHN PAUL II, Address at the Airport, Guinea-Bissau, 27/1/'90, § 7, *Osservatore Romano*, Weekly Edition in English, 1990, no. 7: 9.

[42] Karol WOJTYLA, *Acting Person*, 156ff.; cf. also ibid., 131/2.

[43] POPE JOHN PAUL II, Message for World Peace Day 1987, 8/12/'86, § 4, *AAS* 79 (1987): 49; cf. also idem, Address to the Ambassador of Sweden, 9/2/'87, *IGP2* X-1 (1987): 310/1.

[44] POPE JOHN PAUL II, Address to U.S. Bishops on *Ad Limina* visit, 9/9/'88, § 4, *AAS* 81 (1989): 178.

[45] POPE JOHN PAUL II, Address to Italian Bishops on *Ad Limina* visit, 1/3/'91, § 3, *AAS* 83 (1991): 984.

what God has revealed of himself. The pope states:

> In the present condition of humanity which carries within itself the consequences
> of original sin, whether on the cognitive level or on the practical level, grace is
> necessary, on the one hand, to reach in its fullness what it is possible for reason
> to grasp of God, and on the other hand, to conform one's own behaviour
> coherently to the demands of the natural law. Consequent on this is the fact that
> the various aspects of human life find their most solid foundation and their sure
> guarantee of authenticity in the supernatural order: in particular love, friendship,
> sociality and solidarity, law and socio-political order, and above all freedom,
> which is not real in any context unless it is founded on truth.[46]

He maintains that solidarity "has its roots, not in dubious and passing ideologies but in the perennial truth of the Good News left to us by Jesus."[47]

2. Freedom

When Pope John Paul refers to freedom in the context of solidarity, he is generally referring to external freedom which is supported by solidarity. There are, however, a small number of cases in which he speaks of freedom in a way which makes it clear that it is also to be numbered among the causes of solidarity. He lists freedom among the elementary values which support solidarity and fraternity.[48] External freedom naturally assists solidarity. Solidarity, "when it includes solidarity in truth, freedom, justice, and love...becomes the firm basis for a new world order."[49] Respect for freedom of conscience and religious freedom are inseparable from solidarity,[50] but most important of all is that inner freedom, out of which is drawn love.[51]

---

[46] POPE JOHN PAUL II, Address to Participants in the Ninth International Thomistic Congress, 29/9/'90, § 4, *AAS* 83 (1991): 408.

[47] POPE JOHN PAUL II, Address to Farm-workers and Miners, Oruro, Bolivia, 11/5/'88, § 6, *AAS* 80 (1988): 1570.

[48] POPE JOHN PAUL II, Message for World Communications Day, 24/1/'88, § 5, *AAS* 80 (1988): 1361.

[49] POPE JOHN PAUL II, Address to U.S. Bishops on *Ad Limina* visit, 9/9/'88, § 4, *AAS* 81 (1989): 178.

[50] Cf. POPE JOHN PAUL II, Address to the Ambassador of Tanzania, 12/1/'90, *AAS* 82 (1990): 800.

[51] POPE JOHN PAUL II, *DM*, § 8.

3. Love

Foremost among the causes of solidarity is love, which is a response, in freedom, to the truth about the human person. According to the pope, "solidarity is the concrete face of love."[52] Elsewhere he says that "the most authentic force for development is love which translates itself into operative solidarity."[53] Pope John Paul is quite un-ambiguous about the fact that solidarity lacks meaning unless its foundation is love. In his homily at Santa Cruz airport he says:

> I wish to emphasise also how much solidarity really lacks meaning unless it has love as its foundation. It is the property of solidarity as a virtue which makes us Christians radically different from any other person inspired by a passing ideology. Only a solidarity based on love, and the fruit of love offers any hope of building a stable foundation for the construction of a just and fraternal society.[54]

In other cases where the pope refers to love as the cause of solidarity, it is frequently to the love of God, or to a specifically Christian love that he refers. In the course of an address to workers delegates at Geneva he invites them to struggle for a politic which will realise both their material development and their spiritual progress. He then goes on to say "The leit-motiv which is appropriate here is that of social justice. For the believers whom I represent, this solidarity is rooted in love."[55] In this comment he would appear to be equating solidarity with social justice, and identifying love as their primary motivating force. Elsewhere, the pope speaks of the mutual understanding that is necessary if people are to attain common interests, and explains that this understanding requires of each person that he open himself to the objective consideration of the good of others. He goes on to say, "in this precisely is solidarity, which thus reveals itself as a fundamental expression of the sociality immanent in human nature, and

---

[52] POPE JOHN PAUL II, Address to the Management and Staff of Assicurazioni Generali, 1/12/'90, § 4, *IGP2* XIII-2 (1990): 1351.

[53] POPE JOHN PAUL II, Address to Business People, Naples, Italy, 10/11/'90, § 7, *IGP2* XIII-3 (1990): 1123.

[54] POPE JOHN PAUL II, Homily at Santa Cruz Airport, Bolivia, 13/5/'88, § 8, *IGP2* XI-2 (1988): 1372/3.

[55] POPE JOHN PAUL II, Address to Workers Delegates, Geneva, Switzerland, 15/6/'82, *IGP2* V-2 (1982): 2283/4.

as a particularly significant dimension of Christian love."[56] Finally, at a General Audience in 1988, Pope John Paul speaks of the solidarity of Jesus Christ, and asks in what did it consist. He offers the answer "It is the manifestation of love which has its source in God himself."[57]

On the basis of the above, we can say without doubt that, for John Paul II, love is an efficient cause of solidarity. There are some cases where the pope comes close to saying that love is solidarity.[58] Yet, on the other hand, there are times when it appears that love is seen as being in some way superior to solidarity.

> The person who is a neighbour cannot indifferently pass by the suffering of another; this in the name of fundamental human solidarity, still more in the name of love of neighbour.[59]

This leads us to ask what, if anything, is the difference between the two? We shall tackle this question shortly.

There are, however, a number of other questions arising from the discussion of love as the cause of solidarity. a) What is the difference between the *love* of Christians (i.e., that which comes from, or is inspired by faith in, Christ) and ordinary human *love*? b) In what way does *charity* differ from either or both of these? In answer to the first of these two questions, all we can say at the moment is that both *love* and *Christian love* are acknowledged as causes of solidarity, and no clear distinction is made between them. In order to respond to the second question, we will need to consider what John Paul II says about the relationship between charity and solidarity.

4. Charity

When Pope John Paul refers to charity in the context of solidarity, he frequently indicates that charity is a cause of solidarity. Addressing workers in Paraguay he says: "You must live together in solidarity, because

---

[56] POPE JOHN PAUL II, Address to Representatives of the Association of Catholic Workers, 6/12/'86, § 3, *IGP2* IX-2 (1986): 1856/7.

[57] POPE JOHN PAUL II, Address at General Audience, 10/2/'88, §§ 8/9, *IGP2* XII (1988): 397.

[58] Cf. POPE JOHN PAUL II, *SRS*, § 46.

[59] POPE JOHN PAUL II, *SD*, § 29.

solidarity is a Christian virtue which springs from charity."[60] In the course of another address, on this occasion to the bishops of Italy, the pope says that the initiatives of charity "seek to offer human and fraternal solidarity to migrants from Eastern Europe and from other continents."[61] Once again he appears to argue that solidarity arises out of charity. The Church too is called to respond with solidarity to the many needs of people, as the pope reminds bishops from the U.S.A. "The solidarity about which we speak is that genuine solidarity which is expressed in a spirit of sharing, accompanied by real human feeling, and motivated by supernatural charity."[62]

In the course of an address to the bishops of Piemonte, however, the pope encourages them to teach solidarity which, he says, is "Christian charity as described by the gospel."[63] There are numerous other passages in the same vein in which the pope seems to say that charity and solidarity are simply identified.[64]

Perhaps the most significant statement in terms of clarifying the relationship of charity and solidarity is one in which John Paul II, commenting on an address of Pope Pius XII, indicates in a definitive way the place of solidarity in the social teaching of the church:

> I would remind you of the terms used by Pope Pius XII when, before a world torn apart, he denounced, "the forgetting of that law of human solidarity and charity, dictated and imposed as much by the community of origin and by the equality of rational nature in all men, to whatever people they belong, as by the sacrifice of redemption offered by Christ on the altar of the cross, to his heavenly Father, on behalf of sinful humanity." In this way he expressed the close connection which exists between the human nature created by God in fundamental solidarity, and the power of redeeming love which overcomes the ruptures of sin. In the social teaching of the Church, as you know, solidarity is not separated from charity; it

---

[60] POPE JOHN PAUL II, Homily at Villaricca, Paraguay, 17/5/'88, § 6, *IGP2* XI-2 (1988): 1511.

[61] POPE JOHN PAUL II, Address to Italian Bishops, Vatican, 26/1/'91, § 5, *AAS* 83 1991: 946.

[62] POPE JOHN PAUL II, Address to U.S. Bishops on *Ad Limina* visit, 9/9/'88, § 5, *AAS* 81 (1989): 179.

[63] POPE JOHN PAUL, Address to the Bishops of Piemonte, 31/1/'87, § 4, *AAS* 79 (1987): 1234.

[64] Cf. POPE JOHN PAUL II, *SRS*, § 40; also idem, Address to Government Officials and Diplomatic Corps, Asuncion, Paraguay, 16/5/'88, § 4, *HSSP*, 233; also idem, Address to the Plenary Meeting of the Pontifical Council *Cor Unum*, 19/11/'90, § 2, *AAS* 83 (1991): 674.

would even be an exaggeration to place them in different orders.[65]

This comment would seem to suggest that the law of solidarity and the law of charity are one and the same. It would not be accurate, in John Paul's view to suggest, for example, that charity belongs to the supernatural order and solidarity to the natural order. Yet there is clearly some distinction to be made between charity and solidarity. One indication of what this distinction might be is the pope's comment that, at least in the Christian perspective, solidarity "translates effectively into practice the obligations of evangelical charity."[66] In other words, it would appear that solidarity relates more specifically to the sphere of action or *praxis*, than charity. Another helpful distinction is to be found in the encyclical *Centesimus Annus*, in which Pope John Paul comments that when Pius XI used the "meaningful term" *social charity*, he was in fact referring to the same reality as he himself understands by *solidarity*.[67] It would, therefore, appear that solidarity is distinguished from charity, at least notionally, by the fact that it has to do with relations in society, as opposed to simple interpersonal relations. This would appear to confirm a similar conclusion to which we came in the previous chapter, when examining Wojtyla's concept of solidarity, as outlined in *The Acting Person*.

5. Compassion and Commitment

Having noted that solidarity is characterised by action, our attention now turns to the examination of two elements, each of which is in some sense related to the development of solidarity. These are compassion and commitment. It would appear that, while compassion is helpful in giving rise to solidarity, it often fails because it stops short of action. Commitment, on the other hand, always implies a readiness to act.

In his encyclical on suffering, Pope John Paul gives some attention to the character of the Good Samaritan of the gospel story, and his willingness to stop to help the man who had been attacked by thieves. He says:

This stopping does not mean curiosity but availability. It is like the opening of a

---

[65] POPE JOHN PAUL II, Address to the Fourteenth General Assembly of *Caritas Internationalis*, 28/5/'91, § 2, *AAS* 84 (1992): 293/4.
[66] POPE JOHN PAUL II, Address to Participants in a Conference on Human Work, 20/11/'87, § 2, *IGP2* X-3 (1987): 1161.
[67] POPE JOHN PAUL II, *CA*, § 10.

certain interior disposition of the heart, which also has an emotional expression of its own....Sometimes this compassion remains the only, or principal, expression of our love for and solidarity with the sufferer. Nevertheless, the Good Samaritan of Christ's parable does not stop at sympathy and compassion alone. They become for him an incentive to actions aimed at bringing help to the injured man.[68]

In any other reference to compassion which I have been able to find in the writings and addresses of John Paul II, it is clearly stated that there is considerably more to solidarity than a vague sense of compassion. The classic statement of this view is to be found in *Sollicitudo Rei Socialis*, and it is frequently cited elsewhere in the pope's addresses.

> This (solidarity) then is not a feeling of vague compassion or shallow distress at the misfortunes of so many people, both near and far. On the contrary, it is a firm and persevering determination to commit oneself to the common good; that is to say to the good of all and of each individual, because we are all really responsible for all.[69]

By contrast, Pope John Paul sees solidarity as depending on an "active moral commitment"[70] which amounts to a "firm and persevering determination" to dedicate oneself to the common good.[71] Throughout the addresses and writings of John Paul II, the two terms *commitment* and *determination* are used interchangeably. As we have seen, both commitment and determination are sometimes spoken of as if they were prerequisites of solidarity, but more frequently solidarity is identified with one or other of them. "Solidarity is a firm and persevering commitment to

---

[68] POPE JOHN PAUL II, *SD*, § 28.

[69] POPE JOHN PAUL II, *SRS* 38; cf. also idem, Homily at Maputo, Mozambique, 18/9/'88, § 12, *AAS* 81 (1989): 358; idem, Address to U.S. President George Bush, 27/5/'89, *AAS*, 81 (1989): 1315/6; idem; Address to the Civic Authorities, Rome, 20/1/'90, § 2, *AAS* 82 (1990): 885; idem, Address to Youth, Naples, Italy, 10/11/'90, § 5, *IGP2* XIII-2 (1990): 1078.

[70] POPE JOHN PAUL II, Address to ATAC Transport Workers, Rome, 19/3/'88, § 6, *AAS* 80 (1988): 1337; cf. also idem, Address to Representatives of the Association of Catholic Workers, Vatican, 6/12/'86, § 6, *IGP2* IX-2 (1986): 1858/9; and idem, Address to Canadian Bishops, 27/9/'88, § 5, *AAS* 81 (1989): 201.

[71] POPE JOHN PAUL II, Address to ATAC Transport Workers, Rome, 19/3/'88, § 6, *AAS* 80 (1988): 1337.

the common good."[72] The active nature of this commitment is made clear in another address to workers, this time in Malta.

> The outstanding virtue of the working men and women of Malta should be solidarity: a commitment to the common good; a rejection of selfishness and irresponsibility. We must become responsible for one another. What are needed are concrete acts of solidarity: between employers and employees, between working men and women themselves, with special sensitivity for the poor and the defenceless.[73]

Likewise, solidarity is described as a "firm and persevering determination to commit oneself to the common good."[74] As in the case of *love* and *charity*, so now in the case of *commitment* and *determination*, we see that, while these terms are sometimes used in a way which suggests a causal relationship with solidarity, they are clearly such proximate causes as to make it difficult to distinguish them from that which they cause, namely solidarity. Both determination and commitment imply firmness of purpose and the focussing of action on a particular goal, even to the exclusion of other goals.[75]

6. Work

Pope John Paul frequently refers to solidarity when addressing what he calls the "worker's question." One of his earlier encyclical letters was *Laborem Exercens*, on the question of human work, and the theme of human work was addressed very frequently, especially in the early years of his pontificate. Work pervades the whole of human experience. As we have already seen, it is an aspect of the human condition, of interdepen-

---

[72] POPE JOHN PAUL II, Address to the Citizens, Castel San Giovanni, Italy, 5/6/'88, *IGP2* XI-2 (1988): 1812; cf. also idem, Address to U.S. Bishops on *Ad Limina* visit, 9/9/'88, § 2, *AAS* 81 (1989): 177.
[73] POPE JOHN PAUL II, Address to Workers, Malta, 26/5/'90, § 5, *AAS* 83 (1991): 61.
[74] POPE JOHN PAUL II, Address to U.S. President George Bush, 27/5/'89, *AAS* 81 (1989): 1315/6; cf. also idem, Address to the Diplomatic Corps, Copenhagen, Denmark, 7/6/'89, § 5, *AAS* 81 (1989): 1361; and idem, Address to the Ambassador of Argentina, Vatican, 30/11/'89, *AAS* 82 (1990): 689.
[75] Cf. *The Concise Oxford Dictionary of Current English*, 7th. edition, Oxford: Clarendon Press, 1982. s.v. "**Determination**, n. 1. delimitation, definition; exact ascertainment of amount etc. 2. fixing of purpose, fixed intention; resoluteness;" cf. also s.v."**Commit**, v.t., 2. be doer of (crime, sin, blunder); expose to risk, involve, (character, honour, oneself), pledge oneself by implication, bind (person, oneself to a course of action).... -**ment**, n., (esp.) engagement or involvement that restricts freedom of action."

dence. The pope comments that "work has a precise appropriateness" for stimulating and developing solidarity.[76] I understand this to mean that, because work is so fundamental to the well-being of the person and of society, that the challenge of transforming the interdependence of the workplace into solidarity imposes itself very forcefully on all concerned. There are other situations in life in which the reality and the demands of interdependence can be avoided. A person can choose to live, and to recreate himself, alone and without concern for others, but this is not so easy when it comes to the world of work. Addressing the I.L.O. at Geneva, the pope says: "Within the one community of work, solidarity strives for the discovery of the demands of unity which are inherent in the nature of work, rather than the tendencies towards distinction and opposition."[77]

Addressing the people gathered in St. Peter's Square, John Paul asks, "what is work?" In answer, he explains that it is first and foremost an opportunity for the person to re-discover partnership with God. Then he goes on to say: "Beyond that, work is a means of union and of solidarity, which makes men into brothers, educates them to co-operation, strengthens them in concord, stimulates them in the conquest of things, but above all of hope, freedom, and love."[78]

The world of work is a context in which man, the subject of work, can become depersonalised and degraded. This happens when the other person or group is seen as "just an instrument with a work capacity and physical strength to be exploited at low cost and then discarded when no longer useful."[79] The subject of work is always the same, but the world of work is constantly changing, frequently in a way which is not in the interests of workers. It was such an occurrence, as Pope John Paul says, that gave rise to the "worker question." Even in this apparently negative situation, there is a stimulus for solidarity. The pope explains:

> This question and the problems connected with it gave rise to a just social reaction and caused the impetuous emergence of a great burst of solidarity

---

[76] POPE JOHN PAUL II, Address to the Civic and Ecclesiastical Authorities, Rieti, Italy, 2/1/'83, § 3, *IGP2* VI-1 (1983): 26.

[77] POPE JOHN PAUL II, Address to the I.L.O., Geneva, Switzerland, 15/6/'82, *AAS* 74 (1982): 997.

[78] POPE JOHN PAUL II, Angelus Address, Vatican, 27/9/'81, *IGP2* IV-2 (1981): 307/8; cf. also idem, Address to Youth, Bomako, Mali, 28/1/'90, § 5, *IGP2* XIII-1 (1990): 282.

[79] Cf. POPE JOHN PAUL II, *SRS*, 39.

between workers, first and foremost industrial workers. The call to solidarity and common action addressed to the workers... was important and eloquent from the point of view of social ethics. It was the reaction against the degradation of man as the subject of work... This reaction united the working world in a community marked by great solidarity.[80]

Thus, it appears that work is capable of making an important contribution to the development of solidarity. The pope, however, cautions workers and their unions to avoid falling into the trap of a solidarity which is narrow and exclusive. The challenge to workers is to use the solidarity of the work-place as a stepping-stone to new forms and wider horizons of solidarity.

Working people should not lock themselves into a limited solidarity, which is circumscribed by the interests of the particular category or sector to which they belong, but rather they should keep in mind also the conditions in which others live. True solidarity must always be present wherever the subject of work, that is man, finds himself in conditions of poverty, wretchedness, exploitation, or injustice.[81]

Ultimately solidarity must be envisaged as something which surpasses every political frontier, to accept every worker, because every worker is first and foremost a member of the human family.[82] The common bond of work can be an important contributory factor in the development of this universal vision of solidarity.

7. Communion and Solidarity

One interesting feature in the addresses and writings of Pope John Paul II is the relationship between *communion* and *solidarity*. *Communion* seems to be used in an almost exclusively ecclesial or spiritual context, whereas *solidarity* is used in the context of human society. In two encyclicals, *Dominum et Vivificantem* and *Mulieris Dignitatem*, in which *solidarity* is not used at all, John Paul II uses *communion* quite extensively. The pope would appear to give substance to this distinction when he says:

---

[80] POPE JOHN PAUL II, *LE*, § 8.; cf. also idem, Address to a Workers Conference on *Laborem Exercens*, Vatican, 17/1/'87, § 3, *AAS* 79 (1987): 1197.

[81] POPE JOHN PAUL II, Address to Representatives of the Association of Catholic Workers, 6/12/'87, § 7, *IGP2* IX-2 (1986): 1860; cf. also idem, Address to the I.L.O., Geneva, 15/6/'82, *AAS* 74 (1982): 1000.

[82] Cf. POPE JOHN PAUL, Address to Lancia Motor Workers, Ivrea, Italy, 19/3/'90, § 4, *IGP2* XIII-1 (1990): 702/3.

"If the link that exists between us on the ecclesial plane is called and *is* communion or, better still, the reality of communion, on the plane of ordinary relations and, in general, of associated life, it is and ought to be solidarity."[83] There are also, however, grounds for believing that communion is related to solidarity, as being to action, or theory to praxis. In most of the addresses in which he uses both expressions together, the pope indicates that communion gives rise to solidarity and that it is in solidarity that it finds its practical expression. On the one hand solidarity is rooted in communion.

> Solidarity, in the final analysis, is for us Christians a theological appeal, which has its ultimate foundation, its rootedness, and its definitive norm, in the very reality of the mystery of the communion of God... It translates effectively into practice of the obligations of evangelical charity.[84]

On the other hand, the pope suggests that solidarity allows communion to take on its fullest and most correct meaning.[85] Communion finds its expression in solidarity.

> A true solidarity involves openness to the gift which I can always receive from the other, however poor he may appear to be at first; it becomes an exchange between partners who mutually respect each other's dignity; before God the creator and saviour, it becomes an authentic form of the communion to which all are called.[86]

Against this background, the Church can be understood as "communion in the service of the solidarity of a people."[87]

It would seem clear from the above that, while communion is distinct from solidarity, they are not in any sense opposed. Pope John Paul, over and above the human personal origins and causes of authentic solidarity, has identified another cause, namely the communion of believers which has

---

[83] POPE JOHN PAUL II, Address to Civil and Ecclesiastical Authorities, Rieti, Italy, 2/1/'83, § 3, *IGP2* VI-1 (1983): 25/6.

[84] POPE JOHN PAUL II, Address to Participants in a Conference on Human Work, Vatican, 20/11/'87, § 2, *IGP2* X-3 (1987): 1161; cf. also idem, *SRS*, § 40.

[85] Cf. POPE JOHN PAUL II, Address to Participants in the Fourteenth General Assembly of *Caritas Internationalis*, Vatican, 28/5/'91, § 3, *AAS* 84 (1992): 295.

[86] POPE JOHN PAUL II, Address to a Plenary Meeting of the Pontifical Council *Cor Unum*, 19/11/'90, § 3, *AAS* 83 (1991): 674/5.

[87] Cf. POPE JOHN PAUL II, Homily at Antananariva, Madagascar, 30/4/'89, § 4, *AAS* 81 (1989): 1234.

its source in the communion of God. While this spiritual cause of solidarity is undoubtedly understood as enriching it, and purifying its motivation, I do not think there is any suggestion that it substantially alters the nature of solidarity as praxis.

In this view, I believe I would have the support of Rémi Parent. Parent explains that, historically, the term *solidarity* has not been greatly favoured in Christian circles until relatively recently, partly because of the anti-Christian context in which it developed.[88] It was felt to be in some sense the antithesis of *communion*, or at least a concept which lacked the dignity or spiritual dimension of *communion* or *charity*. According to Parent, this tendency to value *communion* more highly than *solidarity*, arose out of a tension between orthodoxy and orthopraxis.

Solidarity has, in some historical contexts, been associated with a struggle in which the objective was defined in terms of the extermination of the adversary, or the oppression of the oppressor. Thus envisaged, it would certainly be contrary to communion. According to Parent, however, solidarity properly envisaged, is the praxis which holds in their appropriate tension the two theoretical elements of *communion* and *taking-sides-with* the poor, or those who need help of any kind.[89]

C. SOLIDARITY: PRINCIPLE, ATTITUDE, OR VIRTUE

Before we go on to consider the goals of solidarity or the means by which they are attained, it is necessary to pause long enough to acknowledge the central place of the personal subject in the phenomenon of solidarity, and to ask ourselves how solidarity might best be described as an aspect of the moral life of the person.

Solidarity is always personal in character. It may refer to the characteristic stance of an individual person, or of a group of persons, whether a small community, a nation, or even a community of nations. Structures and mechanisms are, in themselves, incapable of solidarity. Solidarity seeks to bring about a better correspondence between the needs of persons and the structures within which they are called to act.[90]

In his encyclical letter *Sollicitudo Rei Socialis*, Pope John Paul says that what makes the exercise of solidarity valid within a society is the

---

[88] Rémi PARENT, ibid., 113.

[89] Cf. Rémi PARENT, ibid., 122, & 127.

[90] POPE JOHN PAUL II, Address to Representatives of the Association of Catholic Workers, 6/12/'86, § 5, *IGP2* IX-2 (1986): 1858.

mutual recognition of each other as persons on the part of the members of society. The person, once recognised, is then seen as *neighbour*. "Solidarity helps us to see the other, whether a person, people or nation...as our neighbour, a helper, to be made a sharer, on a par with ourselves, in the banquet of life."[91] Pope John Paul frequently uses this image, taken from the gospel parable of the Good Samaritan, to express the character of the person in the relationship of solidarity. The implication of this statement, however, goes further than simply the recognition of the other as neighbour; it is, at the same time, an assertion concerning the nature of the subject of solidarity who is also a neighbour. This assertion is expressed more explicitly in an earlier encyclical letter *Salvifici Doloris*. "Who is my neighbour?...It was precisely the Samaritan who showed himself to be the real neighbour of the victim: neighbour means also the person who carried out the commandment of love of neighbour."[92]

In the course of a doctoral dissertation, presented recently to the theology faculty of the Angelicum University, Sr. Vianney Bilgrien focussed attention on the question of solidarity understood as a virtue.[93] In fact Pope John Paul describes solidarity variously as a *duty*, a *principle*, an *attitude*, and a *virtue*. I do not believe that there is any conflict in this use of different terms, but rather that each reflects an aspect of the reality of solidarity. We have already seen that solidarity is a duty, because it is implied by the fact of interdependence. The term *duty* refers to the objective moral goodness of solidarity, the dimension which obliges, even prior to the experience of obligation.

John Paul II frequently refers to solidarity as a principle, which means that it must always be a guiding influence in our lives and our decisions. A principle, however, while it concerns the actions of persons, is in some sense a formula or norm regarded independently of any reference to a particular person. A principle is something proposed, something in the light of which one might act, something which involves criteria, something

---

[91] POPE JOHN PAUL II, *SRS*, § 39.
[92] POPE JOHN PAUL II, *SD*, § 8.
[93] Marie Vianney BILGRIEN, *Solidarity: A Principle, An Attitude, A Duty, Or the Virtue for an Interdependent World*, STD Diss., Rome: Pontifical University of St. Thomas, 1994.

applied, something which has validity.[94] Perhaps it would be correct to say that when the pope calls solidarity a *principle* he focuses attention on its dimension as a general norm for action.

This leaves us with solidarity as *virtue* and solidarity as *attitude*. John Paul II refers to solidarity as *virtue* slightly more frequently than he refers to it as an *attitude*.

> The contrary of that selfish desire which would hinder true development is solidarity. This is the name for the moral virtue found in the human person whose actions are freely and habitually directed to the common good. It should not be confused with a vague feeling of distress at the misfortunes of others: It is rather a readiness to imbue the affairs of our communities and society with the most profound human and spiritual values.[95]

Bilgrien notes that Pope John Paul occasionally uses these two terms together, and wonders whether this implies that the pope understands them as synonyms of each other.[96] It is certainly true that solidarity, irrespective of whether it is presented as an attitude or a virtue, carries the same implications of commitment, of perseverance, and of action.

I believe, however, that the two terms are not used as synonyms for one another. In solidarity, the person, as well as completing an external action, fulfils himself in action. The person and his action form a single cohesive reality, to use the terminology of *The Acting Person*.[97] In other words the solidarity of a person, or indeed a group of persons, has an impact upon the person himself, as well as upon the society or community of which he is a member. When solidarity is described as virtue, it refers to the effect of solidarity on the person himself, his moral growth. Pope John Paul, again referring to the parable of the Samaritan, says:

---

[94] Cf. POPE John Paul II, Address to the Regional Council of Lazio, Italy, 7/2/'87, § 4, *IGP2* X-1 (1987): 287; also idem, Address to Leaders of Culture and Business, Lima, Peru, § 9, *IGP2* XI-2 (1988): 1456/7; also idem, Address to ATAC Transport Workers, Rome, 19/3/'88, § 7, *AAS* 80 (1988): 1337; also idem, Address to Business People, Naples, Italy, 11/11/'90, § 5, *IGP2* XIII-2 (1990): 1112; also idem, Address to Workers, Verona, Italy, 17/4/'88, § 4, *IGP2* XI-1 (1988): 938; and idem, *CA*, § 10.

[95] POPE JOHN PAUL II, Address to the Ambassador of Santa Lucia, 28/10/'91, *AAS* 84 (1992): 960/1.

[96] Cf. Marie Vianney BILGRIEN, ibid., 65; cf. also POPE JOHN PAUL II, *SRS*, § 38; and idem, Address to U.S. Bishops on *Ad Limina* Visit, 9/9/'88, § 3, *AAS* 81 (1989): 178.

[97] Cf. Karol WOJTYLA, *Acting Person*, 149.

> In his good fortune, the poor unfortunate man encountered the "good Samaritan." On the other hand, if the Samaritan had not had the compassion on that person, unknown to him, if he had not bound up his wounds and had not taken care of him, we would not think of him today as "good." It is true: solidarity makes us good.[98]

Solidarity makes us good. Bilgrien, citing Vidal, would appear to support this view. It would not be inaccurate, then, to say that solidarity described as virtue has a particular reference to the personalistic value of action. The first end of solidarity is the goodness of the person who acts.

An attitude, on the other hand, is always towards "the other." Consequently, when the solidarity of a person is described as an attitude, it has a significance which has to do primarily with its outward direction towards other persons, their needs, and the structures of society within which they are called to be and to act.

> Solidarity offers the exciting opportunity of communicating oneself to others in a peaceful and constructive attitude; it allows one to establish stable and coordinated relationships, which correspond to the real needs of persons and of communities; it helps, too, in overcoming those conditions of loneliness and isolation which frequently develop into incommunicability and alienation.[99]

Bilgrien has dealt very fully with the concept of solidarity as virtue, in its theological context. It is not necessary for me, nor would it be within the scope and competence of this work to cover the same ground again. I gratefully refer my readers to her treatment. In conclusion, I would wish simply to suggest that, while it is possible in theory to distinguish between solidarity as virtue and solidarity as attitude, I believe it would be correct to say that in any authentic solidarity the two dimensions will inevitably be found together.

D. OBJECTS AND GOALS OF SOLIDARITY

When it comes to identifying the ends towards which solidarity is directed, it will be helpful to distinguish between its objects, i.e., intermediate ends, and its goals, i.e., long-term ends. Some of the objects will

---

[98] POPE JOHN PAUL II, Address to Youth, Naples, Italy, 10/11/'90, § 5, *IGP2* XIII-2 (1990): 1078.

[99] POPE JOHN PAUL II, Address to the Association of Catholic Workers, Vatican, 6/12/'86, § 3, *IGP2* IX-2 (1986): 1856/7; cf. also idem, Address to the Regional Council of Lazio, 7/2/'87, § 4, *IGP2* X-1 (1987): 287/8.

also be included among the means by which solidarity attains its goals. This means that they will be discussed here under two headings, for the sake of structure and consistency.

1. Justice

One of the most immediate objectives of solidarity is the attainment of justice. According to Pope John Paul, it is only in worldwide solidarity that "enormous and dramatic issues" such as world justice can be dealt with and solved.[100] More specifically, justice is one of the fruits of solidarity identified by the pope in the course of an address to the civic authorities of Reggio Calabria, and the culture of solidarity is indispensable for the promotion of justice.[101]

The pope identifies a need to pursue justice through solidarity on a number of different levels. Addressing a conference on *Laborem Exercens* in 1987, he said that the need "to promote the recognition of inalienable rights and to guarantee conditions of work which conform with justice and equity has caused a great burst of solidarity to spring up among workers."[102] The world of work, however, is an integral part of the social order and, for this reason, a solidarity of the world of work

> will be a solidarity for work, which manifests itself in the struggle for justice and truth in social life...True solidarity seeks to struggle for a just social order in which all tensions can be absorbed and in which conflicts...can be more easily resolved...In order to create a world of justice and peace, solidarity must overturn the foundations of hatred, egoism, and injustice, which all too often are established as ideological principles or the essential law of life in society.[103]

Similarly, the social order is not something which can be totally compartmentalised by political or geographical boundaries, even if these do have the effect of limiting the effect of certain cultural or political

---

[100] POPE JOHN PAUL II, *FC*, § 48; cf. also idem, Address to the Ambassador of Algeria, 4/6/'87, § 4, *IGP2* X-2 (1987): 1958, & idem, Address to the Australian Ambassador, 28/3/'87, *IGP2* X-1 (1987): 853.

[101] Cf. POPE JOHN PAUL II, Address to the Civic Authorities, Reggio Calabria, Italy, 12/6/'88, § 4, *IGP2* XI-2 (1988): 1988/9.

[102] POPE JOHN PAUL II, Address to a Workers Conference on *Laborem Exercens*, Vatican, 17/1/'87, § 3, *AAS* 79 (1987): 1196/7.

[103] POPE JOHN PAUL II, Address to the I.L.O., Geneva, 15/6/'82, *AAS* 74 (1982): 1000/1; cf. also, idem, Address to Residents of the Barrios, Medellin, Colombia, 5/7/'86, § 8, *AAS* 79 (1987): 93/4.

characteristics. "The right path to a world community in which justice and peace will reign without frontiers among all peoples and on all continents, is the path of solidarity, dialogue, and universal brotherhood."[104]

There is one passage in which the pope lists a number of elementary values which support human fraternity and solidarity. One of these is justice.[105] This would, at first sight, suggest that solidarity is in some sense the result of justice rather than the other way around. Among the other elementary values mentioned in the list are peace, and respect for rights, and this would suggest to me that what the pope has in mind here is that justice, like some of these other values, nourishes the further development of solidarity. This would not contradict the fundamental thrust of what I have been saying, namely that justice is one of the immediate goals of solidarity. The virtue of justice supports solidarity in attaining the goals of justice and solidarity.

2. Respect for Persons and their Fundamental Rights

If solidarity is practised authentically, it will demand a deep respect for others.[106] Speaking in Bombay, Pope John Paul comments:

> Where there is true fraternal solidarity, the rights of the weak and the defenceless are not violated; rather the dignity and well-being of all are safe-guarded and promoted. And there can be peace only when there is justice and freedom and respect for the nature of man.[107]

Respect for the poor applies not simply to ensuring that they have the material resources necessary for their survival, but also that their dignity is respected and healed. This, the pope maintains, is a particular concern of the Church.[108] The pope goes as far as to say that "only genuine solidarity...can effectively safeguard the dignity and rights of individuals,

---

[104] POPE JOHN PAUL II, Message for World Peace Day 1986, 8/12/'85, § 4, *AAS* 78 (1986): 283.

[105] Cf. POPE JOHN PAUL II, Message for World Communications Day, 24/1/'88, § 3, *AAS* 80 (1988): 1360.

[106] Cf. POPE JOHN PAUL II, Address to Participants in a Study Week of the Pontifical Academy of Sciences, 27/10/'89, § 6, *IGP2* XII-2 (1989): 1050/1.

[107] POPE JOHN PAUL II, Homily at Bombay, 9/2/'86, § 8, *AAS* 78 (1986): 776; cf. also idem, Address to the Ambassador of Japan, Vatican, 29/4/'88, *AAS* 80 (1988): 1464.

[108] Cf. POPE JOHN PAUL II, Address to Representatives of Charitable Organisations, San Antonio, Texas, 13/9/'87, § 7, *IGP2* X-3 (1987): 472.

and therefore build peace within societies and between nations."[109]

Solidarity will "ensure respect for the cultural, ethnic, and religious groups which form the ensemble of the nation."[110] One social category with which Pope John Paul is particularly concerned, as we have already seen, is the workers. The rights of workers are to be recognised within a framework of solidarity. In the exercise of solidarity "workers' unions have a specific part to play. It is their task to defend the rights of their members through the legitimate means at their disposal, keeping in mind also the rights of other categories of workers."[111] Most fundamental of all, among the rights of workers is the right to seek employment, the right to have space in society to develop their talents and initiative.[112]

In this same spirit of solidarity, nations must respect the rights of their own citizens, as well as the rights of other nations, and this respect must be reciprocated.

> In order to be capable of global solidarity, nations must first of all respect the human rights of their citizens and in turn be recognised by their people as the expression of their sovereignty; secondly nations must respect the full rights of their fellow nations and know also that their rights as a nation will not be disavowed.[113]

The attitude of solidarity, nevertheless, places some limits on the recognition of rights and on the exercise of rights. It is "legitimate rights" which must be recognised, and it is "with due regard to the requirements of the common good that the free exercise of rights is to be guaranteed."[114]

---

[109] POPE JOHN PAUL II, Address to the Ambassador of Zimbabwe, Vatican, 17/1/'91, *IGP2* XIV-1 (1991): 124.

[110] POPE JOHN PAUL II, Address to the Ambassador of Costa Rica, 26/5/'83, Vatican, *AAS* 75 (1983): 835.

[111] POPE JOHN PAUL II, Address to Workers, Malta, 26/5/'90, § 6, *AAS* 83 (1991): 63; cf. also idem, Address to Seafarers, Fishermen and Port Workers, Gaeta, Italy, 25/6/'89, § 4, *IGP2* XII-1 (1989): 1760/1.

[112] Cf. POPE JOHN PAUL II, Address to Lancia Motor Workers, Ivrea, Italy, 19/3/'90, § 4, *IGP2* XIII-1 (1990): 702/3; and idem, Address to Sea-faring people, Gdynia, Poland, 11/6/'87, § 4, *Osservatore*, 1987, no. 30: 7.

[113] POPE JOHN PAUL II, Address to the People of Detroit, U.S.A., 19/9/'87, § 8, *IGP2* X-3 (1987): 672.

[114] Cf. POPE JOHN PAUL II, Address to the Ambassador of Nicaragua, Vatican, 3/1/'91, *AAS* 83 (1991): 755/6; cf. also idem, Address to the President and Members of the Council of the Region of Lazio, Vatican, 20/2/'89, § 5, *AAS* 81 (1989): 959; and idem, Address to the Ambassador of Costa Rica, Vatican, 22/6/'89, *AAS* 82 (1990): 71.

A genuine spirit of solidarity recognises and promotes various categories of rights, cultural and religious as well as material.

> The solidarity about which we speak is...a social concern that embraces all men, women and children in the totality of their personhood, which comprises their human rights, their condition in this world, and their eternal destiny. We cannot prescind from any of these elements.[115]

3. Participation and Collaboration

In the previous chapter we saw that, for Wojtyla, solidarity is the authentic attitude that ensures the orientation of participation to the common good. Participation was described as the adaptation of the person to relations with others. It is the subjective moment of the person's membership of the community of acting. We would expect, therefore, that participation would be one of the objectives of solidarity identified by Pope John Paul II. In effect, an examination of his writings and addresses over the period 1978/94 reveals surprisingly little use or development of the concept of participation in the context of solidarity. Where John Paul does use the term it would appear that participation is a goal of solidarity, but that it also serves as a contributory factor in the development of wider solidarities.

> The solidarity which is woven deep in the interior of a restricted group can favour a more direct participation of the interested parties, (and) can be useful and beneficial, in the measure to which this group remains attentive to the problems of others, concerned for progressively wider solidarities and having in view the realistic conditions for the reinforcement of justice, of liberty, and of peace in the world.[116]

Justice is concerned with giving to each person what is his due. This can not be limited simply to ensuring that everyone can participate equitably in the goods of the world.[117] It also means that every person, group,

---

[115] POPE JOHN PAUL II, Address to U.S. Bishops on *Ad Limina* Visit, 9/9/'88, § 5, *AAS* 81 (1989): 179; cf. also idem, Address to the Ambassador of Tanzania, 12/1/'90, *AAS* 82 (1990): 799/800.

[116] POPE JOHN PAUL II, Address to Parliamentarians of the Western European Union, 30/10/'84, § 2, *AAS* 77 (1985): 363; cf. also idem, Address to Brazilian Bishops on *Ad Limina* Visit, 23/6/'90, § 5, *Osservatore*, 1990, no. 28: 9/10.

[117] Cf. POPE JOHN PAUL II, Address to Representatives of the Association of Catholic Workers, 6/12/'86, § 5, *IGP2* IX-2 (1986): 1858.

or nation must be enabled to find fulfilment through a fully personal participation in the common effort. Participation is not just about having, but also about being and acting. True solidarity involves not only facilitating this participation, but educating people to it.

> It is surely not beyond possibility that in many countries – including the Philip-pines – there might be established a new forum of solidarity, a social pact as it were, between those responsible for public life, those who control the economy, those engaged in education and scientific and technological development, and other forces within society; a pact in which all would agree to work for improved conditions, but in a way that would benefit ever greater numbers of their fellow citizens by educating them for increased participation in economic and civic life.[118]

One concrete situation in which the pope sees the challenge of facilitating the participation of all through solidarity, is the sphere of human work, which ideally is understood as "a singular moment of participation and of generous sharing: in a word, of constructive solidarity."[119] Addressing members of the co-operative movement on the theme of solidarity, Pope John Paul links solidarity and participation, two themes which he says are dear to his heart. He encourages his listeners not to lose sight of the personalistic value of the co-operative movement, which is concretised in the way in which co-operatives facilitate the participation of all.

> In this manner, co-operation becomes attention to problems; service of the most excluded categories, of those who have no work, and therefore no means of sustenance; it is a means of integrating young people into the work force, who are often discouraged by lack of opportunity for involvement; not forgetting of course the marginalisation which we see in the experience of so many of our brothers who find themselves in a position of hardship and exploitation.[120]

One other sphere in which the pope sees a need for participation to be

---

[118] POPE JOHN PAUL II, Address to the Ambassador of the Philippines, 18/5/'91, § 4, *AAS* 84 (1992): 153/4; cf. also idem, *SRS*, § 15, and idem, Address to the Farming Community, Aversa, Italy, 13/11/'90, § 4, *AAS* 83 (1991): 659.

[119] POPE JOHN PAUL II, Address to Representatives of the Association of Catholic Workers, 6/12/'86, § 2, *IGP2* IX-2 (1986): 1856.

[120] POPE JOHN PAUL II, Address to Members of the Confederation of Italian Cooperatives and the Federation of Rural and Trade Credit Unions, 11/11/'89, § 2, *IGP2* XII-2 (1989): 1215.

facilitated by solidarity is that of the reception of large numbers of migrants. It is not enough, the pope says, to allow entry permits to migrants. "It is necessary... to facilitate their real integration in the society which receives them. Solidarity must be the everyday experience of assistance, sharing, and participation."[121] Finally, the pope also argues that the task of government will be easier and more effective when solidarity facilitates the greater participation of all in public affairs.[122]

On various occasions the pope refers to the particular role and competence of the Church in expressing solidarity, and does so in a way which, at one and the same time, claims the right to participate, and recognises the limits of appropriate participation. This would appear to reflect, and apply to the Church as a social group, the understanding of solidarity which we have already seen in *The Acting Person*, as the attitude which moderates participation so that each person or group carries out but does not exceed his/its normal responsibilities.[123] Accordingly, Pope John Paul says: "The Church is called to understand and face a multiplicity of needs that differ among themselves, demonstrating her solidarity and offering her help according to her means and her specific nature."[124]

Participation is more than the simple fact of working alongside others at the same tasks. As I have already said, it refers to the adaptation of the person to relationship with others, both in being and in acting. While Pope John Paul does not develop the concept of participation as fully as one might expect in his writings and addresses, he does refer frequently to *collaboration* as an objective of solidarity, and he describes it in terms which suggest that he understands it as synonymous with participation.[125] The pope comments in one address that "both solidarity and collaboration are means of defending human rights and serving the truth and freedom of

---

[121] POPE JOHN PAUL II, Address to Participants in a World Congress of those engaged in the Pastoral care of Migrants and Travellers, 5/10/'91, § 3, *AAS* 84 (1992): 862.

[122] Cf. POPE JOHN PAUL II, Address to Government Officials and Diplomatic Corps, Asuncion, Paraguay, 16/5/'88, § 4, *HSSP*, 233.

[123] Cf. Karol WOJTYLA, *Acting Person*, 285.

[124] POPE JOHN PAUL II, Address to U.S. Bishops on *Ad Limina* Visit, 9/9/'88, § 5, *AAS* 81 (1989): 179; cf. also idem, *SRS*, § 41.

[125] Cf. POPE JOHN PAUL II, Address to Parliamentarians of the Western European Union, 30/10/'84, § 2, *AAS* 77 (1985): 363; also idem, Address to Government Officials and Diplomatic Corps, Asuncion, Paraguay, 16/5/'88, § 4, *HSSP*, 233.

humanity,"[126] and, elsewhere, replacing *collaboration* with *participation*, he speaks of the role of solidarity in "defending the exercise of democratic freedoms and rights, through adequate structures of participation."[127] The essential relationship between collaboration and solidarity is expressed in very concise terms in the statement: "collaboration is the act proper to solidarity."[128] Elsewhere the pope comments that collaboration is prepared by the principle of solidarity, and that it is one of the first fruits of solidarity.[129] As in the case of participation, the kind of collaboration to which solidarity gives rise is identified as being particularly important in the spheres of work and of international relations.[130]

According to Pope John Paul, "the horizons of an effective solidarity...are vast" because the fruitful work which people do in common, in a spirit of solidarity, is implied by a "conscious and docile collaboration with God."[131]

4. Development

Another important objective of solidarity is the attainment of integral human development. Denis Goulet points out that the architect of the concept of development which was proposed by Paul VI, and commemorated by John Paul II in *Sollicitudo Rei Socialis*, is the French philosopher L.J. Lebret. He outlines Lebret's concept of development, as follows:

> The key moral element in Lebret's concept of development is solidarity, that perceptual and behavioural disposition that binds together the destinies of all human persons, societies, and nations. Solidarity places on the "haves" a moral

---

[126] POPE JOHN PAUL II, Address to U.S. Bishops on *Ad Limina* Visit, 9/9/'88, § 5, *AAS* 81 (1989): 179.

[127] POPE JOHN PAUL II, Address to the Ambassador of Costa Rica, 26/5/'83, *AAS* 75 (1983): 835.

[128] POPE JOHN PAUL II, Address to U.S. Bishops on *Ad Limina* Visit, 9/9/'88, § 5, *AAS* 81 (1989): 179; cf. also idem, *SRS*, § 39.

[129] Cf. POPE JOHN PAUL II, Address to ATAC Transport Workers, 19/3/'88, § 7, *AAS* 80 (1988): 1337; also idem, Address to Participants in the Plenary Meeting of the Pontifical Council of Health-care Administrators, 9/2/'90, *AAS* 82 (1990): 894.

[130] Cf. POPE JOHN PAUL II, Angelus Address, 27/9/'81, *IGP2* IV-2 (1981): 307/8; also idem, Address to Youth, Bomako, Mali, 28/1/'90, § 5, *IGP2* XIII-1 (1990): 282; and idem, Address to the President of Portugal, 27/4/'90, § 6, *AAS* 82 (1990): 1525/6.

[131] POPE JOHN PAUL II, Homily at Villaricca, Paraguay, 17/5/'88, § 6, *IGP2* XI-2 (1988): 1511.

claim, a veritable duty in justice, to assure that the "have nots" of the world come to *have* that minimum supply of essential goods without which they cannot *be* fully human.[132]

According to John Paul II, "the manner and means for the realisation of a politic oriented towards true human development is solidarity."[133] Solidarity must be operative at various different levels because the need for development is experienced on many levels. Speaking to the Regional Council of Lazio, the pope proposes the principle of solidarity as a means of achieving clarity and inspiration for the development of the region.[134] In the course of an address to workers in Australia, Pope John Paul congratulates them for their efforts to promote development in poorer countries, and invites them to offer solidarity to all who are in need, not forgetting the development needs of the less well-off among their fellow Australians.[135]

Particular issues of development, such as the land-question, demand solidarity, as does the attainment of the correct balance between different sectors of the community and of the work-force. The solution of the problems of some should not become the cause of additional problems for others.[136]

Like so many of the themes which we have examined already, development has an important international dimension. Pope John Paul frequently refers to the need for a solidarity which is proportioned to the needs and objectives of global development. In the encyclical *Sollicitudo Rei Socialis*, the pope points out that "nations which historically, economically and politically have the capacity of playing a leadership role" are not "adequately fulfilling their duty of solidarity for the benefit of peoples

---

[132] Denis GOULET, "The Search for Authentic Development," in *The Logic of Solidarity*, ibid., 135; cf. also ibid., 133/6.

[133] POPE JOHN PAUL II, Address to the Civic Authorities, Rome, 20/1/'90, § 2, *AAS* 82 (1990): 885; cf. also idem, Address to the Civic Authorities, Reggio Calabria, Italy, 12/6/'88, § 4, *IGP2* XI-2 (1988): 1988/9; and idem, Address to Business People, Naples, Italy, 11/11/'90, § 5, *IGP2* XIII-2 (1990): 1122.

[134] POPE JOHN PAUL II, Address to the Regional Council of Lazio, Italy, 7/2/'87, § 4, *IGP2* X-1 (1987): 287.

[135] Cf. POPE JOHN PAUL II, Address to Workers, Sydney, Australia, 26/11/'86, § 9, *AAS* 79 (1987): 953.

[136] Cf. POPE JOHN PAUL II, Homily at Villaricca, Paraguay, 17/5/'88, § 5, *IGP2* XI-2 (1988): 1509.

which aspire to full development."[137] Finally, the necessity for authentic global development does not stop short of requiring the engagement of the poorer nations in solidarity among themselves and with the neediest countries of the world.[138]

We tend, perhaps, to associate development with hard-nosed economics. There is certainly a practical economic dimension to the kind of development which solidarity inspires. The pope spells this out in the course of an address in Mozambique.

> Allow me to stress the urgency of this solidarity, envisaged as a speedy and total end to hostilities and the immediate delivery of aid to save a great number of human lives; envisaged as the presentation of short-term aid programmes, for the indispensable reconstruction of the infrastructures of survival and, following that, for the integral development of this beloved country of Mozambique.[139]

The pope does not, therefore, deny the importance of the economic aspect of development. He does, however, insist that the principle of solidarity is at odds with "a narrow and purely material concept of development."[140]

An important personalistic element in the contribution of solidarity is that it requires a model of development which takes account of the needs, and involves the active participation, of the peoples or nations for whom it is intended.[141] It is solidarity that gives development its personal dimension, a dimension which is best expressed by the pope's description of development, in a number of addresses, as a gift between brothers.

> If solidarity gives us the ethical base for appropriate action, then development becomes the offering which brother makes to brother, so that both of them can live more fully in all the diversity and complementarity which are as it were the

---

[137] POPE JOHN PAUL II, *SRS*, § 23; cf. also idem, Homily at Maputo, Mozambique, 18/9/'88, § 12, *AAS* 81 (1989): 358.

[138] Cf. POPE JOHN PAUL II, *SRS*, § 45.

[139] POPE JOHN PAUL II, Address to the Bishops of Mozambique, Maputo, Mozambique, 18/9/'88, § 12, *AAS* 81 (1989): 367.

[140] POPE JOHN PAUL II, Address to Representatives of Business and Cultural Life, Lima, Peru, 15/5/'88, § 9, *IGP2* XI-2 (1988): 1456/7.

[141] Cf. POPE JOHN PAUL II, Address to the Diplomatic Corps, Vatican, 10/1/'87, § 10, *AAS* 79 (1987): 1185.

marks guaranteeing human civilisation.[142]

In conclusion, therefore, authentic human development in all its aspects is clearly an important objective of solidarity.

5. The Common Good

If there is any one statement about solidarity which stands out as a result of its frequent repetition in the addresses of John Paul II, it must be the one which is first found in paragraph thirty-eight of *Sollicitudo Rei Socialis*. It is worth quoting in full because, as well as firmly linking solidarity to the ultimate goal of attaining the common good, it also relates this goal to some of the other themes to which we have been referring. When interdependence becomes recognised as a moral category, Pope John Paul tells us:

> The correct response as a moral and social attitude, as a virtue, is solidarity. This then is not a feeling of vague compassion or shallow distress at the misfortunes of so many people, both near and far. On the contrary, it is a firm and persevering determination to commit oneself to the common good; that is to say to the good of all and of each individual, because we are all really responsible for all.[143]

I limit myself to the four references given in the note below. There are, however, at least twelve addresses in which this same formula, defining solidarity as a commitment in favour of the common good, is repeated. This alone would be sufficient evidence that, for Pope John Paul, the ultimate goal of solidarity is the attainment of the common good.

As the above passage indicates, the common good is the responsibility of all. It is attained in a way that is truly worthy of humanity, by means of "a proper balance between the co-responsibility of the members of society and the commitment of the state."[144] This is the essence of solidarity, that each person or group fulfils his/its appropriate responsibility. While each

---

[142] POPE JOHN PAUL II, Address for World Peace Day 1987, 8/12/'86, § 7, *AAS* 79 (1987): 52; cf. also idem, Address to the Diplomatic Corps, Vatican, 10/1/'87, § 11, *HSSP*, 129; and idem, Address to the Ambassador of Costa Rica, 22/6/'89, *AAS* 82 (1990): 71.

[143] POPE JOHN PAUL II, *SRS*, § 35; cf. also idem, Address to ATAC Transport Workers, 19/3/'88, § 6, *AAS* 80 (1988): 1337; idem, Address to Intelectuals and Business People, Santa Cruz, Bolivia, 12/5/'88, § 3, *IGP2* XI-2 (1988): 1341; idem, Address to Youth, St. Paul's Stadium, Naples, Italy, 10/11/'90, § 5, *IGP2* XIII-2 (1990): 1078.

[144] POPE JOHN PAUL II, Address to Participants in a Convention on the Encyclical Letter *Rerum Novarum*, Vatican, 15/5/'91, § 6, *AAS* 84 (1992): 149.

person is responsible for all, a particular responsibility for overseeing the common good falls upon governmental and juridical structures.[145]

Taking up the theme of Pope John XXIII, John Paul II recognises the need for a "greater international ordering which will watch over the common good of all peoples."[146] This practical solidarity in favour of the universal common good still remains to be fulfilled. At a time when the ending of the cold war has brought hope to many, the international community still seems powerless in the face of regional wars. The present international structures, for all that they have achieved, seem inadequate to the tasks of global development and peace. As the pope commented in *Sollicitudo Rei Socialis*, some of the international structures and organisations "which exist solely for the common good" are in need of urgent reform, either because of their ineffectiveness or because they have actually become a burden on poor nations rather than a help.[147]

The common good is not to be seen as in any way opposed to the true good of the individual person or the component group. Genuine respect for each of the members is the only sound basis for the survival and growth of communities, whether local, national, or international. Solidarity "is a firm and persevering determination to commit oneself to the common good; that is to say to the good of all and of each individual, because we are all really responsible for all."[148]

There are relatively few references to the *civilisation of love* in the addresses and writings of Pope John Paul. In one case, however, the pope indicates that this expression, first used by Pope Paul VI, refers to the same reality as solidarity.[149] This has already been referred to in chapter three. I indicated then that a study of Pope Paul's use of the term would suggest that it would be more properly understood as a result, or goal of solidarity. This view is supported in an earlier address of John Paul II himself, when

---

[145] Cf. POPE JOHN PAUL II, Address to Members of the Union of Catholic Jurists of Italy, 10/12/'88, § 4, *AAS* 81 (1989): 764.

[146] POPE JOHN PAUL II, Address to the Ambassador of Bangladesh, 10/11/'88, *AAS* 81 (1989): 638.

[147] Cf. POPE JOHN PAUL II, *SRS* 43.

[148] POPE JOHN PAUL II, *SRS*, § 38; cf. also idem, Address at the University of Santiago, Chile, 3/4/'87, § 4, *IGP2* X-1 (1987): 1001; and idem, Address to the Ambassador of Zimbabwe, Vatican, 17/1/'91, *IGP2* XIV-1 (1991): 124.

[149] Cf. POPE JOHN PAUL II, *CA* § 10.

he says that the civilisation of love demands the virtue of solidarity.[150] John Paul II also refers on at least two occasions to the *civilisation of work* which proves to be a product of solidarity and collaboration.[151] I would suggest, in the absence of any evidence to the contrary, that the *civilisation of love* and the *civilisation of work* are expressions which correspond to the *common good*.

According to Pope John Paul, "the objective norm of solidarity is...the good of every man and of all men."[152] This calls to mind the fact that the common good is the very *raison d'etre* of every human community or society. The common good, however, is not something concrete or fixed. It is whatever good corresponds to the needs of a particular community and its members and, of course, this varies according to the nature and scope of the community. Furthermore, families as well as other small groups and local communities, which each have their own common good or common interest, are generally members of larger groups, nations, or international communities, which themselves have a broader vision of the common good. It would be impossible within the scope of a work such as this to even name every possible form of the common good. What I intend to do is to examine some of the key expressions of the common good identified by Pope John Paul, and which are clearly among the goals of solidarity.

a. Peace. An element which seems to form part of every expression of the common good is peace. John Paul II indicates that solidarity, through the act of collaboration, is the path to peace. He adapts the motto of Pope Pius XII *opus iustitiae pax*, and argues "one could say, with the same exactness...*opus solidarietatis pax*, peace as the fruit of solidarity."[153]

---

[150] Cf. POPE JOHN PAUL II, Address to Intellectuals and Business People, Santa Cruz, Bolivia, 12/5/'88, § 3, *IGP2*, XI-2 (1988), 1341.

[151] Cf. POPE JOHN PAUL II, Address at Barrios la Concordia, Melo, Uruguay, 8/5/'88, § 9, *IGP2* XI-2 (1988): 1206; cf. also Address to Seafarers, Fishermen, and Port Workers, Gaeta, Italy, 25/6/'89, § 4, *IGP2* XII-1 (1989): 1760/1.

[152] POPE JOHN PAUL II, Address to Workers, Verona, Italy, 17/4/'88, § 4, *IGP2* XI-1 (1988): 938.

[153] POPE JOHN PAUL II, *SRS*, § 39; cf. also idem, Address to the Ambassador of Japan, Vatican, 29/4/'88, *AAS* 80 (1988): 1464; and idem, Address to the Ambassador of Tanzania, 12/1/'90, *AAS* 82 (1990): 799. I have mentioned in an earlier note (cf. Note 7, page 79) the problem of the reluctance of translators to use the Latin substantive *solidarietas* when translating *solidarity* or its equivalents in other European languages. The passage referred to here provides one interesting example of what can happen as a result of this fidelity to classical Latin. In the English version, the pope offers the motto *Opus*

According to Pope John Paul, "solidarity is a factor for peace because it is crucial for development."[154] In an earlier address, he gives a fuller explanation – once again in the context of development – of the reasons why solidarity is so necessary for peace.

> Solidarity is ethical by its nature, because it implies the affirmation of value concerning humanity. For this reason, its implications for human life on our planet and for international relations are also ethical, our common bonds of humanity demand that we live together in harmony and promote that which is good for each other. These implications constitute the reason why solidarity is a fundamental key to peace....In the context of a true solidarity, there is no danger of the exploitation or the evil use of development programmes to benefit the few. Development, moreover, becomes in this way a process which involves the different members of the same human family and enriches them all.[155]

Solidarity has peace as its goal both within nations and on an international level. Solidarity is the basis on which peace can be established in The Lebanon, in Lesotho, and in Nicaragua. "By means of authentic development, a lasting peace can be assured. For this reason, however, it is necessary to create an awareness of solidarity which leads to an integral development, and which protects and oversees the legitimate rights of

---

Solidarietatis Pax, in Latin. Yet, in the official Latin version of the encyclical, and in other places where this motto is cited; it is rendered as *Opus hominum coniunctionis Pax*, cf. *AAS* 80 (1988): 568; also Address to the Bishops of Guatemala, 20/1/'89, *AAS* 81 (1989): 874 This would appear to be rather pedantic. More significantly, the preference for translating *solidarity* into classical Latin, would presuppose that the translators understand the English *solidarity* (or *solidarité*, or *solidarietà*) in the same way that John Paul II does. In fact the contrary seems to be the case at times, especially when they translate solidarity as *necessitudo*, without qualification. This happens on at least nine occasions, cf. *AAS* 73 (1981): 596 & 597; *AAS* 76 (1984): 208 &244; *AAS* 80 (1988): 559; *AAS* 83 (1991): 226, 301, 307, & 309. The term *necessitudo* more closely resembles *interependence* than *solidarity*. For whatever reason an exception to the common practice occurs in the case of *GS*, in which the Latin *solidarietas* is used a number of times; cf. §§ 4.3, 32.4, 57.5, & 90. The same can be found in a definitive passage in *CA*, § 10, where the Pope refers to the "principle of solidarity," which is rendered in the Latin as *principium solidarietatis*, cf. *AAS* 83, 1991, 805.

[154] POPE JOHN PAUL II, Address to U.S. Bishops on *Ad Limina* Visit, 9/9/'88, § 4, *AAS* 81 (1989): 178.

[155] POPE JOHN PAUL II, Address for World Peace Day 1987, 8/12/'86, § 7, *AAS* 79 (1987): 51.

persons."[156] The factors which undermine the peace of a nation are not limited to the realm of pure politics, but generally have socio-economic roots. For this reason, all the people of the nation are called to solidarity, so that there can be peace between the country and the city, and between different sectors of the work force.[157]

In most cases, however, when he refers to peace as the goal of solidarity, the pope is speaking of peace on the international level. This peace, in the first place, involves the settlement of disputes and the ending of hostilities.[158] Constructive neutrality can also be an expression of solidarity, and nations which maintain a position of non-alignment are often in a position to make a valuable contribution to the cause of peace.[159] In the final analysis, however, the peace that comes from solidarity involves far more than simply the absence of war.

> The climate of true peace among nations does not consist in the simple absence of armed conflict, but in a conscientious and effective will to seek the good of all peoples, in such a way that each state, while defining its foreign policy, thinks above all of a specific contribution to the international common good.[160]

b. Food, Shelter, and Health-care. Elements of the common good which are taken for granted in some communities and societies take on a higher profile elsewhere, or even in other sectors of the same society, precisely because they are lacking. Among the most fundamental of these are food, accommodation, and health-care. It is the goal of solidarity to ensure that these essentials are available to all. This link is explicitly stated

---

[156] POPE JOHN PAUL II, Address to the Ambassador of Nicaragua, Vatican, 3/1/'91, *AAS* 83 (1991): 755/6; cf. also, idem, Letter to the Islamic World, concerning the Lebanese People, 7/9/'89, § 5, *AAS* 82 (1990): 82/3; and idem, Address to the Bishops of Lesotho on *Ad Limina* Visit, 15/9/'89, § 4, *AAS* 82 (1990): 728.

[157] Cf. POPE JOHN PAUL II, Homily at Bahia Blanca, Argentina, 7/4/'87, § 7, *IGP2* X-1 (1987): 1131/2; also idem, Address to Farmers, Cuzco, Peru, 3/2/'85, § 3, *AAS* 77 (1985): 876; and idem, Address to the Ambassador of Indonesia, Vatican, 7/11/'91, *AAS* 84 (1992): 965.

[158] Cf. POPE JOHN PAUL II, Homily at Maputo, Mozambique, 18/9/'88, § 12, *AAS* 81 (1989): 358; cf. also idem, Address to the Institutions of the European Community, Luxembourg, 15/5/'85, § 1, *AAS* 78 (1986): 531.

[159] Cf. POPE JOHN PAUL II, Address to the Diplomatic Corps, Vatican, 11/1/'86, § 7, *HSSP*, 113.

[160] POPE JOHN PAUL II, Address at Buenos Aires, Argentina, 6/4/'87, § 3, *HSSP*, 226; cf. also idem, Address to the Diplomatic Corps, Brazilia, Brazil, 30/6/'80, § 1, *HSSP*, 164.

by the pope in Chile, but his challenge to the academic community there has a universal validity. "I invite you all, therefore, men of culture and builders of society, to enlarge and consolidate a current of solidarity which will contribute to assuring the common good: bread, shelter, health, dignity, respect for all the inhabitants of Chile."[161] Addressing delegates at a conference of the U.N. Food and Agricultural Organisation, the pope says:

> Concern must also be voiced about the deterioration of food security in the present world situation. Indeed parallel to the notable increase in world population there has been a recent decline on the world level in the availability of foodstuffs. The result has been a reduction of those reserves which constitute a necessary guarantee against crises of hunger and malnutrition. Similarly in the countries where production is high, this has been artificially reduced by a sector-oriented policy which reflects a closed market calculation. Whatever its domestic value, such a policy is certainly not in harmony with a solidarity open to world needs and acting in favour of those who are most needy.[162]

The pope argues that solidarity will lead to the taking of specific action, particularly in the political and scientific spheres, to ensure both an improvement in food production, and the ready availability of emergency food supplies.[163]

The absence of adequate housing, apart from leaving people at the mercy of the elements, and frequently of disease, also deprives the family of an essential support and focus for its community of life. The pope sees the housing crisis as a concrete example of the failure of solidarity on the part of those who could help and have not done so. It is another practical sphere in which the exercise of solidarity finds its goal. This problem does not affect only the nations of the third world but is "among the specific signs of under-development which increasingly affect the developed

---

[161] POPE JOHN PAUL II, Address at the University of Santiago, Chile, 3/4/'87, § 4, *IGP2* X-1 (1987): 1001.

[162] POPE JOHN PAUL II, Address to Participants in the 25th. Plenary Meeting of FAO, Rome, 16/11/'89, § 6, *AAS* 82 (1990): 672; cf. also idem, Address to the Diplomatic Corps, Vatican, 15/1/'83, § 7, *AAS* 75 (1983): 379; and idem, Address to Workers, Verona, Italy, 17/4/'88, § 6, *IGP2* XI-1 (1988): 940/1.

[163] Cf. POPE JOHN PAUL II, Letter to the Director General of FAO on the Occasion of World Food Day, 10/10/'90, *AAS* 83 (1991): 363; and idem, Address to Participants in a Convention on Population and Food, organised by the Pontifical Academy of Sciences, 22/11/'91, *AAS* 84 (1992): 1119-22.

countries also."[164]

The provision of health-care is but one essential response to the challenge of human suffering, a phenomenon which knows no frontiers of race, class, colour, or creed. As Pope John Paul remarks in *Salvifici Doloris*: "Although the world of suffering exists in dispersion, at the same time it contains within itself a singular challenge to communion and solidarity."[165]

c. Education. It is frequently stated that education is the best means of escape from the cycle of poverty. While the level of education aspired to, both as an individual and a common good, varies from one society to another, the importance of education is universally recognised. Pope John Paul identifies illiteracy and the difficulty or impossibility of obtaining higher education as two among the indices of cultural under-development.[166] Solidarity is the appropriate response to the needy, among whom the pope includes "a child without education."[167] Education is a good to be desired not only because it enables people to find work and to provide for their needs, but also because it contributes to the authentic being of the person.

> To educate is to accompany the person in his growth, in his self-knowledge, in freedom and autonomy, and in responsibility. At the same time, it helps him to be a protagonist in his own growth and to cooperate in the growth of the whole society.[168]

While the responsibility for education ultimately lies with the family,

---

[164] POPE JOHN PAUL II, *SRS*, § 17; cf. also idem, Address to Colombian Bishops on *Ad Limina* Visit, 30/11/'89, § 5, *AAS* 82 (1990): 693; and idem, Address to International Agencies, Nairobi, Kenya, 18/8/'85, § 7, *AAS* 78 (1986): 94.

[165] POPE JOHN PAUL II, *SD*, § 8; cf. also idem, Address to the Diplomatic Corps, N'Djamena, Chad, 1/2/'90, §§ 1 & 3, *AAS* 82 (1990): 822-4; idem, Address to Participants in the Plenary meeting of the Pontifical Council for Pastoral Assistance to Health-Care Workers, 9/2/'90, § 2, *AAS* 82 (1990): 894; and idem, Address during a visit to the Hope Project, Kracow, Poland, 13/8/'91, § 2, *IGP2* XIV-2 (1991): 213/4.

[166] Cf. POPE JOHN PAUL II, *SRS*, § 15.

[167] POPE JOHN PAUL II, Address to the People of the Guasmo Region, Ecuador, 1/2/'85, § 5, *AAS* 77 (1985): 868.

[168] POPE JOHN PAUL II, Address to Civil Leaders and Representatives of Economic and Cultural Life, Asuncion, Paraguay, 17/5/'88, § 6, *AAS* 80 (1988): 1616; also idem, Homily at Bahia Blanca, Argentina, § 7, 7/4/'87, *IGP2* X-1 (1987): 1132.

which is "a community of solidarity," families frequently find themselves deprived of the resources necessary to educate their children, and this is an appropriate sphere of action for a wider solidarity.[169]

d. Work. Finally, as I have already remarked, the phenomenon of work pervades the whole of human experience. We have already seen how work has a particular suitability for promoting solidarity, how it is a privileged context of participation and collaboration, and how it constitutes a particular challenge to the recognition of and respect for rights. Work, or employment, for all these reasons, may also be considered as an aspect of the common good, and a goal of solidarity. Work is a good to be desired because it is a means of subsistence and of participation. Through solidarity among workers, this means of subsistence and participation, in a form worthy of the dignity of workers, can be made more widely available, especially to the less well-off.[170] Exequiel Rivas says: "To offer work to all is probably the most genuine expression of solidarity. In this task nobody can escape his responsibility, while those most responsible are business people and the state through its responsible organisms."[171]

In the course of an address to business-people in Lima, Pope John Paul reminds his listeners that, apart from being a productive activity, a business has to be understood as "a means for the practice of work which realises the human person."[172] It is solidarity which ensures that this aspect of business is not lost to view.

E. THE MEANS BY WHICH SOLIDARITY ACHIEVES ITS OBJECTIVES AND GOALS

At this stage we turn our attention to the means by which solidarity attains its ends. As mentioned above, some of the objectives of solidarity

---

[169] POPE JOHN PAUL II, Homily at Terceira, The Azores, 11/5/'91, § 6, *IGP2* XIV-1 (1991): 1196/7.

[170] Cf. POPE JOHN PAUL II, Address to Workers Delegates, Geneva, 15/6/'82, *IGP2* V-2 (1982): 2283/4; and idem, Christmas Day Greetings, St. Peter's Square, 25/12/'84, *AAS* 77 (1985): 379.

[171] Exequiel RIVAS, "La Solidaridad en la Enseñanza de Juan Pablo II," in *L'Antropologia Solidaristica nella* Centesimus Annus, Papers of an International Conference organised by ASCE and the Diocese of Rieti, 22-27 Oct. 1991, ed. Alfredo Luciani, (Milan: Massimo Editrice, 1992), 226.

[172] POPE JOHN PAUL II, Address to Representatives of Business and Cultural Life, Lima, Peru, 15/5/'88, § 8, *IGP2* XI-2 (1988): 1455/6.

are also its means.

1. Associations and Organisations

The social teaching of the Catholic Church has always emphasised the important contribution of associations and organisations for the development of community and the attainment of the common good. This has already been referred to in chapter three. Pope John Paul, likewise, recognises the possibilities of various types of organisations and co-operative structures, inspired by solidarity. In the area of the local or national economy, co-operatives, business organisations, and trade unions can serve "as a means of protection against commercialisation and the fragmentation of production," and "to defend the just interests of workers."[173] Similarly, the pope sees a role for ethnic organisations, as an expression of the solidarity of a people. He recognises the contribution of the *Romany Union* in seeking recognition for Gypsy people and for their cultural identity, and in claiming a response of solidarity from other citizens in the countries among which they are dispersed.[174]

Charitable organisations of one kind or another serve solidarity in attaining its goals, either in conjunction with statutory bodies or by responding to needs which these bodies have been unwilling or unable to meet.[175] On the international front, as we have already seen, Pope John Paul sees a vital role for organisations which will ensure respect for rights, and contribute to the maintenance of peace. The pope describes such organisations, along with agreements and alliances, as "new forms of solidarity."[176] International organisations which specialise in the spheres of economics and finance can also be mobilised by solidarity as a means for

---

[173] POPE JOHN PAUL II, Address to Workers, Città Castellana, Italy, 1/5/'88, § 5, *AAS* 80 (1988): 1531; cf. also idem, Address to Workers, Malta, 26/5/'90, § 5, *AAS* 83 (1991): 61; and idem, Address to Representatives of the Association of Catholic Workers, 6/12/'86, § 5, *IGP2* IX-2 (1986): 1858.

[174] Cf. POPE JOHN PAUL II, Address to Participants in a Convention on Gypsy Studies, 26/9/'91, § 3, *IGP2* XIV-2 (1991): 658/9.

[175] Cf. POPE JOHN PAUL II, Address to W. German Bishops on *Ad Limina* Visit, 14/11/'89, § 3, *Osservatore*, 1989, no. 49: 6; also idem, Address to the Civic Authorities, Ouagadougou, Burkina Fasu, 29/1/'90, § 5, *AAS* 82 (1990): 819; and idem, Address to Participants in the Plenary Meeting of the Pontifical Council *Cor Unum*, 19/11/'90, § 4, *AAS* 83 (1991): 675.

[176] POPE JOHN PAUL II, Address to the Diplomatic Corps, Vatican, § 3, 14/1/'84, *HSSP*, 86; cf. also idem, Message for World Peace Day 1986, 8/12/'85, § 4, *AAS* 78 (1986): 283; and Address to the Ambassador of the Sudan, 7/1/'88, *IGP2* XI-1 (1988): 50.

development and peace.[177]

2. Subsidiarity which Allows Participation

If associations and organisations of various sizes and scopes are among the means by which solidarity attains its goals, then the basis on which solidarity acts must include the principle of subsidiarity. The close correspondence between solidarity and subsidiarity is confirmed by Pope John Paul on a number of occasions. In a letter addressed to the people of Italy, during the preparations for a general election, Pope John Paul says:

> Love of one's country and solidarity with the whole of humanity do not contra-
> dict man's links with the region and the local community in which he was born,
> and the obligations which he has towards these. Rather, solidarity cuts across all
> the communities in which man lives: the family in the first place, the local and
> regional community, the nation, the continent, the whole of humanity; solidarity
> animates them, bringing about agreement between them according to the
> principle of subsidiarity which attributes to each one of them its due degree of
> autonomy.[178]

3. Diplomacy

Not unrelated to the role of international organisations, is the contribution of international diplomacy as a means of deepening, expressing, and
bringing to fruition the solidarity that exists between the nations of the
world. In the course of an address to diplomats at Harare, the pope
comments: "Each one of you is at the service of your own country's
interests. But the very nature of your profession and your personal experience of other countries and cultures makes you aware of the wider pic-
ture."[179] Elsewhere he reflects on the nature of diplomacy and its suitability
for supporting solidarity in the effort for peace and international

---

[177] Cf. POPE JOHN PAUL II, Address to Participants in the 25th. Plenary meeting of FAO, Rome, 16/11/'89, § 4, *AAS* 82 (1990) 670.

[178] POPE JOHN PAUL II, *Le Responsibilità dei Cattolici di Fronte alle Sfide dell'Attuale Momento Storico*, supplement to *Osservatore Romano*, (Vatican City: Osservatore Romano, 1994), § 7; cf. also idem, Address to Representatives of Business and Cultural Life, Lima, Peru, 15/5/'88, § 8, *IGP2* XI-2 (1988): 1455/6; idem, Address to Government Officials and Diplomatic Corps, Asuncion, Paraguay, 16/5/'88, § 4, *HSSP*, 233; and idem, Address to Participants in the 41st. Social Studies Week, 5/4/'91, § 5, *AAS* 84 (1992): 20.

[179] POPE JOHN PAUL II, Address to the Diplomatic Corps, Harare, Zimbabwe, 11/9/'88, § 3, *HSSP*, 239; cf. also idem, Address to the Diplomatic Corps, Copenhagen, Denmark, 7/6/'89, § 5, *AAS* 81 (1989): 1361.

understanding. "The role of diplomacy is to assist the strengthening of...solidarity by presenting the various positions with clarity and objectivity, and by seeking ways to overcome obstacles without recourse to violence."[180]

4. Solidarity as Struggle and Taking-sides

One of the features of solidarity which is frequently referred to by Pope John Paul in his addresses is the element of struggle. Donal Dorr actually suggests that the word *solidarity* in the writings of John Paul II plays a role which is analogous to the expression *class struggle* in Marxist writings. It is an action-oriented word, but without the negative connotations of the word *struggle*.[181]

Because of the obstacles which interfere with the activity of solidarity, and which we shall shortly be considering, it can never be assumed that justice, development, and peace will be achieved without difficulty. The pope frequently points to the need to struggle against poverty and hunger, and for the establishment of the rights of individuals and of peoples.[182] He also speaks of the need to struggle against unemployment and economic inequity.[183] This struggle demands that we take sides with those who are poor, disadvantaged, and oppressed. "To involve oneself in this commitment to solidarity presupposes taking sides with the most needy people in your country, to defend their rights and attend to their just claims."[184] This taking of sides, which is an element of solidarity, is often expressed in the terminology of preference for the poor.

---

[180] POPE JOHN PAUL II, Address to the Ambassador of Thailand, Vatican, 9/3/'84, *AAS* 76 (1984): 714; cf. also idem, Address to the Ambassador of Sweden, Vatican, 9/2/'87, *IGP2* X-1 (1987): 310/1.

[181] Donal DORR, "The New Social Encyclical," *The Furrow*, 1981: 709/710.

[182] Cf. POPE JOHN PAUL II, Address to the Ambassador of Madagascar, Vatican, 5/1/'87, § 4, *AAS* 79 (1987): 1160; also idem. Address to the Ambassador of Burundi, Vatican, 18/11/'88, *AAS* 81 (1989): 665; and idem, Address to Participants in the 25th. Plenary Meeting of FAO, Rome, 16/11/'89, § 4, *AAS* 82 (1990): 670.

[183] Cf. POPE JOHN PAUL II, Address to Participants in a Congress organised by the Italian Episcopal Conference to mark the Centenary of Rerum Novarum, 2/3/'91, § 4, *IGP2* XIV-1 (1991): 447.

[184] POPE JOHN PAUL II, Address to Civil Leaders and Representatives of Economic and Cultural Life, Asuncion, Paraguay, 17/5/'88, § 6, *AAS* 80 (1988): 1616.

I wish to ask them (all men and women) to be convinced of the seriousness of the present moment and of each one's individual responsibility, and to implement – by the way they live as individuals and as families, by the use of their resources, by their civic activity, by contributing to economic and political decisions, and by personal commitment to national and international undertakings – the measures inspired by solidarity and love of preference for the poor.[185]

The option, or love of preference, for the poor which is inspired by solidarity, is not, however, an option which excludes others. It is, as the term suggests a *preferential* option. On a number of occasions the pope situates this preference for the poor within the broader context of compassion and solidarity towards all.[186] It is also clear that the option for the poor is not to be understood as excluding the poor from participating in the solutions to their own problems. The poor also have something to offer, both to each other and to those who come to their assistance. "A true solidarity involves an openness to the gift which I can always receive from the other, however poor he appears at first; it becomes an exchange between partners who mutually respect each other's dignity.[187]

According to John Paul II, solidarity purifies struggles, ensuring that the struggle *for* the human being and his rights, never becomes a struggle on the part of one person *against* another. Addressing an inter-regional meeting of bishops in southern Africa, the pope insists that "the forms in which...solidarity is realised cannot be dictated by an analysis based on class distinctions and class struggle."[188] As I have mentioned above, Rémi Parent understands solidarity as the attitude which holds the appropriate balance or tension between communion and taking-sides. Communion on its own, without the active element of solidarity, would be less

---

[185] POPE JOHN PAUL II, *SRS*, § 47; cf. also idem, Address to the Diplomatic Corps, Vatican, 12/1/'85, § 2, *AAS* 76 (1985): 646; and idem, Address to Workers, Malta, 26/5/'90, § 6, *AAS* 83 (1991): 63.
[186] Cf. POPE JOHN PAUL II, Address to Bishops of the Philippines on *Ad Limina* Visit, 18/9/'90, § 2, *AAS* 83 (1991): 356; and idem, Address to the Bishops of Taiwan on *Ad Limina* Visit, 15/12/'90, § 3, *AAS* 83 (1991): 734.
[187] POPE JOHN PAUL II, Address to Participants in a Plenary Session of the Pontifical Council *Cor Unum*, 19/11/'90, § 3, *IGP2* XIII-2 (1990): 1235; cf. also idem, Address to the people of the Guasmo Region, Ecuador, 1/2/'85, § 6, *AAS* 77 (1985): 868/9; and idem, *SRS*, § 39.
[188] POPE JOHN PAUL II, Address to the Inter-regional Meeting of southern African Bishops, 15/8/'84, § 3, *AAS* 77 (1985): 159; cf. also idem, Address to Farmers, Cuzco, Peru, 37/2/'85, § 4, *AAS* 77 (1985): 877; and idem, Address to Representatives of the Association of Catholic Workers, Vatican, 6/12/'86, § 4, *IGP2* IX-2 (1986): 1857/8.

troublesome, but it would also lack authenticity, because it would be a limited communion, tending towards exclusivity. On the other hand, taking-sides, without the love that has its source in communion, might have the appearance of being more decisive and more effective, but in the end it also tends to exclude.

Parent proposes six propositions for the development of an appropriate orthopraxis of solidarity. The first proposition is as follows:

> In order that our praxis of solidarity should be truly Christian, communion and taking-sides mutually call for one another. Communion draws out from within itself the taking of sides, without which it tends towards an ideology of such generality as would perhaps save the purity of the concept, but at the expense of a loss of praxis. On the other hand, the taking of sides draws out communion from within itself in order not to be suffocated by individualism...There is no communion which does not call for the taking of sides, nor is there any taking of sides which does not call for communion.[189]

On the occasion of a visit to Vienna in 1983, the pope devoted considerable attention to explaining the implications of Christian solidarity. Having told the workers in his audience that solidarity urges common action, he goes on to remind them that their action must be respectful of persons, even those who hold views which seem to be irreconcilable with their own.

> Christian solidarity is born from the "positive," and not from the "negative." Action based on solidarity strives to eliminate unnecessary suffering imposed by man or nature. Thus it also turns against those who are perhaps interested in perpetuating injustice or evil. The ultimate motive of action should not be the "negative" which may give rise to new oppression, but the "positive" which is liberating....The objective of workers' solidarity should not be victory, triumph, or rule, but redress, improvement, and understanding.[190]

This vision of solidarity as an attitude which, at one and the same time, respects the other, and yet allows the possibility of constructively opposing his actions or his policies, reflects very closely the argument of Wojtyla that opposition may be expressed as an authentic human attitude which, by

---

[189] Rémi PARENT, ibid., 127.

[190] POPE JOHN PAUL II, Address to Workers, Vienna, 12/9/'83, § 6, *Osservatore* 40, 1983: 6. The words used here in the German original are "fur" and "gegen," which would probably be better rendered as "for" and "against." In other words solidarity is always "for." There is no authentic form of solidarity "against."

excluding inappropriate participation, complements the action of solidarity.[191]

The constructive struggle of solidarity is reflected in the pope's own even-handed approach to the two socio-economic systems between which the world has been divided until very recently. He refuses to take sides against one, which might be interpreted as an unqualified endorsement of the other.[192] Speaking of the pope's approach to these systems, Dorr remarks: "The overall impression conveyed by his treatment is that he does not see it as his role to favour one system as against the other, but rather to point out the inadequacies in each."[193] The proposal of a *third way* which would be an alternative to the two existing socio-economic systems is not part of the agenda of John Paul II.

> The Church cannot allow the flag of justice, which is a requirement of the gospel, to be monopolised by any ideology or political trend. Neither does the social doctrine of the Church propose any particular system (economic, social, or political), but, in the light of its fundamental principles, makes it possible to see, above all, the extent to which the existing systems are or are not in conformity with the requirements of human dignity....Nobody has the right to define his *own* particular solution as "catholic," because the principles taught by the Church admit of a plurality of practical applications.[194]

In so far as we are at present considering Pope John Paul's thought on solidarity in a context which includes the Church as a community or society, it is perhaps relevant to refer to his comment on opposition within the Church in the encyclical letter *Veritatis Splendor*. The pope says:

> Dissent, in the form of carefully orchestrated protests and polemics carried on in the media, is opposed to ecclesial communion and to a correct understanding of the hierarchical constitution of the people of God. Opposition to the teaching of the Church's Pastors cannot be seen as a legitimate expression either of Christian freedom or of the diversity of the Spirit's gifts.[195]

This statement obviously has many theological implications, the discussion of which is not within the scope of this work. It is worthy of

---

[191] Cf. Karol WOJTYLA, *Acting Person*, 286/7.

[192] Cf. POPE JOHN PAUL II, *SRS* §§ 21-23 passim.

[193] Donal DORR, "The New Encyclical," ibid., 707.

[194] POPE JOHN PAUL II, Address at Barrios la Concordia, Melo, Uruguay, 8/5/'88, IGP2, XI-2 (1988), 1206.

[195] POPE JOHN PAUL II, *VS*, 113.

note, however, that the pope does not in this case make any distinction between authentic and inauthentic opposition, but considers all opposition to
be inauthentic. From this one must conclude that the Church, while it is a
society in the world, is intended to be considered as specifically different
from the generality of human societies.[196]

5. Dialogue, in a Spirit of Mutual Trust and Respect

While dialogue is a feature of diplomatic activity, it is by no means
restricted to diplomats. In fact dialogue is an essential element of solidarity
in whatever area of human activity it is to be found. It is by means of
dialogue that solidarity purifies struggles and opposition. As John Paul II
remarks: "Solidarity, which finds its origin and its energy in the nature of
human work, and thus in the primacy of the human person over things, will
be able to create the instruments of dialogue and discussion which make
possible the resolution of oppositions without seeking the destruction of the
opponent."[197]

Dialogue is, along with solidarity, a means to achieving justice and
peace.[198] It facilitates the task of government, it allows partners in solidarity
to face up to the requirement of a global economy, and it allows nations to
achieve their legitimate national interests.[199]

If dialogue is to be effective in attaining the goals of solidarity, it must
be undertaken in a spirit of truth. Pope John Paul says: "This spirit of
solidarity is a spirit open to dialogue. It finds its roots in truth and has need
of the truth in order to develop."[200] The truth in dialogue has a double role.
Firstly, it is how I present myself and my position to the other. Secondly it
is how I respond to the other, respecting his integrity, and accepting
whatever is valid in his position. It is in the nature of things that even to

---

[196] Cf. Gregory BAUM, "Structures of Sin" in *The Logic of Solidarity*, ibid., 124/5.

[197] POPE JOHN PAUL II, Address to the I.L.O., Geneva, Switzerland, 15/6/'82, *AAS*
74 (1982): 1000/1; cf. also idem, Address to the Ambassador of India, Vatican, 10/1/'86,
AAS 78 (1986): 640.

[198] Cf. POPE JOHN PAUL II, Address to the Ambassador of the Sudan, Vatican,
7/1/'88, *IGP2* XI-1 (1988): 49.

[199] Cf. POPE JOHN PAUL II, Address to Government Officials and Diplomatic Corps,
Asuncion, Paraguay, 16/5/'88, § 4, *HSSP*, 233; also idem, Address to a UNIAPAC Pilgrim
Group, Vatican, 9/3/'91, § 4, *AAS* 83 (1991): 1034; and idem. Address to Government
Officials and Diplomatic Corps, Ottawa, Canada, 19/9/'84, § 2, *HSSP*, 201.

[200] Cf. POPE JOHN PAUL II, Message for World Peace Day 1987, 8/12/'86, § 4, *AAS*
79 (1987): 49.

undertake dialogue demands a certain basic mutual trust, a trust which is reinforced once it is clear that the dialogue is being carried out in a spirit of truth.[201]

We have already seen that the solidarity of small groups is not to be something exclusive, but rather something which is open to broadening its horizons, so that new and more extensive solidarities may be established.[202] This broadening of solidarity, which facilitates the attainment of the common good, is made possible by dialogue. There is, therefore a kind of cycle of solidarity and dialogue, which explains why dialogue is at times presented as if it were a cause of solidarity.[203]

6. Justice, Respect, and Development

We have already addressed the themes of justice, respect for rights, and development as objectives of solidarity. At this point, without repeating much of what has already been said, we shall briefly consider the role of each as a means by which solidarity achieves its goal or ultimate end.

As far as justice is concerned, we need only recognise that, while it is itself a fruit of solidarity, it is identified by Pope John Paul as being necessary for peace. "Respect and solidarity determine the ways of justice. Peace is the normal fruit of justice."[204] Justice, therefore, follows from solidarity and precedes the attainment of peace. It would not, of course, be wise to speak in absolute terms. Clearly there can be a reasonable degree of peace even while justice remains to be perfected. However the general thrust would appear to be that if solidarity is to give rise to peace, it must first seek justice.

A similar pattern reveals itself when we come to consider respect for personal rights. This respect, itself an objective of solidarity, is identified

---

[201] Cf. POPE JOHN PAUL II, Address to a UNIAPAC Pilgrim Group, Vatican, 9/3/'91, § 4, *AAS* 83 (1991): 1034; and idem. Address to Government Officials and Diplomatic Corps, Ottawa, Canada, 19/9/'84, § 2, *HSSP*, 201.

[202] Cf. POPE JOHN PAUL II, Address to the I.L.O., Geneva, Switzerland, 15/6/'82, *AAS* 74 (1982): 1000.

[203] Cf. POPE JOHN PAUL II, Address to the Diplomatic Corps, Canberra, Australia, 25/11/'86, § 6, *HSSP*, 224; also idem, Address to the Ambassador of Sweden, Vatican, 9/2/'87, *IGP2* X-1 (1987): 310/1; and idem, Message for World Communications Day, 24/1/'88, § 3, *AAS* 80 (1988): 1360.

[204] POPE JOHN PAUL II, Address to the Ambassador of Algeria, Vatican, 4/6/'87, § 4, *IGP2* X-2 (1987): 1958; cf. also idem, Homily at Bombay, 9/2/'86, § 8, *AAS* 78 (1986): 776.

by Pope John Paul as part of the process by which solidarity achieves development. Speaking in his own homeland, he reminds the workers of Gdynia: "We cannot progress, and we cannot speak of any kind of development, if in the name of social solidarity the rights of every person are not respected."[205]

Likewise, development is a means to peace. We have established the fact that authentic development is the fruit of solidarity. It also transpires, however, that it is because it is crucial for development that solidarity is a factor for peace.[206] It follows that, at least in so far as peace is concerned, development is a means by which solidarity achieves its goal. Equally, it is evident from many of the addresses of Pope John Paul that development is an intrinsic part of the process by which solidarity assists people, not simply in obtaining their immediate daily needs in a time of crisis, but also in attaining a security and a relative self-sufficiency in these goods and services.[207]

F. OBSTACLES TO SOLIDARITY

There is, as we have seen, a complex moral process to be accomplished before solidarity arises out of interdependence. Unfortunately, when this moral dimension is ignored or when the process is carried out in a flawed or incomplete way, there arise instead the "diametrically opposed" attitudes of an over-riding desire for profit and a thirst for power, which, when they become established on a global or international level, are expressed in "different forms of imperialism" and the division of the world into blocs sustained by rigid ideologies.[208] It would seem that this negative outcome will be found in either of three situations, a) when the reality of interdependence is not recognised, b) when the truth that interdependence implies certain concrete rights and duties is not recognised, or c) when that truth is ignored in the free personal decision.

---

[205] POPE JOHN PAUL II, Address to the Sea-faring People, Gdynia, Poland, 11/6/'87, § 4, *Osservatore*, 1987, no. 30: 7; cf. also idem, Address to the People of Detroit, U.S.A., 19/9/'87, § 8, *IGP2* X-3 (1987): 672.

[206] Cf. POPE JOHN PAUL II, Address to U.S. Bishops on *Ad Limina* Visit, 9/9/'88, § 4, *AAS* 81 (1989): 178.

[207] Cf. POPE JOHN PAUL II, Address to the Diplomatic Corps, N'Djamena, Chad, 1/2/'90, § 3, *AAS* 82 (1990): 824; also idem, Address to the Bishops of Mozambique, Maputo, 18/9/'88, § 12, *AAS* 81 (1989): 367; and idem, Address for World Peace Day 1987, 8/12/'86, § 7, *AAS* 79 (1987): 52.

[208] POPE JOHN PAUL II, *SRS*, §§ 36 & 38.

Pope John Paul is well aware of the obstacles that present themselves to the realisation of solidarity. Through his life-time he has experienced some of them at close quarters. In more recent years he has become acquainted with their manifestation in a more global context. Addressing the Swedish ambassador, he says:

> In the modern world, obstacles to solidarity abound, obstacles arising from racial prejudice or religious intolerance, or resulting from ideologies and systems which spawn hatred, distrust and conflict. In the face of these obstacles we must be convinced of the value and real effectiveness of solidarity and fraternal collaboration.[209]

As we have seen already, solidarity is hampered either when there is a lack of awareness of the implications of interdependence or when this awareness is ignored in the free decision, in preference for an individualism which is closed to others and to their needs. Pope John Paul, on a number of occasions, counterposes solidarity and individualism. Speaking to young people in Madagascar, he tells them: "Your personality will not mature unless you smash the individualism which makes you flee from others."[210]

1. Thirst for Profit and Power

Individualism is manifested in two attitudes which are diametrically opposed to solidarity, namely an over-riding desire for profit and a thirst for power. These in turn give rise to experiences and structures which together form a culture which is opposed to the culture of solidarity, and thus in conflict with the common good. While individualism conveys an image of a person standing alone and sealed off from others, the attitude of individualism can, of course, be the attitude of a group or of a nation. One expression of the individualism of the group is racism. Reflecting on the state of Western Europe at a time when Eastern Europe was emerging from the domination of totalitarian regimes, the pope remarks: "Alongside generous spurts of solidarity, a real concern for the promotion of justice, and a constant preoccupation with effective respect for human rights, one

---

[209] POPE JOHN PAUL II, Address to the Ambassador of Sweden, 9/2/'87, *IGP2* X-1 (1987): 310.

[210] POPE JOHN PAUL II, Address to Youth, Antananariva, Madagascar, 29/4/'89, § 2, *IGP2* XII-1 (1989): 982; cf. also idem, Address to the Ambassador of Norway, 20/1/'86, § 4, *IGP2* IX-2 (1986): 158; and idem, Homily at Terceira, The Azores, 11/5/'91, § 6, *IGP2* XIV-1 (1991): 1196/7.

is constrained to recognise the presence and diffusion of counter-values such as egoism, hedonism, racism and practical materialism."[211]

Pope John Paul quite frequently links the two themes of the all-consuming desire for profit and the thirst for power in his addresses. On reflection this is not simply because these are two attitudes which are diametrically opposed to solidarity, and it is convenient to mention them together. There is considerable interplay between these two attitudes in reality, because power is frequently a means to profit, and profit – especially excessive profit – is frequently a means to power. For this reason, I will follow the lead of Pope John Paul and consider the two attitudes together.[212]

It is important to be clear at the outset concerning the cause of the problem. There is nothing wrong with power in itself. All power, like wealth, has a social purpose, and John Paul II reminds us that this implies a duty to use power and wealth for the common good.[213] This assertion of the social purpose of power and wealth is undoubtedly related to the understanding, to which we have already referred, that the world's resources have a universal destination. Similarly, the pursuit of profit in itself is not unjust. In fact the profit motive at some level is clearly an important factor in economic development. The pope, however, questions the level of profit and the manner in which it is made.

> To pursue profit is not in itself unjust, provided profit is obtained in a licit way and by means of a correct management of the company. To seek reasonable profit is, besides, in keeping with the right of "economic initiative." But profit must not be made into an absolute criterion: it is only a rule of efficiency, which must be subjected to the restrictions of the principle of solidarity.[214]

The difficulty, then, is with an attitude of desire for power or profit, which is such that it would deny or unjustly limit the participation of others.

According to John Paul II, solidarity "is based on the solid conviction

---

[211] POPE JOHN PAUL II, Address to the Diplomatic Corps, Vatican, 13/1/'90, § 9, *AAS* 82 (1990): 863; cf. also idem, Christmas Day Greetings, 25/12/'84, *AAS*, 77 (1985), 380; and idem, Message for World Communications Day, 24/1/'88, § 3, *AAS* 80 (1988): 1360.

[212] Cf. POPE JOHN PAUL II, *SRS*, § 37.

[213] Cf. POPE JOHN PAUL II, Address to the Ambassador of the Philippines, 18/5/'91, § 4, *AAS* 84 (1992): 154.

[214] POPE JOHN PAUL II, Address to Business-people, Naples, 11/11/'90, § 5, *IGP2* XIII-2 (1990): 1122.

that what is hindering full development is that desire for profit and that thirst for power already mentioned."[215] These attitudes, as the pope remarks, are to be found not only in individuals but in nations and in blocs of nations too. This favours the establishment of what the pope calls the "structures of sin." He says "if certain forms of modern imperialism were considered in the light of these moral criteria, we would see that, hidden behind certain decisions, apparently inspired only by economics and politics, are real forms of idolatry: of money, ideology, class, technology."[216]

As we have already seen, authentic human development is oriented towards the attainment of the common good. It follows that what hinders such development, is opposed to the good, and is in fact contributing to what is evil. Pope John Paul recognises this when he says:

> Structural reform must be accompanied by moral reform, because the deepest roots of social evil are of a human nature, that is to say, on the one hand the exclusive desire for profit and, on the other, the thirst for power. Given that the roots of social evils are of this order, it follows that they cannot be overcome except on the moral level, that is to say by a conversion, by passing from behaviour inspired by uncontrolled egoism to an authentic culture of solidarity.[217]

We are once again presented, therefore, with struggle as an intrinsic element of solidarity. It is not a struggle against other persons, but the struggle of a person with himself, and of a society with its own values and structures. True dialogue focuses attention on "the aspirations for solidarity present in all people's hearts. It means abandoning the divisive kind of thinking that defends personal privilege and power."[218] Addressing the issue of external debt, the pope conjures up the image of a ship caught in a violent storm to convey the urgency of the struggle to overcome the evil of excessive profit with the good of solidarity. A solution to debt must be sought and initiated, in the light of the principle of solidarity, "with the end of avoiding shipwreck on the rocks of egoism, of profit at all costs, or

---

[215] Cf. POPE JOHN PAUL, *SRS*, § 38.

[216] Cf. POPE JOHN PAUL, *SRS*, § 37.

[217] POPE JOHN PAUL II, Address to Participants in a Convention on the Encyclical Letter *Rerum Novarum*, 15/5/'91, § 7, *AAS* 84 (1992): 150.

[218] POPE JOHN PAUL II, Address to the Ambassador of Malawi, Vatican, 13/4/'89, *AAS* 81 (1989): 1130; cf. also idem, Address to the Ambassador of Ecuador, Vatican, 5/1/'89, *AAS* 81 (1989): 846.

of a narrow and purely material concept of development."[219]

The pope's analysis is not ultimately a negative or unduly pessimistic one, because he is preoccupied with presenting solidarity as the way of overcoming the longing for profit and the thirst for power.[220] Solidarity in fact surpasses every abuse of power, as well as the deficient understanding of work as purely a means to profit.[221]

2. Alienation and Associated Phenomena

The disordered desire for profit and power has its concrete expression in a variety of experiences and structures, all of which constitute obstacles to solidarity and to the attainment of the common good. As I have already suggested this twin attitude tends, in two very practical ways, to exclude the appropriate participation of others. It becomes, consequently, the cause of alienation.

The pope remarks that the whole person, even beyond the framework of productive labour, is affected by the economic and political system. Commenting that the authentic destiny of humanity and the truth about the person have received scant respect in Eastern Europe in recent decades, he suggests that a closer examination of the West will also reveal "alongside an impoverishment of values, other forms of exploitation and alienation. A society is alienated," he continues, "when, in the forms of its social organisation, of its production and consumption, it makes more difficult the gift of self which man is called to make, and the constitution of solidarity among men."[222]

The pope refers critically to the individualism which is so often associated with consumer societies, and the way in which consumerism and materialism conflict with the recognition of the true meaning of the

---

[219] POPE JOHN PAUL II, Address to Representatives of Business and Cultural Life, Lima, Peru, 15/5/'88, § 9, *IGP2* XI-2 (1988): 1456/7.

[220] Cf. POPE JOHN PAUL II, Address to Workers, Verona, Italy, 17/4/'88, § 4, *IGP2* XI-1 (1988): 938; cf. also idem, *SRS*, § 38.

[221] Cf. POPE JOHN PAUL II, Message for World Communications Day, 24/1/'88, § 3, *AAS* 80 (1988): 1361; also idem, Address to Lancia Motor Workers, Ivrea, Italy, 19/3/'90, § 4, *IGP2* XIII-1 (1990): 702/3.

[222] POPE JOHN PAUL II, Address to Participants in a Congress organised by the Bishops' Commission of the European Community, 11/10/'91, § 4, *IGP2* XIV-2 (1991): 804/5.

person.[223] Through this individualism, man is threatened with alienation both from the work of his own hands and intellect, and from the environment in which he lives.[224]

There are a number of other addresses in which the pope, while not using the term *alienation* is clearly referring to phenomena which are associated with that reality, whether self-inflicted or otherwise. He speaks of "the collapse of the family structure, the scattering of its members, especially the youngest, and the subsequent sicknesses found among them – the abuse of drugs, alcoholism, casual sexual encounters, exploitation by others."[225] Speaking to the Italian bishops in 1991, he refers to the marks of sickness and death in society.

> The negative birth-rate, which has reached an alarming level, and which is leading to the ageing of the population and the creation of a generation gap; the frequent recourse to divorce and marital separation; the easy acceptance of the plague of abortion, which atrophies the moral sense and undermines the capacity for welcoming and protecting life at every stage; the high number of suicides; the frightening proliferation of drugs; the worrying phenomenon of useless road-deaths on Saturday nights; the emergence of new and insidious forms of poverty; the spread of sicknesses which find fertile soil in lifestyles which deny the truth of the person. In this context, there is a risk that solidarity is more stated than lived; tolerance can deteriorate into lack of interest and lack of commitment; mutual respect can be degraded into closed egoism and moral relativism.[226]

These phenomena are surely, in many cases, to be understood as expressions of a deep yearning for authentic participation which people have either rejected for themselves, or which has been denied them by others, because of the influence of inauthentic social attitudes or structures. In each case the pope refers to the need for a lived solidarity to overcome this sense of dissipation and lack of purpose.

> Solidarity offers the exciting opportunity of communicating oneself to others in

---

[223] Cf. POPE JOHN PAUL II, Address to the Ambassador of Norway, Vatican, 20/1/'86, § 4, *IGP2* IX-2 (1986): 158; also idem, Address to W. German Bishops on *Ad Limina* Visit, 14/11/'89, § 3, *Osservatore*, 1989, no. 49: 6; and idem, Address to the Diplomatic Corps, Vatican, 13/1/'90, § 9, *AAS* 82 (1990): 863.

[224] Cf. POPE JOHN PAUL II, *RH*, § 15.

[225] POPE JOHN PAUL II, Address for World Peace Day 1987, 8/12/'86, § 8, *AAS*, 79 (1987), 54.

[226] POPE JOHN PAUL II, Address to the Italian Bishops on *Ad Limina* Visit, 1/3/'91, § 3, *AAS* 83 (1991): 984.

a peaceful and constructive attitude; it allows one to establish stable and coordinated relationships, which correspond to the real needs of persons and communities; it helps too in overcoming those conditions of loneliness and isolation which frequently develop into incommunicability and alienation.[227]

3. Perverse Structures, Super-development, and Under-development

When society is motivated by the desire for excessive profit, or "having," the result is an imbalance in development. The stronger sectors and nations absorb resources, becoming richer and, therefore, more powerful, while the weaker increasingly find themselves deprived of what they need, and at the mercy of the strong, economically, politically, and even culturally.

Pope John Paul makes a distinction between *super-development* and *under-development*, neither of which is authentic, because both prevent the proper realisation of the person.

> There are some people – the few who possess much – who do not really succeed in "being" because, through a reversal of the hierarchy of values, they are hindered by the cult of "having;" and there are others – the many who have little or nothing – who do not succeed in realising their basic human vocation because they are deprived of essential goods.[228]

Super-development, then, is not merely a matter of *having*, or even *having* in abundance. It is the fruit of a culture in which *having* takes precedence over *being*. On the other hand, the pope identifies three particular indicators of under-development: the housing crisis, unemployment or underemployment, and international debt. He notes that the first two of these are also evident in the underdeveloped sectors of many highly developed countries.[229] The gap between developed and developing countries is not a static one but an ever-widening one, because wealth offers advantages which support further development, while exploitation hinders development.[230]

Gradually mechanisms and structures develop, oriented towards greater

[227] POPE JOHN PAUL II, Address to the Association of Catholic Workers, 6/12/'86, § 3, *IGP2* IX-2 (1986): 1856/7, cf. also Address to Participants in a Congress organised by the Italian Episcopal Conference to Mark the Centenary of *Rerum Novarum*, 2/3/'91, § 2, *IGP2* XIV-1 (1991): 447.
[228] POPE JOHN PAUL II, *SRS*, § 28.
[229] Cf. POPE JOHN PAUL II, *SRS*, §§ 17-19.
[230] Cf. POPE JOHN PAUL II, *SRS*, § 14.

profit. Some of them may even have been set up for good reasons related to development, but perverted by the all-consuming nature of the desire for profit, together with a narrow vision of development. These mechanisms often appear to function automatically, and create the impression of being outside of personal control.[231] Exequiel Rivas identifies the concept of "perverse mechanisms" as something absolutely new which John Paul II has introduced into the social teaching of the Church. These mechanisms, he argues, are considered perverse because they impede free human activity. Yet it would be a mistake to think that they are outside personal control. What makes them immoral is precisely the fact that they are manipulated by the developed nations to their own advantage.[232] Gregory Baum, likewise, notes that, while John Paul II is "aware of the unconscious, non-voluntary, quasi-automatic dimension of social sin...the greater emphasis in his analysis of social sin lies on personal responsibility."[233] This is not the place to attempt to deal with "social sin" as a theological concept. It is important, however, to advert to Pope John Paul's conviction that even the structures which undermine free personal action and constitute an obstacle to solidarity are in some sense the result of personal agency.

One of the classic expositions of the "perverse mechanisms" is the description by John Steinbeck of how farm families from the mid-West of the United States were dispossessed of their land by the banks and the large enterprises, and subsequently exploited by fruit farmers and oppressed by the state authorities in California, where they had gone seeking to earn a living. What is hopeful in this description is that, even in the depths of poverty and in the face of death, the human spirit is not broken and the final act is an act of human solidarity between the poorest of the poor.[234] Under-development is an obstacle to solidarity, because it acts against the attainment of the common good. Pope John Paul describes under-development as a danger for world peace.[235]

---

[231] Cf. POPE JOHN PAUL II, *SRS*, §§ 16, 36.

[232] Exequiel RIVAS, ibid., 221; cf. POPE JOHN PAUL II, *SRS*, §§ 17, 35, & 40.

[233] Gregory BAUM, "Structures of Sin," in *The Logic of Solidarity*, ibid., 115. Baum suggests that the teaching of John Paul II has a certain affinity with the emphasis on personal agency in the sociology of Max Weber.

[234] Cf. John STEINBECK, *The Grapes of Wrath*, (New York: Penguin Modern Classics, 1951), 30-33, & 415/6.

[235] Cf. POPE JOHN PAUL II, Address to the Diplomatic Corps, Vatican, 11/1/'86, § 8, *HSSP*, 113; also idem, Address at Buenos Aires, Argentina, 6/4/'87, § 3, *HSSP*, 226.

4. The Opposition of Blocs and the Arms Race

The most immediately obvious attitude which underlies the opposition of blocs on the international front is the thirst for power. As Pope John Paul explains, however, the existence of two opposing blocs, which became evident in the aftermath of the second world war, is rooted in the existence of opposing ideologies, which promote "antithetical forms of the organisation of labour and of the structures of ownership, especially with regard to the so-called means of production."[236] As Baum explains, both systems are seen by Pope John Paul as hostile to solidarity.

> According to *Sollicitudo*...certain faults of the Marxist theory are shared by the theory of liberal capitalism: both theories rely exclusively on enlightened self-interest...Both theories entertain an "economistic" view of human beings, both look upon economic behaviour as following certain laws and hence as determined, both regard economics as an exact science, and both reject the entry of traditional values, such as justice and solidarity, into the logic of the economy.[237]

The opposition of the blocs is not, therefore, distinct in any real sense from the great questions of work and development, including that of profit.

The systems based on these economic roots, however, very quickly came to view one another with apprehension, and this led to the militarisation of the opposition between them. The pope continues:

> It was inevitable that by developing antagonistic systems and centres of power, each with its own forms of propaganda and indoctrination, the ideological opposition should evolve into a military opposition and give rise to two blocs of armed forces, each suspicious and fearful of the other's domination.[238]

It is possible to discern in this description the erosion of the trust which is so essential if solidarity is to be authentic; in other words if, through dialogue, it is to broaden its horizons, rather than remaining closed and exclusive. It is also possible to see how the development of military opposition places at risk that peace which is so central to the common good of each nation, and to the universal common good which is the goal of solidarity.

The need to have power and to dominate is manifested in the way in

---

[236] POPE JOHN PAUL II, *SRS*, § 20.
[237] Gregory BAUM, "Liberal Capitalism," in *The Logic of Solidarity*, ibid., 85.
[238] POPE JOHN PAUL II, *SRS*, § 20.

which the opposition of blocs has been played out ideologically and militarily in those developing countries which, for reasons of economic dependence and strategic location, have found themselves within the spheres of influence of one or other of the two blocs. Pope John Paul comments:

> The tension between East and West is not in itself an opposition between two different levels of development, but rather between two concepts of the development of individuals and peoples, both concepts being imperfect and in need of radical correction. This opposition is transferred to the developing countries themselves, and thus helps to widen the gap already existing on the economic level between North and South.[239]

The link between ideological and military opposition on the one hand, and under-development on the other, is quite evident. As the pope explains, many developing nations have been caught up in, and overwhelmed by, ideological conflicts. Money which should have been used for development has been diverted in order to sustain conflicts, and an excessive preoccupation with security has deadened "the impulse towards united cooperation for the common good."[240]

Many developing countries become impoverished because they devote an excessive proportion of their own income to military expenditure. Pope John Paul argues, however, that the failure to alleviate the misery of impoverished peoples is also a direct result of the fact that such a high level of resources is invested in arms and military equipment by the nations of the developed world.[241]

Profit-at-any-cost is an obstacle to solidarity. Yet frequently the business of the manufacture and supply of arms is a point of coincidence between the thirst for power on the part of one enterprise or nation, and the unscrupulous desire for profit on the part of another. The pope says:

> The value of solidarity and the common good must also guide the relations between enterprise and society both in the national and in the international context. There are instruments which should not be produced, or the production of which must be rigorously controlled. The first example is that of arms... Even

---

[239] POPE JOHN PAUL II, *SRS*, § 21.

[240] ibid., § 22; and cf. ibid., § 21.

[241] Cf. POPE JOHN PAUL II, *SRS*, § 23; and also idem, Address to the Ambassador of Australia, 28/3/'87, *IGP2* X-1 (1987): 853.

here, the law of profit cannot be considered as supreme.[242]

In December 1989, just as many of the totalitarian regimes of the so-called Soviet bloc were beginning to crumble dramatically before the eyes of the world, Pope John Paul welcomed President Mikhail Gorbaciov of the U.S.S.R. to the Vatican. The pope spoke of the possibility that a common concern for humanity might lead "not only to the overcoming of international tensions and to an end of the opposition of blocs," but could also "give birth to a universal solidarity especially in relation to the developing countries."[243] Writing in 1991, the pope comments on the unprecedented ending of the opposition of the blocs. He remarks that the overturning of the European order sanctioned by the Yalta conference was achieved, not by means of another war as many had feared, but by peaceful persistence.[244] The implication of this is that the authentic human attitude of solidarity triumphed over the ideologies based on the diametrically opposed attitude of the thirst for power.

The ending of the "classical" opposition of the two blocs, each with its imperialist tendencies is indeed a step in the right direction. Peaceful solutions have since put an end to various other long-standing conflicts too, precisely because of the willingness of people to engage in dialogue in a spirit of trust. Events in and between some of the former Eastern bloc countries, as well as in other parts of the world, remind us, however, that the thirst for power which gave rise to the opposition of the blocs and to the arms race, is still a factor in both intra-national and international relations. A further problem, deriving in some sense from the ending of the opposition between the blocs, is the question which arises for arms manufacturers and dealers as to how they can continue to make profit unless they find new markets for their products, with all the implications which this might have for world peace.

5. War, Poverty, and Debt

It may at first sight seem a little unusual to consider war alongside poverty and debt, in a study of the obstacles to solidarity. These realities,

---

[242] POPE JOHN PAUL II, Address to Workers, Verona, Italy, 17/4/'88, § 6, *IGP2* XI-1 (1988): 940/1; cf. also idem, *SRS*, § 24.

[243] POPE JOHN PAUL II, Address to President Mikhail Gorbaciov, Vatican, 1/12/'89, § 5, *AAS* 82 (1990): 698.

[244] Cf. POPE JOHN PAUL II, *CA*, § 24.

however, are the logical conclusion of a social order dominated by the
unbridled desire for profit and thirst for power, of which we have already
spoken. War and poverty alike are causes of death; war and indebtedness
alike bring nations and entire regions of the world to their knees. These
phenomena are invariably found together, just as the desire for profit and
the thirst for power so often operate in tandem. Pope John Paul frequently
links these themes. He comments that "poverty and hunger, especially
among millions of refugees,... and the suffering inflicted by armed conflict,
are signs of a deep imbalance in the human heart."[245]

Struggles are necessary, as we have seen, but war is an inhuman
struggle because it is against the other person. As such it places the civil
co-existence at risk.[246] War sows the seeds of division, and this in itself is
enough to make it clear that war can never be compatible with true
solidarity.[247] Speaking of civil war in Angola and The Lebanon, as well as
of the Gulf War of 1991, the pope refers to the vast numbers of people left
in a situation of need as a result of war; need for food and shelter and many
other essentials of life; need which is in conflict with the common good.[248]
There is evident today, according to John Paul II, the beginnings of a
movement beyond the situations of war and injustice, a movement to
establish a web of solidarity. Solidarity is a duty imposed by fidelity to the
memory of those who have been and remain the victims of conflict. The
establishment of solidarity, however, requires a struggle against the logic
of war.[249]

If war destroys peace, which is a central element of the common good,

---

[245] POPE JOHN PAUL II, Address to the Ambassador of Iran, 20/6/'91, *AAS* 84 (1992):
307; cf. also idem, Address to the Ambassador of Australia, Vatican, 28/3/'87, § 7, *IGP2*
X-1 (1987): 624; and idem, Address at Buenos Aires, Argentina, 6/4/'87, § 3, *HSSP*, 226.

[246] Cf. POPE JOHN PAUL II, Address to the President of Italy, Vatican, 2/6/'84, *AAS*
76 (1984): 956.

[247] Cf. POPE JOHN PAUL II, Address at a Meeting of Cardinals and Bishops of the
Middle East, Vatican, 4/3/'91, §§ 5/6, *AAS* 83 (1991): 1024/5; and also idem, Address to the
Bishops of Angola, and the Prince Islands and St. Thomas Islands on *Ad Limina* Visit,
5/9/'91, § 2, *AAS* 84 (1992): 575.

[248] Cf. POPE JOHN PAUL II, ibid.; and also idem, Message to the Secretary General
of the United Nations, 21/3/'91, *AAS* 84 (1992): 76.

[249] Cf. POPE JOHN PAUL II, Address to Participants in a Congress organised by the
Italian Episcopal Conference to Mark the Centenary of *Rerum Novarum*, 2/3/'91, § 2, *IGP2*:
XIV-1 (1991): 447; also idem, Address to the Ambassador of the Lebanon, 17/12/'90, § 2,
AAS 83 (1991): 738/9; and idem, Address to the Ambassador of Algeria, 4/12/'89, *AAS* 82
(1990): 700.

personal poverty and international debt make short work of what is left. The struggle to be waged against poverty is a struggle of solidarity. "True solidarity must always be present wherever the subject of work, that is man, finds himself in conditions of poverty, wretchedness, exploitation, or injustice."[250] The pope speaks of poverty, famine, and deprivation as "terrible violations of solidarity" and remarks that the causes of these phenomena are not purely natural. "World opinion must more correctly assess the economic, social, and political factors which create or maintain situations of deprivation which all too often are fatal."[251] This is a clear reference to the attitudes of desire for excessive profit and thirst for power, together with the structures and mechanisms which are built on these attitudes.

Towards the beginning of this chapter, we saw that the reality of debt is among the phenomena which give rise to an awareness of interdependence and demand a response of solidarity. Now as we draw towards the conclusion of our analysis, it transpires that the failure to respond in a spirit of solidarity is frequently the cause of deeper and even more intractable indebtedness on the part of the poorer nations. The situation of international debt constitutes an obstacle to solidarity because debt undermines development. The popes remarks on this issue to the Bolivian Ambassador can be applied universally where debt cripples development.

> The social and human cost associated with this crisis of indebtedness, means that this situation cannot be considered in purely economic or monetary terms. For this reason it is necessary to promote new forms of international solidarity which, in a climate of mutual trust and co-responsibility, will make it possible to set in motion both long and short term measures, to ensure that the legitimate aspirations of so many Bolivians to the development which is their right, will not be frustrated.[252]

Because it slows down the rhythm of development, debt creates social and

---

[250] POPE JOHN PAUL II, Address to Representatives of the Association of Catholic Workers, Vatican, 6/12/'86, § 7, *IGP2* IX (1986): 1860; cf. also idem, Address to the Ambasssador of Madagascar, Vatican,5/1/'87, § 4, *AAS* 79 (1987): 1160.
[251] POPE JOHN PAUL II, Address to Participants in the Plenary Meeting of the Pontifical Council *Cor Unum*, 19/1/'90, § 2, *AAS* 83 (1991): 674.
[252] POPE JOHN PAUL II, Address to the Ambassador of Bolivia, Vatican, 23/2/'90, § 2, *AAS* 82 (1990): 894.

international tensions, and undermines peace.[253]

G. CONCLUSIONS AND DEFINITIONS

It will be clear from all that has gone before that the concept of solidarity in the thought of Pope John Paul II is a very rich one. It remains now for us to draw some conclusions concerning the links between this concept, and the concept elaborated in the writing of Karol Wojtyla, and to attempt to answer some of the questions which have arisen in the course of this chapter.

1. Continuity between Karol Wojtyla and John Paul II

On the level of terminology and central concepts, there is an obvious continuity between the treatment of *solidarity* in the writings of Karol Wojtyla and that which we have seen in the writings and addresses of Pope John Paul II. As I have noted, the term *participation* is not as widely used as one might expect, given its importance as an objective of solidarity, and as a means to the common good in *The Acting Person*. The same concept, however, would appear to be expressed in the term *collaboration*, which is given a totally positive meaning, as the act proper to solidarity.

The presentation of solidarity as action-oriented belongs to both the papal and the pre-papal material. The theme of *work* is closely linked with the concept of solidarity in both periods, as is the concept of the personal subject of solidarity as *neighbour*, the concept of *dialogue*, and the identification of the *common good* as the goal which is served by solidarity. On the other hand, the concept of global *development* as an objective of solidarity and a means of attaining the common good, would appear to be specific to the papal material, and this would be explained by the shift in perspective offered by the global nature of the papal ministry. In general, I would suggest that the exploration by John Paul II of many concrete aspects of the common good, and of those factors which conflict with it, gives the concept of solidarity a more practical emphasis than it has in the pre-papal writings of Wojtyla. The papal material, likewise, expands more fully on the attitudes, structures, and conditions arising from the individualism of persons and groups, which constitute an obstacle to

---

[253] Cf. POPE JOHN PAUL II, Address to the Ambassador of Brazil, Vatican, 2/4/'90, § 5, *AAS*, 82 (1990), 1388/9; also idem, Address to the Ambassador of Australia, Vatican, 28/3/'87, *IGP2* X-1 (1987): 853.

solidarity. These differences are no doubt contributed to by the broader context within which the papal material is developed.

2. Solidarity and Christian Solidarity

In the material which I have studied, Pope John Paul frequently refers to solidarity in a Christian context, and eight times he actually uses the expression Christian solidarity. I have not, however, come across any evidence to suggest that Pope John Paul thinks of *Christian solidarity* as being in any way opposed to or radically other than *solidarity* as a human reality. On two of the occasions on which he uses the term *Christian solidarity* it is part of the larger expression *human and Christian solidarity*, suggesting that the two are compatible and that they operate, in some sense, together.[254] It is perhaps worth recalling that John Paul II sees solidarity as rooted in love, both human love and divine love. I believe that it would not be inaccurate to suggest that, when the pope speaks of solidarity without reference to the spiritual/theological dimension he is speaking of an attitude or virtue which is motivated by authentic human love. On the other hand, when he refers to the Christian dimension of solidarity, he is speaking of an attitude or virtue which is motivated by divine love as well as human love, but certainly not to the exclusion of human love. It would be possible, in this perspective, to think of Christian solidarity as something which transcends a purely human solidarity, not in the sense that it is necessarily more authentic or more committed, but in the sense that its scope is more profound.

The distinction between Christian solidarity and human solidarity raises the question as to whether the definition of virtue can be applied to Christian solidarity alone, or whether it applies equally to human solidarity. Pope John Paul frequently refers to the Christian virtue of solidarity.[255] On the other hand, many of his references to solidarity as virtue involve no specific reference to the Christian context, and two at least would seem to exclude it. Addressing a group of intellectual and business people in Bolivia, the pope tells them that "to be a leader in the political, cultural, or

---

[254] Cf. POPE JOHN PAUL II, Address to Youth, Cochabamba, Bolivia, 11/5/'88, § 3, *AAS* 80 (1988): 1576; and also idem, Address to Youth, Naples, Italy, 10/11/'90, § 5, *IGP2* XIII-2 (1990): 1078.

[255] Cf. POPE JOHN PAUL II, *SRS* § 40; also idem, Address to Government Officials and Diplomatic Corps, Asuncion, Paraguay, 16/5/'88, § 4, *HSSP*, 233; and idem, Homily to Workers, Villaricca, Paraguay, 17/5/'88, § 6, *IGP2* XI-2 (1988): 1511.

indeed, any other order, not alone does not exclude, but actually requires the virtue of solidarity."[256] It seems unlikely that some quality which is required by anyone who seeks to be a leader could be claimed as the sole preserve of explicit Christians. I mention this lest there appear to be any suggestion that Pope John Paul II's identification of solidarity as a virtue in some sense tends to restrict it to or monopolise it for Christians.

While on the subject of virtue, I refer to Bilgrien's assertion that, since charity is a theological virtue, and since solidarity is a virtue for all, solidarity cannot be considered a part of charity.[257] It remains clear, nonetheless, that Pope John Paul does present solidarity as something which springs from and is intimately related to charity; something which is neither separate from nor in a different order to charity. If that presents a difficulty with regard to the understanding of theological virtue, then that is a difficulty which ought perhaps to be considered by theologians.

3. Love and Charity

As I have indicated, Pope John Paul II states that solidarity springs from charity, and is rooted in love. The question arises as to whether charity refers specifically to Christian solidarity, and love to human solidarity. A study of the various passages in which the pope uses these terms in the context of solidarity reveals that there is no clear boundary between the two terms. In roughly three-quarters of the cases in which Pope John Paul uses the term *charity* with reference to solidarity, he is speaking either of Christian solidarity, or at least in an ecclesial context. On the other hand, while the term *love* is frequently used when solidarity is referred to without any specific religious implication, it is also used quite regularly where the religious connection is explicit.

4. Solidarity as a Synthesis of Personalism and Communalism

Solidarity is presented in the thought of Pope John Paul II as a synthesis of personalism and communalism, in a dual sense. In the first place, solidarity is the *attitude or virtue of individual persons and of personal communities, acting together*, in a spirit of subsidiarity, in order to attain the common good. As we have seen, it is the role of the state, or

---

[256] POPE JOHN PAUL II, Address to Intellectuals and Business People, Santa Cruz, Bolivia, 12/5/'88, § 3, *IGP2*, XI-2 (1988), 1341; also idem, Address to the Ambassador of Santa Lucia, 28/10/'91, *AAS* 84 (1992): 960.

[257] Cf. Marie Vianney BILGRIEN, ibid., 204.

the community in the broader sense, to oversee, to co-ordinate, and where necessary to assist directly the activity of the individual person. It is solidarity that ensures the appropriate balance of participation, and which sees to it that both the subjectivity of the person and of society are safeguarded at all times.[258]

Secondly, solidarity is an attitude or virtue which *considers the needs both of individual persons and of personal communities*, and seeks to find a way in which these can be responded to in harmony and with equity. Dorr explains:

> John Paul's teaching on solidarity is designed to plug a notable gap that often arises when personal development is put at the heart of a system of morality. This gap is the one between the individual and the others with whom that person is linked in any way. If *right* or *good* means what is good for *me*, how does that fit in with what is good for persons around me, whose needs often seem (at least at first sight) to be in competition with mine?[259]

As we have seen, this dimension of solidarity is expressed in the capacity of solidarity to be, at one and the same time, an expression of communion and an active taking-of-sides with those whose needs are greatest. Solidarity is a commitment "to the good of all and of each individual."[260]

5. Definition

I wish to conclude this chapter by formulating a definition of solidarity, based on the examination of Pope John Paul's writings and addresses which we have just completed. I believe we can say:

Solidarity is a virtue of persons and communities who, in each human situation, are actively committed to the good of each person and of all. It is the attitude which leads persons and communities to seek together the common good, that is peace, along with the material, cultural, and spiritual conditions necessary to live as persons, through engaging in dialogue in a spirit of truth and trust, through seeking justice and respecting rights, through promoting the appropriate participation of all, and through the gradual achievement of authentic human development. Solidarity is a moral duty based on the fact of human interdependence and

---

[258] Cf. POPE JOHN PAUL II, *LE*, § 6.
[259] Donal DORR, "Solidarity and Integral Human Development," ibid., 146/7.
[260] POPE JOHN PAUL II, *SRS*, § 38.

fundamental human equality. For believers it finds an additional foundation in communion with God. Solidarity comes into being when that interdependence together with its implications, and that communion, are recognised in a spirit of truth, and translated into action through a free and loving commitment which endures over time. Because of the various individualist attitudes and structures which undermine solidarity, and the conditions that flow from these, solidarity will inevitably involve an element of struggle, which is always for the realisation of the person, and never against other persons.

Concluding Comments

It only remains for us now to consider briefly what conclusions may be drawn concerning the concept of *solidarity* developed in the thought of Karol Wojtyla.[1]

A. A SYNTHESIS OF
PERSONALISM AND COMMUNALISM

It is consistently affirmed in the thought of Wojtyla that solidarity, whether it is considered as a duty, a virtue, or an attitude, is a characteristic of persons. Structures cannot have or offer solidarity. Communities and nations are in solidarity because they are made up of persons. It might not seem necessary to emphasise this, yet the absence of the person at the heart of Durkheim's concept of solidarity is the significant lacuna in his theory. Likewise, the essential criticism of both liberal capitalism and Marxist socialism is that they allow human functions to take the place of human persons.

The human person is, nonetheless, called to transcend himself in co-existence and co-acting. It is precisely because of the power and the urgency of this call to community that the need exists to ensure that the person is not swallowed up in the community. Solidarity, as understood by Karol Wojtyla can properly be called "a synthesis of personalism and communalism," because it is the attitude which recognises, not only that there is no conflict between the good of the person and the good of the community, but that these goods can really only be achieved together. It seems to me that everything else that Wojtyla says about solidarity is capable of being understood in this framework.

We have seen that Wojtyla recognises two types of inter-personal relation, the personal and the social, and two corresponding profiles of participation. *I–You* participation is personal, but it offers the basis for the constitution of community. Likewise, *We* participation is communal, but it is also constitutive of the person in the sense that the person finds himself more fully in the community. Neither form of participation can, therefore, be adequately understood without the other. The task of ensuring that these two profiles of participation are realised in their appropriate balance is one

---

[1] For the purposes of these concluding comments, which are synthetic by nature, I will, for the sake of convenience, refer to Karol Wojtyla / Pope John Paul II simply as Wojtyla.

which is achieved through the dynamic of solidarity.

In both his pre-papal and his papal material, Wojtyla speaks of solidarity as an attitude which is oriented to the common good. He emphasises, however, that the common good should not be simply identified with the good of the community. The common good is the coincidence of the personal good and the communal good. It is the full development of the whole person and of all people. This understanding of the common good is consistent with the view that solidarity is a synthesis of personalism and communalism.

In his study of the person in action, Wojtyla refers to two important developments which go hand-in-hand, namely integration and transcendence. The mature person is an integral cohesive unit and, at the same time, constantly seeks fulfilment in self-transcendence. Considering the person specifically as a community member, we can say that solidarity is the key factor in the process of integration and transcendence. The person retains his own integrity and his own interiority, but he is constantly drawn beyond himself and his individualist tendencies to think and act as a community member. The integration and the transcendence of the person in community are essentially linked. If the person loses his own identity in the community, he is no longer integrated, and there is no participation in any real sense. If, on the other hand, the person loses himself in his interiority, to use the terminology of Mounier, there is no transcendence and, as a consequence, no participation. In either case, both the person and the community are at a loss.

Another aspect of solidarity closely related to the above is its dependence on truth. The truth with which Wojtyla is concerned is, first and foremost, the truth about the human person, and this truth contains both personalist and communalist elements. The person is, on the one hand, free, responsible, and incapable of being replaced by another person. On the other hand, persons are interdependent and the person only fulfils himself when his freedom and responsibility lead him to place his uniqueness at the service of others in community. Wojtyla's criticism of liberal Capitalism and of Marxist socialism, is concerned with the failure of each to recognise the totality of this truth about the human person.

There are a number of other issues which consistently surface in the thought of Wojtyla on solidarity, and which fit into the framework of this synthesis. One is his insistence that genuine solidarity is not closed or limited. In other words, it does not attempt to set boundaries or frontiers to the extension of the community on the pretext of defending the person. The more immediate and local solidarities of groups, nations, and particular sectors of the work-force help to make the reality of community more concrete and accessible, and in this way they lay the ground-work for a more extensive solidarity. They can, however, also obscure the truth that all human community is ultimately based on the recognition of the other as *neighbour*, as a personal subject like myself, over and above the other more limited bonds of community. When this more expansive communal dimension is denied, solidarity loses its authenticity because, while ensuring the participation of some, it acts as a vehicle for the exclusion of others. The good of each person can only be promoted when the community is expanded to include every person.

What Wojtyla has to say about opposition and taking-sides also fits into the framework of solidarity understood as a synthesis of personalism and communalism. Solidarity seeks to ensure the adequate participation of all, for the good of the community. In general, solidarity demands that each one should play his own part, and that nobody should overstep the limits of his responsibility. An exception is made, however, when another person is impeded for some reason from adequately playing his own part. This could happen because of poverty, sickness, deficiencies in education, or indeed as a result of a deliberate policy of exclusion. In such cases, taking-sides is a way of supporting the person who is in need, both for his own good and for the good of the whole community. Taking-sides in this sense is never taking-sides *against* someone, and for this reason it is not in conflict with communion. Opposition, likewise, is the response of solidarity when it seems that the action of the community will exclude the person, or that the action of the person will damage the community. This kind of constructive opposition serves both the person and the community.

We have seen that Wojtyla describes solidarity, both in his pre-papal and papal material, in terms which are consistent with calling it a virtue. As a virtue, solidarity is closely related to both charity (love) and justice, having its roots in the former and having the latter as one of its immediate objectives. As I have suggested in Chapter five, when solidarity is described as a virtue, it is with reference to the impact which it has on the moral growth of the person. When it is described as an attitude, however, it refers primarily to the impact of solidarity on relations with others, on the community. Wojtyla's reference to solidarity both as a virtue and as an attitude is, therefore, consistent with the view that solidarity is a synthesis of personalism and communalism.

B. THE VALUE OF
WOJTYLA'S CONCEPT OF SOLIDARITY

It transpires from our study that the concept of solidarity is quite well established, both in secular social philosophy and in the philosophy underlying the social teaching of the Church. Karol Wojtyla was ideally placed to take into his own thought elements of various traditions, both ancient and more recent. His concept of solidarity reveals traces of the thought of Aristotle and Aquinas, Scheler and Mounier, as well as the influence of a century of Catholic social thought. What is new about Wojtyla's concept of solidarity?

Wojtyla emphasises the value of human work as a privileged moment of solidarity, and he is no stranger to the concept of human interdependence. In this he has much in common with Durkheim. As we have seen, however, he diverges from Durkheim in his insistence that it is the person who gives value to the work, and not the function that gives social value to the person.

Wojtyla's thought on the person in community has much in common with that of Scheler. His concept of solidarity, however, reveals an immediate link between the personal act and the personalistic value of the act. His concept of *person* is more cohesive than that of Scheler. Unlike Scheler, he emphasises the place of duty and personal responsibility in solidarity. While recognising the value of compassion as an expression of solidarity, he refuses to identify the two.

As I have indicated, many of the elements of Wojtyla's concept of solidarity are evident in the earlier social teaching of the Church, and in particular in the thought of Paul VI. Wojtyla's work represents a development of this social teaching in a number of ways. In the first place, he brings to the social teaching of the Church the benefit of his own philosophical approach. Without in any sense being a phenomenologist, he uses what is helpful in the phenomenological method to gain access to the person in his relations with others. As a result, his concept of solidarity presents itself as personal praxis rather than theory. Wojtyla brings to the social teaching of the Church the benefit of his own experience of life under both fascist and Marxist collective systems. Coming from a former Eastern bloc country, he is also in a position to offer a unique perspective on the limitations of liberal capitalism as a system of social organisation.

Finally, not content with speaking about a solidarity without frontiers, Wojtyla uses the concept of solidarity to overcome the significant frontier between Christians and those of other faiths, between believers and non-believers. By means of his open and inclusive use of the concept of solidarity, Wojtyla completes a process initiated by John XXIII. Solidarity proclaims the possibility, and indeed the necessity, of participating with others, "as neighbours" and "helpers" in addressing the problems and needs of the whole of humanity, in an attempt to realise the universal common good.

How practical or useful is the concept of solidarity? Solidarity is not a political theory or a system of social organisation. In so far as it is rooted in metaphysical realities such as love, truth, and freedom, solidarity can not be legislated for, although certain legal and social structures would undoubtedly facilitate it, while others would undermine it. The practicality of solidarity is something altogether different. Solidarity is practical because it is a dynamic principle of action, which enables a person to find support in community for his individual commitment to the common good, and to lend his support to a similar commitment on the part of other persons. In solidarity, the commitment of all the community members is greater than the sum of their individual commitments.

C. AREAS WHICH MAY MERIT FURTHER STUDY

As we have seen, Wojtyla consistently argues that opposition can only be authentic, and can only purify solidarity, when it is an opposition to evil and to the structures of evil. Once it becomes an opposition to other persons it undermines solidarity. Wojtyla also consistently rejects the logic of war and violence as the product of attitudes which are diametrically opposed to solidarity. In war, and in armed struggle of every kind, those who are engaged in the fighting and, increasingly, non-combatants as well, tend to be assigned a kind of collective identity as members of the nation or community to which they belong. Psychologically, it would appear that the first step in armed combat is often the depersonalisation of the "other." Wojtyla never goes as far as to say that there is no such thing as a just war. The logic of solidarity would, however, seem to imply just such a conclusion. This position would, however, be open to criticism on the grounds that opposition or taking sides can scarcely be effective if the sanction of physical resistance is excluded. This is a question which would merit further examination.

When the issue of the dignity of women and their role in society is addressed, it is generally examined from the perspective of equality. As we have seen, for Wojtyla as well as for Scheler and Mounier, the notion of the equality of persons is something of a "double-edged sword." The equality of persons is a concept which may help to prevent unjust discrimination, but it may also act in such a way as to exclude honest and appropriate discrimination, in the strict sense of the word. It seems that the concept of solidarity might be quite helpful in developing a better appreciation of the dignity of women and of the appropriate participation of men and women in society. This is because the concept of solidarity affirms the fundamental equality in dignity of every person, both as a personal subject, an "I," and as "other." Dialogue and participation are undertaken, in solidarity, on the basis that to be an "other" person is good, and to be and act with the "other" adds to the total of goodness. This theme is treated in *Mulieris Dignitatem*, and also in *Love and Responsibility*, but interestingly the concept of solidarity is not used in either case. The position of women in society, and the unique role of women in development, would merit further examination in the light of the concept of solidarity.

Bibliography

This bibliography includes only material which has been cited in notes.

A. REFERENCE WORKS

BROWN, Raymond E., and James C. Turro. "Canonicity," §§ 87-9, *Jerome Biblical Commentary*, vol. 2. (Englewood Cliffs N.J.: Prentice Hall, 1968), 515-534.

SILLS, David, L. *International Encyclopaedia of the Social Sciences*, in 17 vols. (London: Collier-Macmillan, 1968).

B. PRIMARY SOURCES[1]

1. Books

JOHN PAUL II, Pope. *Crossing the Threshold of Hope*, London: Jonathan Cape, 1994.

WOJTYLA, Karol. *Valutazioni sulla Possibilità di Costruire L'Etica Cristiana Sulle Basi del Sistema di Max Scheler*. Rome: Logos, 1980.

_____. *Love and Responsibility*. London: Collins, 1981.

_____. *Alle Fonti di Rinnovamento: Studio sull Attuazione del Concilio Vaticano II*. Vatican City: Libreria Editrice Vaticana, 1981.

_____. *Persona e Atto*. Vatican City: Libreria Editrice Vaticana, 1982.

_____. *I Fondamenti dell'Ordine Etico*, second edition. Vatican City, Edizioni CSEO / Libreria Editrice Vaticana, 1989.

---

[1]The material of Karol Wojtyla / Pope John Paul II is entered under the publication name of the author, the effect being that the material is treated as it would be if John Paul II and Karol Wojtyla were two distinct authors. *John Paul II, Pope* comes before *Wojtyla, Karol* for reasons of alphabetical order only, and it is not intended to imply that there is any lack of continuity in the thought of our subject.

2. Articles

WOJTYLA, Karol. "Participation et Alienation," in *The Yearbook of Phenomenological Research: Analecta Husserliana*, Vol. 6, 61-74. Dordrecht: D. Reidel, 1977.

_____. "Teoria-Prassi: Una Tema Umano e Cristiano," *Incontri Culturali (Rome)*, 10 (1977): 31-41.

_____. "The Acting Person," in *The Yearbook of Phenomenological Research: Analecta Husserliana*, Vol. 10, 3-367. Dordrecht: D. Reidel, 1979.

_____. "The Person: Subject and Community," *The Review of Metaphysics*, XXXIII, 2 , No. 30, Dec. 1979: 273-308.

_____. "Thomistic Personalism," in *Person and Community: Selected Essays*, Catholic Thought from Lublin, 4, translated by Theresa Sandok, OSM, New York: Peter Lang, 1993: 165-176.

_____. "The Problem of the Theory of Morality," in *Person and Community: Selected Essays*, Catholic Thought from Lublin, 4, translated by Theresa Sandok, OSM. New York: Peter Lang, 1993, 129-161.

3. Encyclical Letters and Major Documents of Pope John Paul II

JOHN PAUL II, POPE. *Redemptor Hominis*. London: CTS, 1980.

_____.*Dives in Misericordia*. London: CTS, 1980.

_____.*Familiaris Consortio*. London CTS, 1981.

_____.*Laborem Exercens*. London: CTS, 1981.

_____.*Salvifici Doloris*. London: CTS, 1984.

_____.*Dominum et Vivificantem*. London: CTS, 1986.

_____.*Sollicitudo Rei Socialis*. London: CTS, 1988.

_____.*Mulieris Dignitatem*. Dublin: Veritas, 1988.

_____.*Redemptoris Missio*. Vatican City: Libreria Editrice Vaticana, 1991.

_____.*Centesimus Annus*. Vatican City: Libreria Editrice Vaticana, 1991.

_____.*Veritatis Splendor*. Vatican City: Libreria Editrice Vaticana, 1993.

4. Written Messages of Pope John Paul II
JOHN PAUL II, POPE. Message to the Inter-Regional Meeting of Southern African Bishops, 15/8/'84, *Acta Apostolicae Sedis* 77 (1985): 157-160.

_____. Message for World Peace Day (1986), 8/12/'85, *Acta Apostolicae Sedis* 78 (1986): 278-288.

_____. Message for World Peace Day (1987), 8/12/'86, *Acta Apostolicae Sedis* 79 (1987): 45-57.

_____. Message for World Communications Day, 24/1/'88, *Acta Apostolicae Sedis* 80 (1988): 1358-1361.

_____. Letter to all Catholic Bishops concerning the Situation in The Lebanon, 7/9/'89, *Acta Apostolicae Sedis* 82 (1990): 60-63.

_____. Letter to the Islamic World, concerning the Lebanese People, 7/9/'89, *Acta Apostolicae Sedis* 82 (1990): 82-83.

_____. Letter to the Director General of FAO, on the Occasion of World Food Day, 10/10/'90, *Acta Apostolicae Sedis* 83 (1991): 361-363.

_____. Message to the Secretary General of the United Nations, 21/3/'91, *Acta Apostolicae Sedis* 84 (1992): 75-76.

_____. *Le Responsibilità dei Cattolici di fronte alle Sfide dell'Attuale Momento Storico*, (Letter to the People of Italy), 13/1/'94, Supplement to *Osservatore Romano*. Vatican City: Osservatore Romano, 1994.

5. Addresses and Homilies of Pope John Paul II
JOHN PAUL II, POPE. Address to the Presidency of the European
Parliament, 5/4/'79, *Acta Apostolicae Sedis* 71 (1979): 604-606.

_____. Address to the Diplomatic Corps, Brasilia, Brazil, 30/6/'80, *The
Holy See at the Service of Peace*, ed. Sr. Marjorie Keenan, 164-166.
Vatican City: Pontifical Council for Justice and Peace, 1988.

_____. Angelus Address, St. Peter's Square, 27/9/'81, *Insegnamenti di
Giovanni Paolo II* IV-2 (1981): 307-313. Vatican City: Libreria Editrice
Vaticana, 1982.

_____. Address to the I.L.O., Geneva, 15/6/'82, *Acta Apostolicae Sedis*
74 (1982): 992-1006.

_____. Address to Workers Delegates, Palais des Nations, Geneva,
15/6/'82, *Insegnamenti di Giovanni Paolo II* V-2 (1982): 2283-2285.
Vatican City: Libreria Editrice Vaticana, 1983.

_____. Address to Civil and Ecclesiastical Authorities, Rieti, Italy,
2/1/'83, *Insegnamenti di Giovanni Paolo II* VI-1 (1983): 23-27. Vatican
City: Libreria Editrice Vaticana, 1984.

_____. Address to the Diplomatic Corps, Vatican, 15/1/'83, *The Holy See
at the Service of Peace*, ed. Sr. Marjorie Keenan, 71-82. Vatican City:
Pontifical Council for Justice and Peace, 1988.

_____. Address to Ambassador of Costa Rica, 26/5/'83, *Acta Apostolicae
Sedis* 75 (1983): 834-835.

_____. Address to Workers, Vienna, 12/9/'83, *Osservatore Romano*,
Weekly Edition in English, Vatican City, 1983, no. 40, 5-6.

_____. Address to the Ambassador of Senegal, 9/1/'84, *Acta Apostolicae
Sedis* 76 (1984): 576-579.

_____. Address to the Ambassador of Thailand, 9/3/'84, *Acta Apostolicae
Sedis* 76 (1984): 713-714.

_____. Address to the President of Italy, 2/6/'84, *Acta Apostolicae Sedis* 76 (1984): 955-958.

_____. Address to Government Officials and Diplomatic Corps, Ottawa, Canada, 19/9/'84, *The Holy See at the Service of Peace*, ed. Sr. Marjorie Keenan, 201-206. Vatican City: Pontifical Council for Justice and Peace, 1988.

_____. Address to Parliamentarians of the Western European Union, 30/10/'84, *Acta Apostolicae Sedis* 77 (1985): 362-364.

_____. Christmas Day Greetings, St. Peter's Square, 25/12/'84, *Acta Apostolicae Sedis* 77, 1985: 377-381.

_____. Address to the Diplomatic Corps, Vatican, 12/1/'85, *The Holy See at the Service of Peace*, ed. Sr. Marjorie Keenan, 93-105. Vatican City: Pontifical Council for Justice and Peace, 1988.

_____. Address to the People of the Guasmo Region, Ecuador, 1/2/'85, *Acta Apostolicae Sedis* 77 (1985): 866-869.

_____. Address to Farmers, Cuzco, Peru, 3/2/'85, *Acta Apostolicae Sedis* 77 (1985): 874-881.

_____. Address to the Institutions of the E.C., Luxembourg, 15/5/'85, *Acta Apostolicae Sedis* 78 (1986): 531-536.

_____. Address to the Ambassador of India, 10/1/'86, *Acta Apostolicae Sedis* 78 (1986): 639-641.

_____. Address to the Diplomatic Corps, Vatican, 11/1/'86, *The Holy See at the Service of Peace*, ed. Sr. Marjorie Keenan, 106-119. Vatican City: Pontifical Council for Justice and Peace, 1988.

_____. Address to the Ambassador of Norway, Vatican, 20/1/'86, *Insegnamenti di Giovanni Paolo II* IX-1 (1986), 156-159. Vatican City: Libreria Editrice Vaticana, 1987.

_____. Address at the Raj Ghat Monument, Delhi, India, 1/2/'86, *Acta*

Apostolicae Sedis 78 (1986): 737-740.

_____. Homily at Bombay, India, 9/2/'86, *Acta Apostolicae Sedis* 78 (1986): 771-777.

_____. Address to the Diplomatic Corps, Canberra, Australia, 25/11/'86, *The Holy See at the Service of Peace*, ed. Sr. Marjorie Keenan, 223-225. Vatican City: Pontifical Council for Justice and Peace, 1988.

_____. Address to Workers, Sydney, Australia, 26/11/'86, *Acta Apostolicae Sedis* 79 (1987): 949-953.

_____. Address to Representatives of the Association of Catholic Workers, 6/12/'86, *Insegnamenti di Giovanni Paolo II* IX-2 (1986), 1855-1860. Vatican City: Libreria Editrice Vaticana, 1987.

_____. Address to the Ambassador of Madagascar, Vatican, 5/1/'87, *Acta Apostolicae Sedis* 79 (1987): 1158-1161.

_____. Address to the Diplomatic Corps, Vatican, 10/1/'87, *The Holy See at the Service of Peace*, ed. Sr. Marjorie Keenan, 120-130. Vatican City: Pontifical Council for Justice and Peace, 1988.

_____. Address to Workers Conference on *Laborem Exercens*, 17/1/'87, *Acta Apostolicae Sedis* 79 (1987): 1195-1201.

_____. Address to the Bishops of Piemonte, 31/1/'87, *Acta Apostolicae Sedis* 79 (1987): 1230-1235.

_____. Address to the Regional Council of Lazio, 7/2/'87, *Insegnamenti di Giovanni Paolo II* X-1 (1987): 285-288. Vatican City: Libreria Editrice Vaticana, 1988.

_____. Address to the Ambassador of Sweden, Vatican, 9/2/'87, *Insegnamenti di Giovanni Paolo II*, X-1 (1987): 310-312. Vatican City: Libreria Editrice Vaticana, 1988.

_____. Address to the Ambassador of Australia, 28/3/'87, *Insegnamenti di Giovanni Paolo II*, X-1 (1987): 852-854. Vatican City: Libreria Editrice

Vaticana, 1988.

_____. Address at the University of Santiago, Chile, 3/4/'87, *Insegnamenti di Giovanni Paolo II*, X-1 (1987): 998-1006. Vatican City: Libreria Editrice Vaticana, 1988.

_____. Homily at Punta Arenas, Chile, 4/4/'87, *Insegnamenti di Giovanni Paolo II*, XI-1 (1987): 1034-1042. Vatican City: Libreria Editrice Vaticana, 1988.

_____. Address at Buenos Aires, Argentina, 6/4/'87, *The Holy See at the Service of Peace*, ed. Sr. Marjorie Keenan, 226-227. Vatican City: Pontifical Council for Justice and Peace, 1988.

_____. Homily at Bahia Blanca, 7/4/'87, Argentina, *Insegnamenti di Giovanni Paolo II*, X-1 (1987): 1125-1133. Vatican City: Libreria Editrice Vaticana, 1988.

_____. Address to the Ambassador of Algeria, 4/6/'87, *Insegnamenti di Giovanni Paolo II*, X-2 (1987): 1956-1960. Vatican City: Libreria Editrice Vaticana, 1988.

_____. Address to the Sea-faring people, Gdynia, Poland, 11/6/'87, *Osservatore Romano*, Weekly Edition in English, Vatican City, 1987, no.30, 7-8.

_____. Address to Representatives of Charitable Organisations, San Antonio, Texas, 13/9/'87, *Insegnamenti di Giovanni Paolo II*, X-3 (1987), 466-473. Vatican City: Libreria Editrice Vaticana, 1988.

_____. Address to the People of Detroit, U.S.A., 19/9/'87, *Insegnamenti di Giovanni Paolo II*, X-3 (1987): 662-674. Vatican City: Libreria Editrice Vaticana, 1988.

_____. Address to Participants in a Conference on Human Work, 20/11/'87, *Insegnamenti di Giovanni Paolo II*, X-3 (1987): 1159-1165. Vatican City: Libreria Editrice Vaticana, 1988.

_____. Address to the Ambassador of The Sudan, 7/1/'88, *Insegnamenti di Giovanni Paolo II*, XI-1 (1988): 49-51. Vatican City: Libreria Editrice Vaticana, 1989.

_____. Address at the General Audience, Vatican, 10/2/'88, *Insegnamenti di Giovanni Paolo II*, XI-1 (1988): 394-398. Vatican City: Libreria Editrice Vaticana, 1989.

_____. Address to ATAC Transport Workers, Rome, 19/3/'88, *Acta Apostolicae Sedis* 80 (1988) 1333-1339.

_____. Address to Workers, Verona, Italy, 17/4/'88, *Insegnamenti di Giovanni Paolo II*, XI-1 (1988): 936-942. Vatican City: Libreria Editrice Vaticana, 1988.

_____. Address to the Ambassador of Japan, 29/4/'88, *Acta Apostolicae Sedis* 80 (1988): 1464-1466.

_____. Address to Workers, Civita Castellana, 1/5/'88, *Acta Apostolicae Sedis* 80 (1988): 1527-1532.

_____. Address at Barrios la Concordia, Melo, Uruguay, 8/5/'88,*Insegnamenti di Giovanni Paolo II*, XI-2 (1988): 1200-1207. Vatican City: Libreria Editrice Vaticana, 1990.

_____. Address to Farm Workers and Miners, Oruro, Bolivia, 11/5/'88, *Acta Apostolicae Sedis* 80 (1988): 1566-1572.

_____. Address to Youth, Cochabamba, 11/5/'88, Bolivia, *Acta Apostolicae Sedis* 80 (1988): 1573-1580.

_____. Address to Intellectuals and Business People, Santa Cruz, Bolivia, 12/5/'88, *Insegnamenti di Giovanni Paolo II*, XI-2 (1988): 1339-1348. Vatican City: Libreria Editrice Vaticana, 1990.

_____. Homily at Santa Cruz Airport, Bolivia, 13/5/'88, *Insegnamenti di Giovanni Paolo II*, XI-2 (1988): 1365-1374. Vatican City: Libreria Editrice Vaticana, 1990.

_____. Address to Representatives of Business and Cultural Life, Lima,

Peru, 15/5/'88, *Insegnamenti di Giovanni Paolo II*, XI-2 (1988): 1448-1458. Vatican City: Libreria Editrice Vaticana, 1990.

_____. Address to Government Officials and Diplomatic Corps, Asuncion, Paraguay, 16/5/'88, *The Holy See at the Service of Peace*, ed. Sr. Marjorie Keenan, 231-234. Vatican City: Pontifical Council for Justice and Peace, 1988.

_____. Address to Civil Leaders and Representatives of Economic and Cultural Life, Asuncion, Paraguay, 17/5/'88, *Acta Apostolicae Sedis* 80 (1988): 1612-1618.

_____. Homily at a Mass for Workers, Villaricca, Paraguay, 17/5/'88, *Insegnamenti di Giovanni Paolo II*, XI-2 (1988): 1505-1514. Vatican City: Libreria Editrice Vaticana, 1990.

_____. Address to the Citizens of Castel San Giovanni, Italy, 5/6/'88, *Insegnamenti di Giovanni Paolo II*, XI-2 (1988): 1811-1813. Vatican City: Libreria Editrice Vaticana, 1990.

_____. Address to the Civil Authorities, Reggio Calabria, 12/6/'88, *Insegnamenti di Giovanni Paolo II*, XI-2 (1988): 1986-1989. Vatican City: Libreria Editrice Vaticana, 1990.

_____. Address to U.S. Bishops on *Ad Limina* Visit, 9/9/'88, *Acta Apostolicae Sedis* 81 (1989): 176-181.

_____. Address to the Diplomatic Corps, Harare, Zimbabwe, 11/9/'88, *The Holy See at the Service of Peace*, ed. Sr. Marjorie Keenan, 238-241. Vatican City: Pontifical Council for Justice and Peace, 1988.

_____. Address to the Bishops of Mozambique, 18/9/'88, *Acta Apostolicae Sedis* 81 (1989): 359-368.

_____. Homily at Maputo, Mozambique, 18/9/'88, *Acta Apostolicae Sedis* 81 (1989): 350-359.

_____. Address to Canadian Bishops on *Ad Limina* Visit, 27/9/'88, *Acta Apostolicae Sedis* 81 (1989): 198-202.

_____. Address to a Plenary Session of the Council of Europe, Strasbourg, 8/10/'88, *Acta Apostolicae Sedis* 81 (1989): 683-686.

_____. Address to the Ambassador of Bangladesh, 10/11/'88, *Acta Apostolicae Sedis* 81 (1989): 637-639.

_____. Address to the Ambassador of Burundi, Vatican, 18/11/'88, *Acta Apostolicae Sedis* 81 (1989): 663-665.

_____. Address to members of the Union of Catholic Jurists of Italy, 10/12/'88, *Acta Apostolicae Sedis* 81 (1989):763-766.

_____. Address to the Ambassador of Ecuador, 5/1/'89, *Acta Apostolicae Sedis* 81 (1989): 845-847.

_____. Address to the Bishops of Guatemala on *Ad Limina* Visit, 20/1/'89, *Acta Apostolicae Sedis* 81 (1989): 869-876.

_____. Address to the President and Members of the Council of the Region of Lazio, 20/2/'89, *Acta Apostolicae Sedis* 81 (1989): 958-960.

_____. Address to the Ambassador of Malawi, 13/4/'89, *Acta Apostolicae Sedis* 81 (1989): 1129-1131.

_____. Address to Youth, Antananariva, Madagascar, 29/4/'89, *Insegnamenti di Giovanni Paolo II*, XII-1 (1989): 980-990. Vatican City: Libreria Editrice Vaticana, 1991.

_____. Homily at Antananariva, Madagascar, 30/4/'89, *Acta Apostolicae Sedis* 81 (1989): 1231-1237.

_____. Address to U.S. President George Bush, 27/5/'89, *Acta Apostolicae Sedis* 81 (1989): 1314-1316.

_____. Address to the Diplomatic Corps, Copenhagen, Denmark, 7/6/'89, *Acta Apostolicae Sedis* 81 (1989): 1357-1361.

_____. Address to the Ambassador of Costa Rica, 22/6/'89, *Acta Apostolicae Sedis* 82 (1990): 70-72.

_____. Address to Seafarers, Fishermen and Port Workers, Gaeta, 25/6/'89, *Insegnamenti di Giovanni Paolo II*, XII-1 (1989). Vatican City: Libreria Editrice Vaticana, 1990, 1758-1762.

_____. Address to the Bishops of Lesotho on *Ad Limina* Visit, 15/9/'89, *Acta Apostolicae Sedis* 82 (1990): 276-280.

_____. Address to Participants in a Study Week of the Pontifical Academy of Sciences, 27/10/'89, *Insegnamenti di Giovanni Paolo II*, XII-2 (1989): 1046-1051. Vatican City: Libreria Editrice Vaticana, 1991.

_____. Address to Workers, Taranto, Italy, 28/10/'89, *Acta Apostolicae Sedis* 82 (1990): 577-581.

_____. Address to Members of the Confederation of Italian Cooperatives, and the Federation of Rural and Trade Credit Unions, 11/11/'89, *Insegnamenti di Giovanni Paolo II*, XII-2 (1989): 1213-1216. Vatican City: Libreria Editrice Vaticana, 1991.

_____. Address to W. German Bishops on *Ad Limina* Visit, 14/11/'89, *Osservatore Romano*, Weekly Edition in English, Vatican City, 1989, no.49, 6.

_____. Address to the Participants in the 25th. Plenary Meeting of FAO, Rome, 16/11/'89, *Acta Apostolicae Sedis* 82 (1990): 670-674.

_____. Address to the Ambassador of Argentina, 30/11/'89, *Acta Apostolicae Sedis* 82 (1990): 688-690.

_____. Address to Colombian Bishops on *Ad Limina* Visit, 30/11/'89, *Acta Apostolicae Sedis* 82 (1990): 690-695.

_____. Address to President Mikhail Gorbaciov, 1/12/'89, *Acta Apostolicae Sedis* 82 (1990): 696-699.

_____. Address to the Algerian Ambassador, 4/12/'89, *Acta Apostolicae Sedis* 82 (1990): 699-701.

_____. Address to the Ambassador of Tanzania, 12/1/'90, *Acta*

Apostolicae Sedis 82 (1990): 798-800.

_____. Address to the Diplomatic Corps, Vatican, 13/1/'90, *Acta Apostolicae Sedis* 82 (1990): 860-870.

_____. Address to the Civic Authorities, Rome, 20/1/'90, *Acta Apostolicae Sedis* 82 (1990): 884-887.

_____. Address at the Airport of Praia, Cape Verde, 25/1/'90, *Insegnamenti di Giovanni Paolo II*, Vol. XIII-1 (1990): 178-184. Vatican City: Libreria Editrice Vaticana, 1992.

_____. Address at the Airport at Guinea-Bissau, 27/1/'90, *Osservatore Romano*, Weekly Edition in English, Vatican City, 1990, no. 7, 7-9.

_____. Address to Youth, Bomako, Mali, 28/1/'90, *Insegnamenti di Giovanni Paolo II*, XIII-1 (1990): 279-283. Vatican City: Libreria Editrice Vaticana, 1992.

_____. Address to the Civic Authorities, Ougadougou, Burkina Fasu, 29/1/'90, *Acta Apostolicae Sedis* 82 (1990): 816-821.

_____. Address to the Diplomatic Corps, N'Djamena, Chad, 1/2/'90, *Acta Apostolicae Sedis* 82 (1990): 821-825.

_____. Address to Participants in the Plenary Meeting of the Pontifical Council of Health-care Administrators, 9/2/'90, *Acta Apostolicae Sedis* 82 (1990): 839-899.

_____. Address to the Ambassador of Bolivia, 23/2/'90, *Acta Apostolicae Sedis* 82 (1990): 943-945.

_____. Address to Workers at the Lancia Plant, Ivrea, Italy, 19/3/'90, *Insegnamenti di Giovanni Paolo II*, XIII-1 (1990): 699-705. Vatican City: Libreria Editrice Vaticana, 1992.

_____. Address to the Ambassador of South Korea, 30/3/'90, *Acta Apostolicae Sedis* 82 (1990): 983-985.

Bibliography 255

_____. Address to the Ambassador of Brazil, 2/4/'90, *Acta Apostolicae Sedis* 82 (1990): 1386-1389.

_____. Address to the President of Portugal, 27/4/'90, *Acta Apostolicae Sedis* 82 (1990): 1522-1526.

_____. Address to Workers, Malta, 26/5/'90, *Acta Apostolicae Sedis* 83 (1991): 59-64.

_____. Address to Brazilian Bishops on *Ad Limina* Visit, 23/6/'90, *Osservatore Romano*, Weekly Edition in English, Vatican City, 1990, no. 28, 9-10.

_____. Address to the Diplomatic Corps, Dar-es-Salaam, Tanzania, 1/9/'90, *Acta Apostolicae Sedis* 83 (1991): 209-213.

_____. Address to Bishops of the Philippines on *Ad Limina* Visit, 18/9/'90, *Acta Apostolicae Sedis* 83 (1991), 355-358.

_____. Address to Participants in the IX International Thomistic Congress, 29/9/'90, *Acta Apostolicae Sedis* 83 (1991): 404-410.

_____. Address to Youth, St. Paul's Stadium, Naples, Italy, 10/11/'90, *Insegnamenti di Giovanni Paolo II*, Vol. XIII-2. Vatican City: Libreria Editrice Vaticana, 1990: 1075-1080.

_____. Address to Business-people, Naples, Italy, 11/11/'90, *Insegnamenti di Giovanni Paolo II*, XIII-2 (1990). Vatican City: Libreria Editrice Vaticana, 1990, 1118-1124.

_____. Address to the Farming Community, Aversa, Italy, 13/11/'90, *Acta Apostolicae Sedis* 83 (1991): 657-660.

_____. Address to the Participants in the Plenary Meeting of the Council *Cor Unum*, 19/11/'90, *Acta Apostolicae Sedis* 83 (1991): 673-675.

_____. Address to the Management and Staff of Generali, 1/12/'90, *Insegnamenti di Giovanni Paolo II*, XIII-2 (1990): 1350-1351. Vatican City: Libreria Editrice Vaticana, 1992.

_____. Address to the Ambassador of Venezuela, 15/12/'90, *Acta Apostolicae Sedis* 83 (1991): 729-732.

_____. Address to the Bishops of Taiwan on *Ad Limina* Visit, 15/12/'90, *Acta Apostolicae Sedis* 83 (1991): 732-737.

_____. Address to the Ambassador of The Lebanon, 17/12/'90, *Acta Apostolicae Sedis* 83 (1991): 738-740.

_____. Address to the Ambassador of Nicaragua, 3/1/'91, *Acta Apostolicae Sedis* 83 (1991): 754-756.

_____. Address to the Ambassador of Zimbabwe, 17/1/'91, *Insegnamenti di Giovanni Paolo II*, XIV-1 (1991): 123-125. Vatican City: Libreria Editrice Vaticana, 1993.

_____. Address to Italian Bishops on *Ad Limina* Visit, 26/1/'91, *Acta Apostolicae Sedis* 83 (1991): 943-947.

_____. Address to Italian Bishops on *Ad Limina* Visit, 1/3/'91, *Acta Apostolicae Sedis* 83 (1991), 982-987.

_____. Address to Participants in a Congress organised by CEI to mark the Centenary of Rerum Novarum, 2/3/'91, *Insegnamenti di Giovanni Paolo II*, XIV-1 (1991): 446-448. Vatican City: Libreria Editrice Vaticana, 1993.

_____. Address at a Meeting of Cardinals and Bishops of the Middle East, 4/3/'91, *Acta Apostolicae Sedis* 83 (1991): 1024-1027.

_____. Address to a UNIAPAC Pilgrim Group, 9/3/'91, *Acta Apostolicae Sedis* 83 (1991): 1031-1034.

_____. Address to participants in the 41st, Social Studies Week, 5/4/'91, *Acta Apostolicae Sedis* 84 (1992): 17-21.

_____. Homily at Terceira, Azores, Portugal, 11/5/'91, *Insegnamenti di Giovanni Paolo II*, XIV-1 (1991), 1192-1198. Vatican City: Libreria Editrice Vaticana, 1993.

_____. Address to those participating in a Convention on the Encyclical Letter Rerum Novarum, 15/5/'91, *Acta Apostolicae Sedis* 84 (1992): 144-151.

_____. Address to the Ambassador of The Philippines, 18/5/'91, *Acta Apostolicae Sedis* 84 (1992): 152-155.

_____. Address to Participants in the Fourteenth General Assembly of Caritas Internationalis, 28/5/'91, *Acta Apostolicae Sedis* 84 (1992): 293-296.

_____. Address to the Ambassador of Iran, 20/6/'91, *Acta Apostolicae Sedis* 84 (1992): 306-308.

_____. Address during a Visit to the Hope Project, Cracow, 13/8/'91, *Insegnamenti di Giovanni Paolo II*, XIV-2 (1991): 211-217. Vatican City: Libreria Editrice Vaticana, 1993.

_____. Address to the Bishops of Angola, and the Prince Islands and St. Thomas Islands, on *Ad Limina* Visit, 5/9/'91, *Acta Apostolicae Sedis* 84 (1992): 576-579.

_____. Address to Participants in a Convention on Gypsy Studies, 26/9/'91, *Insegnamenti di Giovanni Paolo II*, XIV-2 (1991): 656-659. Vatican City: Libreria Editrice Vaticana, 1993.

_____. Address to Participants in a World Congress of those involved in the Pastoral Care of Migrants and Travellers, 5/10/'91, *Acta Apostolicae Sedis*, 84 (1992), 860-863.

_____. Address to Participants in a Congress organised by the Bishops' Commission of the European Community, 11/10/'91, *Insegnamenti di Giovanni Paolo II*, XIV-2 (1991): 803-806. Vatican City: Libreria Editrice Vaticana, 1993.

_____. Address to the Ambassador of Santa Lucia, 28/10/'91, *Acta Apostolicae Sedis* 84 (1992): 959-961.

_____. Address to the Ambassador of Indonesia, 7/11/'91, *Acta*

Apostolicae Sedis 84 (1992): 963-966.

_____. Address to the Participants in a Convention on Population and Food, organised by the Pontifical Academy of Sciences, 22/11/'91, *Acta Apostolicae Sedis* 84 (1992): 1118-1123.

C. SECONDARY SOURCES

1. Books
ARISTOTLE. *Nicomachean Ethics*, in *The Works of Aristotle*, Vol. 2, translated by W.D. Ross, Great Books of the Western World, ed. Robert Maynard Hutchins, no.9. Chicago: Encyclopaedia Brittanica, 1952.

BENJAMIN, Jean-Marie. *Jean Paul II: L'Octobre Romain*. Paris: Editions France-Empire, 1979.

BUTTIGLIONE, Rocco. *Il Pensiero di Karol Wojtyla*, Milan: Jaca Book, 1982.

CICERO, Marcus Tullius. *Laelius De Amicitia*, ed. G.B. Bonino. Turin: Paravia, 1936.

CRAIG, Mary. *Man from a Far Country*. London: Hodder and Stoughton, 1979.

DUPUY, Maurice. *La Philosophie de Max Scheler. Son Evolution et son Unité*, in two volumes. Paris: Presses Universitaires de France, 1959.

DURKHEIM, Emile. *Les Regles de la Méthode Sociologique*. Paris: Alcan, 1919.

_____.*Sociologie et Philosophie*. Paris: Alcan, 1924.

_____. *De la Division du Travail Social*, 7th. ed., Paris: Presses Universitaires de France, 1960.

EPICTETUS, *Discourses*, translated by George Long, in *Lucretius,*

Epictetus, Marcus Aurelius, Great Books of the Western World, no. 12, ed. Robert Maynard Hutchins. Chicago: Encyclopaedia Brittanica, 1952.

FRANKL, Viktor E., *Man's Search for Meaning*, New York: Washington Square Press, 1984.

KELLY, Eugene. *Max Scheler*. Boston: Twayne, 1977.

LONERGAN, Bernard. *De Constitutione Christi Ontologica et Psychologica*, Rome: Gregorian University Press, 1974.

_____. *Insight*. London: Darton, Longman and Todd, 1983.

LURIA, A.R. *Higher Cortical Functions in Man*. London: Tavistock, 1966.

MARCUS AURELIUS, *Meditations*, translated by George Long, in *Lucretius, Epictetus, Marcus Aurelius*, Great Books of the Western World, no. 12, ed., Robert Maynard Hutchins. Encyclopaedia Brittanica, 1982.

MERSCH, Emile. *Le Corps Mystique du Christ. Etudes de Theologie Historique*, with a preface by Fr. J. Lebreton. Paris: Desclee, 1936.

MOIX, C. *La Pensee d'Emmanuel Mounier*. Paris: Editions du Seuil, 1960.

MOUNIER, Emmanuel. *Le Personnalisme*, second edition. Paris: Presses Universitaires de France, 1951.

_____. *Révolution Personnaliste et Communautaire*, in *Oeuvres de Mounier*, Vol. 1. Paris: Editions du Seuil, 1960.

_____. *De La Propriété Capitaliste à la Propriété Humaine*, in *Oeuvres de Mounier*, Vol. 1, Paris: Editions du Seuil, 1960.

_____. *Traité du Caractère*, in *Oeuvres de Mounier*, Vol 2. Paris: Editions du Seuil, 1961.

_____. *Qu'est ce que le Personnalisme?*, in *Oeuvres de Mounier*, Vol. 3. Paris: Editions du Seuil, 1962.

_____. *Le Communisme Parmi Nous*, in *Oeuvres de Mounier*, Vol. 4, Paris: Editions du Seuil, 1963.

MULCAHY, Richard E., *The Economics of Heinrich Pesch*. New York: Henry Holt, 1952.

MUNERA VELEZ, Dario. *Personalismo Etico de Participacion de Karol Wojtyla*. Medellin: Universidad Pontificia Bolivariana, 1988.

NOTA, John. *Max Scheler, the Man and his Work*. Chicago: Franciscan Herald Press, 1983.

PADELLARO, Nazzareno. *A Portrait of Pius XII*, translated by Michael Derrick. London: Catholic Book Club, 1956.

RANLY, Ernest W. *Scheler's Phenomenology of Community*. Martinus Nijhoff, The Hague, 1966.

SCHELER, Max. *The Nature of Sympathy*, translated by Peter Heath, with a general introduction to Max Scheler's works by W. Stark, London: Routledge and Kegan Paul. New Haven: Yale University Press, 1954.

_____. *Das Ressentiment im Aufbau der Moralen*, in *Gesammelte Werke*, Vol. 3, ed. Maria Scheler. Berne: Francke, 1955.

_____. *On the Eternal in Man*, translated by Bernard Noble. London: SCM Press, 1960.

_____. *Formalism in Ethics and non-Formal Ethics of Values*. A new attempt toward the Foundation of an Ethical Personalism, translated by Manfred S. Frings and Roger L. Funk. Evanston: Northwestern University Press, 1973.

SENECA, Lucius A. *Epistulae ad Lucilium*, Vol. 1. Pisa: Giardini, 1983.

STEINBECK, John. *The Grapes of Wrath*. (New York: Penguin Modern Classics, 1951).

THOMAS AQUINAS. *Summa Theologiae*, in 3 Vols. New York: Benziger

Bros. Inc., 1948.

UTZ, Alfred, F. *Entre le neo-liberalisme et le neomarxisme. Recherche philosophique d'une Troisieme Voie.* Paris: Beauchesne, 1976.

WILLIAMS, George H. *The Mind of John Paul II: Origins of his Thought and Action.* New York: Seabury, 1981.

2. Encyclical Letters and Major Church Documents Prior to Pope John Paul II

JOHN XXIII, POPE. *Mater et Magistra,* in *Proclaiming Justice and Peace,* eds. Michael Walsh and Brian Davies. London: Collins 1991.

_____. *Pacem in Terris,* in *Proclaiming Justice and Peace,* eds. Michael Walsh and Brian Davies. London: Collins 1991.

LEO XIII, POPE. *Rerum Novarum,* Centenary Study Edition, with introduction and notes by Joseph Kirwan. London: CTS, 1991.

PAUL VI, POPE. *Populorum Progressio,* in *Proclaiming Justice and Peace,* eds. Michael Walsh and Brian Davies. London: Collins 1991.

_____. *Octagesimo Adveniens,* in *Proclaiming Justice and Peace,* eds. Michael Walsh and Brian Davies. London: Collins 1991.

_____. *Evangelii Nuntiandi,* in *Proclaiming Justice and Peace,* eds. Michael Walsh and Brian Davies. London: Collins 1991.

PIUS XI, POPE. *Quadragesimo Anno,* in *Proclaiming Justice and Peace,* eds. Michael Walsh and Brian Davies. London: Collins 1991.

PIUS XII, POPE. *Summi Pontificatus,* Latin text, in *Acta Apostolicae Sedis,* 31 (1939): 413-453.

_____. *Summi Pontificatus,* English text, in *Acta Apostolicae Sedis,* 31 (1939): 538-564.

_____. *Mystici Corporis Christi.* London: CTS, 1943.

SECOND VATICAN ECUMENICAL COUNCIL, *Pastoral Constitution on the Church in the Modern World: Gaudium et Spes*, in *The Documents of Vatican II*, ed. Walter M. ABBOTT. London: Geoffrey Chapman, 1966.

WORLD SYNOD OF BISHOPS. *Justice in the World*, (Document of the Third Synod, 30th. Sept. – 6th. Sept. 1971), in *Proclaiming Justice and Peace*, eds. Michael Walsh and Brian Davies. London: Collins 1991.

3. Written Messages and Letters of Other Popes
PAUL VI, POPE. Message for World Peace Day, 1977, 8/12/'76, *Insegnamenti di Paolo VI* XIV (1977): 1021-1028. Vatican City: Libreria Editrice Vaticana, 1977.

4. Articles
AUBERT, Roger. "L'Encyclique *Rerum Novarum*, Point d'Aboutissement d'Une Lente Maturation," in *De* Rerum Novarum *a* Centesimus Annus, 5-26. Vatican City: Conseil Pontificale *Justice et Paix*, 1991.

BAUM, Gregory. "Liberal Capitalism," in *The Logic of Solidarity: Commentaries on Pope John Paul II's Encyclical* On Social Concern, eds. Gregory Baum and Robert Ellsberg, 75-89. New York: Orbis Books, 1989.

_____. "Structures of Sin," in *The Logic of Solidarity: Commentaries on Pope John Paul II's Encyclical* On Social Concern, eds. Gregory Baum and Robert Ellsberg, 110-126. New York: Orbis Books, 1989.

CAMPANINI, Giorgio. "Capitalismo, Socialismo, 'terza via'," *Quaderno Filosofico*, 8 (1983): 213-224.

COLOMBO, Arrigo. "La 'Terza Via', una Proposta Ambigua," *Quaderno Filosofico*, 8 (1983): 173-185.

CONLEY, John J. "The Philosophical Foundations of the Thought of Pope John Paul II: A Response," in *The Thought of Pope John Paul II*, ed. John M. Mc. Dermott, 23-28. Rome: Gregorian University Press, 1993.

DELOGU, Antonio. "Non vi è terza (nè altra) via nell' 'Esprit' di Mounier", *Quaderno Filosofico*, 8 (1983): 186-201.

DORR, Donal. "The New Social Encyclical," *The Furrow*, 32 (1981), no. 11: 705-710.

_____. "Solidarity and Integral Human Development," in *The Logic of Solidarity: Commentaries on Pope John Paul II's Encyclical* On Social Concern, eds. Gregory Baum and Robert Ellsberg, 143-154. New York: Orbis Books, 1989.

DUNLOP, Francis N. "Scheler's Idea of Man. Phenomenology v Metaphysics in the Late Works" *Aletheia*, 2 (1981): 220-234.

GOREVAN, Patrick, "Max Scheler: Phenomenology and Beyond," in *At The Heart of the Real: Philosophical Essays in honour of Archbishop Desmond Connell*, ed. Fran O' Rourke, 285-294. Dublin: Academic Press, 1992.

GOULET, Denis. "The Search for Authentic Development," in *The Logic of Solidarity: Commentaries on Pope John Paul II's Encyclical* On Social Concern, eds. Gregory Baum and Robert Ellsberg, 127-142. New York: Orbis Books, 1989.

HARVANEK, Robert F. "The Philosophical Foundations of the Thought of Pope John Paul II," in *The Thought of Pope John Paul II*, ed. John M. Mc. Dermott 1-21. Rome: Gregorian University Press, 1993.

HEBBLETHWAITE, Peter. "Husserl, Scheler and Wojtyla. A Tale of Three Philosophers," *Heythrop Journal*, 27 (1986): 441-445.

IBANA, Rainer R.A. "The Essential Elements for the Possibility and Necessity of the Principle of Solidarity, according to Max Scheler", *Philosophy Today*, 33 (1989), No. 1: 42-55.

KALINOWSKI, Georges. "Karol Wojtyla face à Max Scheler, où l'origine de *Osoba i Czyn*," *Revue Thomiste*, 80 (1980): 456-465.

_____. "La Pensée Philosophique de Karol Wojtyla, et la Faculté de Philosophie de l'Université Catholique de Lublin," *Aletheia*, 4 (1988): 198-216.

LAND, Philip S. and Peter J. HENRIOT. "Towards a New Methodology in Catholic Social Teaching," in *The Logic of Solidarity: Commentaries on Pope John Paul II's Encyclical* On Social Concern, eds. Gregory Baum and Robert Ellsberg, 65-74. New York: Orbis Books, 1989.

MATTEUCCI, Ivana. "Sull'Epistemologia Sociologica di Durkheim: note introduttive," *Studi Urbinati/B*, 61 (1988): 463-477.

MAZOWIECKI, Tadeusz. "Sur le Personnalisme et le Dialogue," *Esprit*, 432 (1974): 241-247.

NELSON, Ralph. "Emmanuel Mounier between Proudhon and Marx," *Science et Esprit*, 31 (1979): 207-228.

PARENT, Rémi. "Solidarité, Communion, Parti-pris," *Studia Moralia*, 31/1 (1993): 103-131.

RIVAS, Exequiel, "La Solidaridad en la Ensenanza de Juan Pablo II," in *L'Antropologia Solidaristica nella* Centesimus Annus, Papers of an International Conference organised by ASCE and the Diocese of Rieti, 22-27 Oct. 1991, ed. Alfredo Luciani, 215-228. Milan: Editrice Massimo, 1992.

ROGGERONE, Giuseppe. "Temi da Riprendere," *Quaderno Filosofico* (Lecce) 8 (1983): 225-228.

SCHOOYANS, Michel. *"Centesimus Annus* et la *Sève Généreuse* de *Rerum Novarum," De* Rerum Novarum *a* Centesimus Annus, 27-72. Vatican City: Conseil Pontificale *Justice et Paix*, 1991.

SEIFERT, Joseph. "Karol Cardinal Wojtyla (Pope John Paul II) as philosopher and the Cracow-Lublin School of Philosophy", *Aletheia*, 2 (1981): 130-199.

SEIGEL, Jerrold. "Autonomy and Personality in Durkheim: An essay on Content and Method," *Journal of the History of Ideas*, 48 (1987): 483-507.

SERVERIN, Evelyne. "Propos sur l'Utilité. les Valeurs du Crime chez Marx et Durkheim," *Archives de Philosophie du Droit*, 26 (1981): 183-198.

SOBRINO, Jon. "Bearing with One Another in Faith," in J. Sobrino and J. Hernandez-Pico, *Theology of Christian Solidarity*, 1-45. New York: Orbis, 1985.

SPADER, Peter H. "Person, Acts and Meaning: Max Scheler's Insight," *The New Scholasticism*, 59 (1985): 200-212.

STYCZEN, Tadeusz. "Reply to Georges Kalinowski," *Aletheia*, 4 (1988): 217-255.

URICOECHEA, F. "La Theorie de la Solidaritè de Durkheim. Une Critique," *Cahiers Internationaux de Sociologie*, 66 (1979): 115-123.

VACEK, Edward V. "Contemporary Ethics and Scheler's Phenomenology of Community," *Philosophy Today*, 35 (1991), no. 2: 161-174.

WILDER, Alfred op. "Community of Persons in the thought of Karol Wojtyla," *Angelicum* 56 (1979): 211-244.

ZABLOCKI, Janusz. "The Reception of the Personalism of Mounier in Poland," Translated by Aleksandra Rodzinska, *Dialectics and Humanism*, 5 (1978): 145-162.

5. Addresses and Homilies of Other Popes

PAUL VI, POPE. Address to Mark the Closing of the Holy Year, 25/12/'75, in *Insegnamenti di Paolo VI* XIII (1975): 1564-1568. Vatican City: Libreria Editrice Vaticana, 1976.

PIUS XII, POPE. Radio Message to Celebrate the Fiftieth Anniversary of *Rerum Novarum*, 1/6/'41, *AAS* 33 (1941), 216-227.

_____. Christmas Message, 23/12/'50, *Acta Apostolicae Sedis*, 43 (1951): 49-59.

_____. Radio Message to Participants at the Congress of Christian Associations of Italian Workers, Milan, 1/5/'56, *Relations Humaines et Société Contemporaine: Synthèse Chrétienne Directives de S.S. Pie XII*, eds. Alfred F. UTZ and J.F. GRONER (French edition translated by A.

SAVIGNAT and H. Th. CONUS), 3 vols. 3440-3447. Paris / Fribourg: Editions St. Paul, 1956/63.

_____. Address to Participants at the First Congress of the International Association of the Economic Sciences, 9/9/'56, *Acta Apostolicae Sedis* 48 (1956) : 670-674.

_____. Address to Participants at an International Meeting of Catholic Organisations of Small and Medium-Sized Businesses, 8/10/'56, *Acta Apostolicae Sedis* 48 (1956): 798-801.

_____. Christmas Message, 23/12/'56, *Acta Apostolicae Sedis* 49 (1957): 5-22.

_____. Address to Participants at the General Assembly of the National Association of Italian Farmer's Health Savings Schemes, 16/5/'57, *Relations Humaines et Société Contemporaine: Synthèse Chrétienne Directives de S.S. Pie XII*, eds. Alfred F. UTZ and J.F. GRONER, (French edition translated by A. SAVIGNAT and H. Th. CONUS), 3 vols, 3215-3219. Paris / Fribourg: Editions St. Paul, 1956/63.

_____.Christmas Message, 22/12/'57, *Acta Apostolicae Sedis*, 50 (1958): 5-24.

_____.Address to the International Consultative Commission of the Entrepreneurs of the Chemical Industry, 10/1/'58, *Relations Humaines et Société Contemporaine: Synthèse Chrétienne Directives de S.S. Pie XII*, eds. Alfred F. UTZ and J.F. GRONER, (French edition translated by A. SAVIGNAT and H. Th. CONUS), 3 vols, 3514-3517. Paris / Fribourg: Editions St. Paul, 1956/63.

6. Doctoral Dissertations

BILGRIEN, Marie Vianney. *Solidarity: A Principle, an Attitude, a Duty?: Or the Virtue for an Interdependent World*, STD Dissertation. Rome: Pontifical University of St. Thomas, 1994.

LATUSEK, Pawel. *Incontro tra il Personalismo e il Marxismo in Polonia,*

Ph.D. Dissertation. Rome: Pontifical Gregorian University.

O'DONOVAN, C.P. *Person as Subsistent in the Early Teaching of St. Thomas Aquinas*, Ph.D. Dissertation. Rome: Pontifical Gregorian University, 1967.

WOODS, Thomas, *A European Community of Nations in the Teaching of Pius XII*, D.C.L. Dissertation. Rome: Pontifical Lateran University, 1962.

Index